MISSING CLASS

STRENGTHENING SOCIAL MOVEMENT GROUPS BY SEEING CLASS CULTURES

BETSY LEONDAR-WRIGHT

ILR PRESS
an imprint of
CORNELL UNIVERSITY PRESS
Ithaca and London

First published 2014 by Cornell University Press
First printing, Cornell Paperbacks, 2014

Printed in the United States of America

Library of Congress Cataloging-in-Publication Data

Leondar-Wright, Betsy, author.
    Missing class : strengthening social movement groups by seeing class cultures / Betsy Leondar-Wright.
        pages cm
    Includes bibliographical references and index.
    ISBN 978-0-8014-5256-7 (cloth : alk. paper) —
    ISBN 978-0-8014-7920-5 (pbk. : alk. paper)
    1. Social classes—United States. 2. Social movements—
United States. 3. Speech and social status—United
States. 4. Class consciousness—United States.
    5. Intercultural communication—United States. I. Title.
    HN90.S6L465   2014
    303.48'40973—dc23   2013040673

Cornell University Press strives to use environmentally responsible suppliers and materials to the fullest extent possible in the publishing of its books. Such materials include vegetable-based, low-VOC inks and acid-free papers that are recycled, totally chlorine-free, or partly composed of nonwood fibers. For further information, visit our website at www.cornellpress.cornell.edu.

Cloth printing   10 9 8 7 6 5 4 3 2 1
Paperback printing 10 9 8 7 6 5 4 3 2 1

To Felice Yeskel
1954–2011
My inspiration to explore class,
my colleague in fighting classism,
and my beloved friend

CONTENTS

Tables and Figures

ONLINE TABLES AND APPENDIXES

Available at www.classism.org/missing-class-tables-figures

MISSING CLASS

Introduction

Activist Class Cultures as a Key to Movement Building

For its annual goal-setting meeting, the Tri-
City Labor Alliance (TLA), an urban coalition of unions and their allies,
brought in an outside facilitator, Zoe, a college-educated white woman from
a professional-middle-class (PMC) background who was respected by many
members.[1]

At the beginning of the meeting, Zoe made a very long statement using
many phrases that had no concrete referent (no action, person, organization,
time, or place specified), such as *category of goals, proactive, review the process, participation in mobilization, leadership development opportunities*, and *strategic planning*. She mentioned only a very few potential concrete goals, such as making
sure that the construction of a new mall used only union labor.

Then Zoe wrote three general questions on a big sheet of paper and instructed the sixty members to break into a dozen small groups and "put these
recommendations into the context of these benchmarks." The small group
I joined, five older human services workers, chatted about electoral candidates, state budget cuts, grandchildren, and retirement parties, virtually ignoring Zoe's questions. During the report-backs, only one of the small groups
seemed to have stayed on topic and come to agreement on all three questions;
not coincidentally, it was the only group composed entirely of teachers.

All the small groups with industrial and service workers did not cooperate
with the process to some degree. No report-backs included Zoe's general

terms "benchmark," "process," "mobilization," or "strategy/strategic." Instead, the members of working-class unions spoke more concretely, even when making broad political points: they mentioned candidates to support; they suggested incentives to activate inactive members; and they named adversaries such as the union-busting mall developer.

In the discussion that followed, whenever members spoke, Zoe restated their points in more general terms; for example, she categorized a proposed phone tree as "mobilization." While most members spoke either at the macro level of political issues (such as "health care") or at the micro operational level (such as a suggestion to call a member to see if he had a firefighter retirees' phone list), only Zoe and two other white PMC labor leaders spoke at the intermediate level of organizational development.

At the end of the meeting, Zoe described the discussion as "unclear," and two top TLA leaders said it hadn't helped the executive committee prioritize ways to build the organization. Clearly, the dedicated labor activists at this meeting had two very different approaches to social change.

It was not that working-class union members felt animosity toward Zoe or other college-educated labor leaders. In fact, TLA members generally felt a strong sense of solidarity and enthusiasm for the group. One industrial worker, Slim, when asked about the annual goal-setting meeting, said admiringly of Zoe's role, "Sometimes you need somebody that's like, second chair, that's thinking. You know, like for years we used to say the labor movement didn't have enough intellectuals. . . . Today we got a lotta intellectuals in the labor movement, but you know, being a thinker wasn't something encouraged in the labor movement, and strategizing and all that."

This was not a story of cross-class conflict or hostility but of class subgroups operating from two different playbooks and thus accomplishing less. Nor did TLA members of different classes seem to literally misunderstand each other's words, despite speaking in two such different ways. Members in each class used the style of expression that was habitual for them and persistently raised the topics they prioritized. It was as if two parallel conversations happened, with the result that the TLA did not get a clear agreement on goals.

The TLA story illustrates the purpose and focus of this book. Class-culture differences often hamper movement building in ways more subtle than outright interclass clashes or misunderstandings. Lack of class awareness prevents activists from noticing how class dynamics play out and so keeps them from effectively bridging class differences.

Researching Class-Culture Differences in Social Change Groups

Why have there been so few cross-class, multiracial mass movements in US history? This perennial question has been answered in many ways. But gradually I have come to the conclusion that understanding activists' class-culture differences is one necessary precondition for mass movement building in the United States today.

Over and over again during my thirty years of progressive activism, I have experienced rifts along class lines. I'll mention just a few of many examples. Middle-class people who opposed nuclear power on environmental grounds missed many chances to work with working-class groups that were more focused on electricity prices or job loss. In the movement for pay equity, middle-class feminists sometimes framed the issue differently than did unions. In the struggle over the gutting of the welfare safety net, low-income women's groups did not get support from most middle-class feminists. The movement against corporate globalization came together for one glorious moment in Seattle in 1999; but afterward the unions went their way, and the student groups, faith-based groups, and environmentalists went theirs. Differences in self-interest only partially explain these failures of solidarity; in each case there seemed to be cultural differences as well.

I wrote a small section on activist class-culture differences in my book *Class Matters: Cross-Class Alliance Building for Middle-Class Activists* (2005) using anecdotal evidence; and when I brought up this topic on a book tour, I got very strong reactions. People questioned me heatedly, argued with my particulars, enthused, gave me their own culture-clash stories, reprinted and circulated the class-culture section of my website more than any other, and encouraged me to write more about activist class cultures. Only this topic made the temperature in the room rise.

The most common request was for hard evidence of exactly what _are_ the cultural differences among activists of various classes. What proof did I have that class was related to any particular differences in activists' ways of operating? I realized that I couldn't answer that question without social science research, without a rigorous analysis of a big sample of activists.

So I went to graduate school at Boston College, and with help from some dynamite sociologists I did field research on varied activist groups in 2007 and 2008. I ended up with almost one hundred transcripts of meetings and interviews with members of twenty-five left-of-center groups in five states. This book describes the class-culture differences I discovered in analyzing those transcripts.

is this enough

But before I get into specifics, I want to make the case that looking through a class lens at the internal workings of social change groups is worth the trouble. In the next chapter I tell five stories of groups' problems three ways: first focused on the group's movement tradition, then on members' race and gender, and finally on members' social class. This exercise reveals what is added when participants' class life stories are known.

"Class" is a concept shrouded in fog in our supposedly classless society. Think about the Occupy movement's slogan "We are the 99 percent": an admirable basis for class unity, but what vast differences in life experience it obscures between, say, the 10th and 80th income percentiles. Class is often regarded only as a feature of the macroeconomy; by contrast, race and gender have both macro *and* *micro* dimensions in the progressive lexicon: identities, stereotypes, cultures, and organizational dynamics, not only structural inequities. What does the microlevel of class entail? To shed more light on this confusing topic, in chapter 2, I look at ideas about class identities and class cultures that help explain the micropolitics of activist groups.

At heart, this book is a comparison, not of twenty-five groups, but of the four major class categories I found among 362 meeting participants. Most of us frequently guess wrong about our acquaintances' class backgrounds and current class status. In doing this analysis, I had a special lens into social change groups, watching their conversations and their dynamics while holding members' class indicators in mind. In chapter 3 I introduce the commonalities within each class. I profile the movement traditions into which the twenty-five groups fall in chapter 4. For a surprisingly large number of attitudes and behaviors, I found that class *does* predict how an activist may think or act, more so than race, age, or gender. The subtle interplay between how things are done in each movement tradition and the effects of individual members' class predispositions paints a complex picture of why activists tend to think and act as they do.

The following five chapters each add a new layer to this understanding of intersecting class cultures and movement traditions. In interviews, activists repeatedly raised the same few concerns about problems within their groups. Since one goal of this book is to help social change groups grow and thrive, each of these five chapters about my research findings focuses on one of these common organizational problems: (1) low turnout, (2) inactive members, (3) disagreements over antiracism, (4) overtalking, and (5) offensive behavior by activists. Class dynamics are woven into each of these troubles, and resolving them requires understanding class-culture differences. These problem-solving implications apply to other kinds of organizations as well, such as workplaces, schools, and social services agencies.

In addition to shedding more light on how group troubles operate, something else turned out to vary by activists' class: speech style. As soon as I used a class lens to review the recordings and transcripts, one thing became glaringly obvious: lifelong-working-class activists (that is, those who had not experienced upward mobility into the middle class since a childhood in the working class or in poverty) talked differently than college-educated activists. Humor, vocabulary, wordiness, and use of swear words and insults all varied significantly by class. The speech differences themselves were not usually problematic to groups, but knowing class speech codes could deepen understanding of class dynamics. Therefore, I have interspersed among the chapters six brief "class speech differences" interludes that illuminate the group troubles in adjacent chapters.

Every class culture brings strengths to the coalition table, and recognizing class differences can help activists tap into all available strengths. In particular, lifelong-working-class and impoverished activists' contributions may be slighted if class-privileged activists wear blinders that allow them to value only certain cultural capital. In a country with a working-class majority (Zweig 2011), a mass movement must be built with working-class cultural strengths in its bones. One of my goals with this book is to demonstrate to readers that more open discussion of class identities and class dynamics could be transformative for future social movements.

PART I

Class Diversity among Activists

CHAPTER 1

Why Look through a Class Lens?

Five Stories through Three Lenses

Small voluntary groups run into trouble: there are internal conflicts, difficult decisions, and clashes with other groups. Where can members turn for ideas on how to set things right? They may turn to their movement traditions. They may frame problems in terms of race or gender, or turn to practices from their ethnic roots or their gender identities. Or they may draw from their class cultures—but usually much less consciously, without naming them as class.

Any story of small-group troubles can be told in these three ways: through the lens of movement traditions, through a race and/or gender lens, or through a class lens. The goal of this chapter is to persuade readers that it is worthwhile to look through a class-culture lens.

In this chapter I introduce five of the twenty-five groups included in this book by telling one brief story of an intragroup problem in three ways: framing the story in terms of movement traditions; looking through a race and gender lens; and revealing participants' class identities to see new patterns and hypothesize about class cultures. In each case, something new is learned by looking through the class lens—usually something not articulated by the participants themselves because of the scarcity of class discourse among activists in the United States today.

To begin to illustrate the value of adding the class lens, here's one very small incident.

First Story: The Long-Underwear Dilemma

A core member of the Parecon Collective, Rupert, began wearing an unusual garment that left little to the imagination. Several members were disturbed to learn that he wore his colorful, slinky long underwear when representing the collective to the public, but they didn't say anything directly to him.

1. Movement Tradition Lens: Can Anarchists Put Social Pressure on Each Other?

The Parecon Collective defined itself as radical and antiauthoritarian, and many members identified themselves as anarchists. This antiauthoritarian political tendency was the fastest-growing subculture among young white activists in the 1990s and the first decade of the twenty-first century (Starr 2005; Kutz-Flamenbaum 2010).

To Parecon members, autonomy was a core value, which any kind of peer pressure threatened to violate. They didn't mind having procedures for their shared work, although they joked about how often they failed to follow them. But in an area as personal as clothing, where many prided themselves on being unconventional, it wasn't comfortable to try to influence someone to become more mainstream. What to do?

Two members spoke privately to Olivia, a member who was a personal friend of Rupert, asking her to intervene. In response, she teased him during a meeting, laughing as she said, "I can't believe you're wearing underwear!" Rupert replied, "They're pants! I don't know what you're talking about." To which Olivia said, "You'd wear those! You're pushing boundaries, dude! Amazing!" The next time I saw Rupert, he was wearing jeans.

Olivia bringing up the clothing problem so lightly allowed the group to avoid imposing its norms in a heavy way that might trigger concerns about hierarchy and authoritarian control. Other members' view on the long underwear was able to hold sway, without the majority dictating to the minority.

In their interviews, both Rupert and Olivia laughed about this incident and reiterated that they are close friends. As a nonhierarchical relationship, friendship was a more acceptable basis on which anarchists could apply pressure than a leader/follower relationship. In this case the friendship bond worked well to transmit some group feedback to a member who had violated an unspoken norm without requiring unacceptable levels of collective control.

2. Adding the Race and Gender Lens to the Long-Underwear Dilemma

Unusual clothing that flouts mainstream standards is a valued subcultural marker among anarchists and other young radicals, but women use it far more often than men. While anarchist men might sport dreadlocks or tattoos, their clothing tends to differ from mainstream male styles only in being used and/or all black, not by dramatically different types of garments than most mainstream men wear. Rupert seemed to have been violating gender norms by being so revealing and eccentric.

Olivia stood out in the mostly male Parecon Collective for her flamboyant postmodern pastiche of retro garments, an art form practiced by many of her age, gender, and subculture. By wearing his colorful long johns, Rupert was dressing a little like her. Thus it's not surprising that she was the one asked by two plain-dressing men to speak with him. Did those two men also ask Olivia to carry their feedback to Rupert not only because of their friendship, and not only because of her bohemian clothing, but because of her gender as well? Women are sometimes expected to handle tricky interpersonal situations in mixed-gender groups (Tannen 1990 and 1994).

Everyone in this situation was white. Discomfort with directly expressing criticism or conflict has been described as more typical of whites than of some other ethnic groups, such as African Americans (Kochman 1981; Bailey 1997). While the Parecon Collective joked around a lot, the joking didn't usually involve rough teasing of anyone in the room. In a mixed-race or all-black group, might Rupert have heard people's reactions to his long-underwear pants the first moment he walked in wearing them, instead of a month later?

The race and gender lens suggests these interesting questions. What more could a class lens add?

3. Adding the Class Lens: Indirectness versus Bluntness

Olivia was not just Rupert's friend, and not just one of the few women in the Parecon Collective, but she was also a lifelong-poor person, one of only two people in the core group who wasn't raised by college-educated homeowner parents. Olivia had been recruited to the Parecon Collective by a working-class woman who explicitly said she wanted another woman from a working-class background to keep her company in the group but who had since quit. Olivia's willingness to be jokingly blunt about a touchy subject was a resource to the group—a resource that may have come from her low-income roots and her lack of socialization into professional norms. Teasing is a much more common form of humor among working-class and poor activists than among any other class.

Two studies of US white and black men's values found that upper-middle-class (UMC) men emphasized getting along with everyone and diplomacy (Lamont 1992), while working-class men valued blunt honesty (Lamont 2000).

During meetings, the Parecon Collective appeared to be a casual, friendly, youthful group, sprawled on worn couches, laughing together at Republicans, religious people, and consumers of corporate products. But interviews with members revealed a startling level of unspoken conflict. A founding member, Edrin, was messing up a core aspect of their work and never showed up to meetings to discuss the situation—and Olivia believed that no one had ever confronted him about it directly. She said, "We often talk about this behind his back [*laughs*] . . . he's really hard to talk to. We've tried, we've tried like, we decided he should [do his role a certain way], and then he just doesn't do it. . . . I think he should be required to come to a meeting every six months or something at least . . . he's just like not even there." But Edrin was often present in a far corner of the group's space when she and other active members were there. He successfully avoided interacting with them.

Is such conflict avoidance fully explained by the other lenses? Is it sufficient to say that there's a reticent cultural style in some US anarchist groups? Can we completely understand why Parecon members didn't approach Rupert directly but asked Olivia to do it for them by noting that the conflict avoiders were white men? Perhaps—but below we will find that conflict avoidance is most common among people who grew up in the lower part of the professional-middle-class (PMC) range.

Today's movement traditions have grown from distinct class roots, and one hypothesis explored in this book is that today's anarchist subculture (as opposed to, say, the Spanish anarchists of the 1930s) has some strongly PMC class-cultural aspects. Most anarchist groups are prefigurative, intending to "be the change you want to see in the world" by manifesting the opposite of oppressive mainstream society in their practices. But could such conflict avoidance be one way that some anarchist groups don't manage to escape the downside of their predominantly PMC backgrounds? This question is addressed in the book's analysis of other antiauthoritarian groups.

Next I'll look at two more small kerfuffles through the same three lenses, then move on to a major conflict that threatened a group's effectiveness, and finally profile a huge fight that ended one group's existence.

Second Story: Reacting to Criticism from Within

This story took place in a very different setting, a grassroots community group in a low-income area of a big city. At one Women Safe from Violence (WomenSafe) meeting, a member who wasn't part of the core group, Randall, raised a criticism of a recent public presentation by leaders Elaine and Bette. He said, "I don't want to be hypercritical of the group, but we were half-assed! It went off on weird tangents. We should put it on a video or a DVD, because the speaker gets into random stuff. We were not smooth, we were all over the frickin' place."

Several members reacted negatively as Randall spoke, both verbally and with body language. One interrupted him to say coldly, "I don't know how many of [those programs] you've done!" The chair said indignantly, "Do you think it was [WomenSafe's] fault?" Bette shouted, "I was there! We *have* a video! There was no TV to show it on that time! . . . You kept interrupting, that was the problem!" And then in a calmer voice but still vehement she added, "Sometimes we're not as perfect as we like, but your interpretation is *quite wrong!*"

After a pause, another member, Adaline, suggested scheduling an organizational evaluation session to go over the substance of Randall's critique. The members who had been so vehement a moment before calmly agreed with her. Why such a different reaction to Adaline than to Randall? Why could some members hear a suggestion for group self-evaluation from one person but not another?

1. Movement Tradition Lens: Family Mutual Aid and Pride in Being Nonprofessional

WomenSafe members prided themselves that their group was run by the very people who had needed the group's help, who then became empowered to find collective as well as individual solutions. The founder, Elaine, told me, "I call it constituent-led organizing—and it's frickin' magic. . . . Those who lead the group are those affected by the issue."

Randall's criticism offended the core members because it suggested that the do-it-ourselves ethic of the group wasn't effective. By talking about creating prepackaged technological tools such as a DVD, he was suggesting a slicker style, a mode more like a social service agency than an activist mutual-aid group.

As with many community groups, family ties seemed to be the model on which WomenSafe was based. Mutual self-defense of the family was the group's main mode, both in its program work and in its internal workings. Randall positioned himself as an outsider attacking the family, referring to "the speaker" in the third person and saying "half-assed." Adaline spoke more gently, from a "we" position within the family.

2. Race/Gender Lens: White Guys are Welcome If They Stay Low-Key

Randall as a white male was not welcome to critique a majority-female group. Adaline as a white woman was welcome to make the same points. Those reacting defensively to Randall's criticism were women of three races, closing ranks in the face of a white man's attack. Another white man, Eugene, was a respected core member who was repeatedly elected to the board—but unlike Randall, Eugene was very quiet, doing his share of the work but not speaking much at meetings. It seems that white men were welcome as long as they didn't dominate.

3. Adding a Class Lens: Closing Ranks or Introspective Processing?

There were just two people whose parents had graduate degrees at this meeting: Randall and Adaline. Their shared perspective that there might be something amateurish and ineffective about the group's public presentations may have come from their more elite class-cultural roots. Organizational development is often the turf of people from PMC backgrounds, so it's not surprising that they were the two who suggested an evaluation process. They may also have felt more entitled to be critical.

Most of the women who sprang to the presenters' defense were lifelong-working-class or lower-middle-class people. Loyally closing ranks around leaders seems to be part of working-class culture, in particularly within grass-roots community organizations. How widespread a class-cultural trait this is will be explored in chapter 6.

Adaline, a middle-aged Jewish woman, was the only member present who had a four-year college degree. Her reaction to Randall was different from the other women's, not only in that she agreed with him more but also in how she framed the disagreement differently, in terms of group process and organizational introspection: "There is room for [WomenSafe] to look at itself. We could look at our presentations, go over 'when you said that' or 'this is how to do that better.' This defensiveness about did we mess up is not helpful. I've seen very little processing and analyzing in this group, or talk about how to improve [WomenSafe]."

After a pause, the chair, Laci, responded, "Totally. It's good to criticize ourselves," and Kristal said, "Maybe at the next meeting." Adaline's culturally PMC perspective, oriented more toward group introspection by "processing and analyzing," influenced other group members to modify their usual mode of closing ranks around the leaders.

Third Story: Workers Argue Unsuccessfully with the Organizer's Idea

Another small disagreement happened in a meeting of the Local 21 Organizing Committee. The chair, Lynette, a substitute staff organizer, insisted that the members plan a party; but all the workers who had been elected to a coordinating group argued with her that a skill-training session would attract more potential members. One member, Alonzo, shouted at the organizer, put on his hat, and dramatically strode toward the door as if to walk out, before returning to the meeting.

1. Movement Tradition Lens: Top-Down Labor Tradition Collides with Democratic Expectations

Local 21 was part of a huge international union, which staffed this organizing committee to try to unionize certain low-paid service workers. The agendas for the organizing-committee meetings were set by Local 21 managers, not by organizers or workers. Democratic decision-making power by rank-and-file workers is not a universal union practice (Early 2009). Before unionization, an organizing campaign is even more likely to be centrally controlled by union management. Organizing staffers are caught between their mission of mobilizing workers and the directives they get from their supervisors. Lynette put the party on the agenda as a question, as if the members would be making the decision. But when they objected to the plan, she had to admit to them that it was a done deal, with only details of time and place left to be worked out.

The meeting I observed was during Lynette's last week as union staff, as she had just resigned. She told me that she hated her job. The next Local 21 Organizing Committee meeting I observed was led by a different organizer, Owen. He also expressed frustration with the constraints of his job, with his subordination to orders from above and with how little say workers had in the unionization campaign.

But from the union management's point of view, a streamlined, cost-effective process modeled on past unionization victories no doubt made sense. Their lean organizing system has been proven effective by successful unionization at many workplaces. Controversies about the best method for reviving the labor movement continue to rage on (Early 2011; Yates et al. 2008).

Alonzo's frustration was with how low turnout had been at recent meetings and events, down to one-tenth the number of a few months earlier. He urgently wanted the union drive to succeed and was angry that the union seemed to be making mistakes in recruiting workers. The staff and the rank-and-file members seemed to agree on the goal but not always on the methods. In his interview he affirmed the right of the Local 21 staff to tell him and other workers what to do, even while he expressed his disagreement with some of their decisions.

2. The Race and Gender Lens on the Party versus Skill-Training Argument

Lynette was white, and at this meeting she was chairing a virtually all-black group. A few months later, when an energetic black man, Owen, replaced the white organizer, member turnout picked up dramatically.

Demographically matching the organizer to the constituency is a time-honored practice in community and labor organizing. Perhaps black workers were more resistant to a white organizer and more inspired by a black organizer. When Lynette drew members out via questions, she did get some cooperation, but they resisted whenever she pushed or insisted, in a way that no one resisted Owen as chair.

There was a gender difference in how workers expressed their disagreement with Lynette's top-down party plan. The women resisted through passive noncooperation: one did a word-find puzzle on her lap; there were side conversations about astrology and food. Small, almost surreptitious signs of resistance included catching eyes and uttering a distinctive African American women's sound of disparagement, a soft high-to-low "MMp-mmp-mmp."

Alonzo, the one black man present, reacted differently. His body language was very active; he got up, paced, put on his hat, and walked almost to the door. When he was frustrated, he shouted "Lynette!" and repeated emphatically that workers would come "if it's related to their job! If it's related to their job!" When Lynette plowed on with party details, Alonzo teased her so exuberantly that she laughed for the first time that evening: "Lynette! I going to marry you, because you never give up! Jesus! She *never* gives up, man!" His participation in the meeting was full of bravado, sometimes performed for the researcher in the room, very different from the women staying quietly in their chairs. (See Heath 1983 for a sociolinguistic analysis of black male socialization encouraging more performative speech compared with quieter forms of verbal creativity for black women.)

3. Adding the Class Lens: Classism as the Elephant under the Carpet

Lynette was raised by college-educated parents and had a four-year college degree; the workers' education varied from dropping out in middle school to two-year degrees. The dynamic between this organizer and the members was not just that of race but class as well.

The reasons that Lynette met such resistance went beyond the substance of the party-planning disagreement. I cringed listening to how she spoke to the members in a condescending, kindergarten-teacher tone. She made the following comments while the party was under discussion: "I don't know why you're against trying something new"; "They have the right attitude in [another city]—[*shouting*] *They* have the right attitude"; "You guys just can't seem to lighten up!" [*while pointing her finger rhythmically at Alonzo*]; and, worst of all, "Behave yourself! Why does Janelle *do* this every month? No wonder she told me to do this meeting!"

Given that the experienced members had solid evidence backing up their position that workers would turn out for training to improve their prospects for a pay raise (they pointed out that a prior skills workshop had drawn an overflow crowd), there was no reason for her to belittle their opinion, even though she wasn't authorized to approve it.

The moments when Alonzo shouted and walked away, and the moments when other members didn't cooperate with Lynette, were usually immediately after her most condescending comments. At one point Alonzo complained about workers not turning out despite his phone calls, and Lynette advised, "Alonzo, you have to be prepared for that, and not take it personally, not take it to heart, and just keep persisting with it . . . that's what you have to do." In his most direct response to her patronizing tone, he responded sarcastically, "Thank you, Lynette. Every time [when I make recruitment calls] I'm going to call Lynette. And every time I call Lynette and tell Lynette [about] who don't come to meetings, and Lynette, they still don't show up. Lynette, it's *for* them!" His two decades of greater age and more years of union organizing experience compared with Lynette's credentials added weight to his sarcasm.

Mocking laughter, consistent with a working-class culture of teasing and rough humor, greeted the details of Lynette's proposal, such as the low budget allotted for party expenses.

Lynette didn't succeed as a union organizer, not just because organizational policies limited her flexibility, not just because she was a white person organizing a mostly black constituency, but also because she had condescending attitudes expressed in verbal classism.

Now we move on to two broader and more divisive conflicts within groups.

Fourth Story: Dealing with a Dominating Personality When No One Is Supposed to Dominate

The Action Center (AC) was an ad hoc direct action group preparing for protest at one of the 2008 major-party political conventions. The core group of about twenty-five put a strong emphasis on shared leadership and strict consensus decision making. Thus several informants saw it as a problem that one member, Dirk, talked frequently and aggressively in meetings, acted independently without consulting the group, kept key information secret, and in other ways dominated like an unaccountable leader.

One central member, Gail, said that something he did was a "power grab, hierarchy . . . don't tell me that that man isn't the leader of the group. . . . I don't think anybody could look at that meeting and not say Dirk's running this whole damn group."

1. Movement Tradition Lens: Can Anarchists Tell Each Other What to Do?

What are the implications of having an antiauthoritarian ideology for how a group runs itself? I encountered two quite different perspectives among convention protestors and other anarchism-influenced groups, two subcultural strains whose historical roots are explored further in chapter 4.

First, a structured group-process tradition, rooted in prefigurative movements of the 1970s and 1980s and influenced by pagan spirituality, holds that in order to run a group without hierarchy, many agreements about procedures must be forged and observed with rigorous discipline (Epstein 1991: 271–72; Cornell 2011). Strictly rotating facilitation and consensus decision making are what keep informal hierarchies from developing in this view. Counter to the stereotype, anarchism in this tradition means more rules than most groups have, not fewer.

The second type of anarchist perspective, rooted in the punk subculture, puts the highest value on no one coercing anyone else. Consensus decision making is important in this view because the rights of an individual with a minority opinion cannot be violated by a majority decision. If individual autonomy is sacrosanct, then rules for decision making can't be more than simply suggestions without creating an internal contradiction. Dirk's behavior implied a more extreme version of this view, along the lines of "no one tells me what to do."

Some Action Center members described being torn between these two interpretations of their values. One member, Dallas, put the tension in terms of "negotiating constraints and agreements on how do we balance personal autonomy versus our responsibility to a community."

As the week of the political convention approached and out-of-town activists began to arrive, the challenges of planning with an ever-expanding open group threw more members into the structured-process faction. Rules about who had the right to make what decisions proliferated; so did conversations about how many rules were too many. Some reluctantly, some eagerly,

Action Center members discussed adding more delegation of authority and more conditions on decision-making roles.

Dirk's independent streak stood out more conspicuously as the group became more structured. A retreat was held to deal with internal dynamics, with Dirk's behavior as a major topic. At the retreat, the group did role playing and small group exercises designed to teach them how not to dominate each other. But the tools of the structured-process tradition couldn't solve the problem that some members had a fundamental disagreement with that tradition.

2. Race and Gender Lens: Calling Out Domination

Most Action Center core members shared a gender analysis, which most interviewees summarized in the word "patriarchy." Men who made sexist comments, talked a lot, or used power in unaccountable ways were described as patriarchal. There was controversy over how to deal with a patriarchal man, but the most common procedure seemed to be for a small group of men to meet with him privately and "call out" his unacceptable behavior. Interviewees told me of two such confrontations, one with a man named Canton who talked about wanting multiple wives, and one with Dirk, who became agitatedly defensive during this session of male-on-male criticism.

When Dallas was asked, "Has anyone driven you crazy at a meeting?," he answered in terms of the oppressive use of power:

> Generally Dirk is the only one who drives me crazy. I'm one of the few people who will call him on it, take a bad-guy role. I enjoy working with him one-on-one, but in the group he's not that aware—no, he is aware, but he uses his power: "I'm autonomous and you can't infringe on my personal" . . . "I don't want to wait five seconds 'cause that's oppressive to me." We could do more to call out oppressive behaviors.

For Dallas, it was valid to object to being dominated on the basis of a social identity but invalid to object to being constrained by the group's agreements for sharing airspace (the opportunity to talk).

Dallas, Gail, and others seemed discouraged that nothing was working to improve Dirk's behavior, not the role-playing and discussions about sharing airspace at the retreat, not the confrontation by other white men, not rules about how information and decision making must be shared. Those were the methods they believed would work to reduce sexist or racist domination, yet in Dirk's case, they didn't seem to be working.

3. Adding a Class Lens: Invisible versus Imagined Working-Class Members

The assumption of several Action Center interviewees was that most members came from middle-class backgrounds and that their current low incomes (living on part-time jobs to free up time for protest planning, or in some cases squatting and dumpster-diving) were voluntary. For example, when Dallas was asked about the social class of Action Center members, he said, "I guess we all come from a similar class background. All went to college or plan to go—we all had the opportunity."

Of the white men who took Dirk aside, those for whom I have demographic data were from PMC or UMC backgrounds and had college degrees. Those I spoke with presumed that Dirk was just like them, formed by entirely dominant social identities, conditioned to be dominating and thus needing antioppression education to learn how not to dominate.

But unbeknownst to most Action Center interviewees, Dirk was almost the group's only working-class-background active member. While almost all of their parents had graduated from college and earned salaries, Dirk's parents had high school diplomas and earned hourly wages. Dirk had attended a nonresidential public college, but he had worked only at blue-collar jobs since.

Talking dominant to dominant wasn't working in part because, with regard to class, they were actually dominants scolding a subordinate. While Dirk's hyper, aggressive, and reportedly manipulative behavior was not typical of any demographic category, including working-class activists, it's possible that peers with working-class backgrounds similar to his could have been more successful in reining him in.

Gail, a very class-conscious middle-class white woman, was the only person I spoke with who suspected Dirk's working-class background, and she associated it with his outspokenness:

> The strength of Dirk is . . . he is willing to blurb out what isn't very popular to say. . . . The little bit I know about Dirk and his background is he said at one point, "Well, I'm [part of a traditionally working-class white ethnic group]," and I think he is relatively working class and has an ethnic identity, and so I think his willingness to blurb out stuff is a strength actually. I like that about him, you know. But . . . he can get kind of brutal at times too.

When I asked Gail to tell me about the class makeup of the group, she said she thought working-class people were more likely to be suspected of being police infiltrators (agents paid to spy on direct action groups). She guessed that those suspicions were due to classist stereotypes of people who didn't come from the same background as most of the group. She named one man, Canton, and one woman, Minnie, as two people with working-class styles who had been suspected of being infiltrators, probably unfairly in her opinion.

Two Action Center interviewees told me that when a delegation of other white men confronted Canton and one of them accused him of being an infiltrator because he was so quiet and always took notes, Canton began to cry and said that he was quiet because he was intimidated by the other members, who had so much more education and knew so much more political analysis. Some judged this display of internalized classism as sincere, and the group decided not to kick him out.

But when court documents later revealed who the paid infiltrators were, Canton and Minnie were on the list. They had been hired by law enforcement authorities to spy on the group and collect evidence for criminal charges. Far from being the politically unsophisticated person he portrayed himself as, Canton understood the antioppression values of the group well enough to successfully con members by winning their sympathy for being working class. Thus a class lens sheds light on a problem of utmost concern to groups like the Action Center: how to detect and protect themselves from infiltrators without poisoning the group with pervasive suspicion of all newcomers.

This bizarre drama epitomizes the state of confusion about class in the left today. The group's actual working-class member was invisible to them; as a problem person, he was dealt with by methods based on the presumption that he shared their privileged background, which didn't work. Meanwhile, a person presumed to be working class won an undeserved free pass from suspicion of treachery, thanks to manipulating the group's class sympathies.

In other groups, too, there were many misunderstandings of who came from which class background. Simply learning more about members' life stories would enable many groups to better understand their internal class dynamics.

Fifth Story: A Faith-Based Group Splits over Strategic Paths

The Citywide Interfaith Coalition mobilized religious congregations on poverty issues in a major urban area. An executive board member, Jeremiah, came to a meeting of a subgroup, the Workforce Development Task Force, with the intention of chewing them out for straying from the strategic path the board had laid out. Conflict broke out, with raised voices and an unresolved disagreement about next steps. This rift was so severe that some longtime members quit the coalition after this meeting, and the task force was disbanded.

1. Movement Tradition Lens: Community Organizing Clashes with Professional Advocacy

The Interfaith Coalition used a community-organizing methodology that was a faith-based variation on the Alinsky (1971) practices of the Industrial Areas Foundation (Bobo, Kendall, and Max 2001). The membership voted on issue priorities once a year; particular public officials were targeted, and mass accountability sessions were staged to confront them and to demand prede- cided reforms. This method had brought the coalition some notable successes in past years, but not in the current year. Member turnout had dwindled. The targeted official had failed to show up for the recent accountability session. The resulting demoralization was the context for the infighting.

Jeremiah, a fervent believer in the coalition's community-organizing methodology, had come to the meeting to scold the group for doing too little to punish the official for not showing up and to ask them to return to the preset strategy and to drop their alternative approach.

The Workforce Development Task Force had been formed to work on a technical policy issue prioritized by membership vote at the coalition's last annual convention.[1] While some task force members were clergy or mem- bers of religious congregations, most had a professional job related to the is- sue, such as staffing a social services agency. Two had specialized expertise in the technical aspects of development projects, including the chair, Brandon, who worked as a loan administrator at a for-profit lender. Thus the task force fit into the movement tradition of professional nonprofit advocacy, very dis- similar from the Alinsky organizing tradition of the Interfaith Coalition's umbrella group.

Task force members brought energetic excitement to this meeting be- cause allies on the county commission had decided to set up a Community Benefits Advisory Board and had asked some of them to serve on it. Their assessment was that some of their long-stalled legislative priorities might have some hope of enactment at the county level.

But Jeremiah had a very negative reaction to the idea of working through an advisory board and shifting the focus to the county level. In his interview, he attributed the task force's autonomous action to their "ignorance" of how the Interfaith Coalition operated. He told the group they didn't have the authority to change their target or tactics.

Several task force members reacted angrily to Jeremiah's criticism. They saw him as blocking progress by rigidly adhering to the preset plan, even when it wasn't working. The clash of political approaches, professional advocacy versus community organizing, became explicit at times in the group's discussion at the meeting:

> SHERMAN: The [advisory board] is intended to include people with expertise, and it should. . . . Now we have to . . . make sure that the people with expertise are community-minded people . . . and share our values and that there's room for community representatives, and this does not preclude that.
>
> JEREMIAH: I think you might be confusing the term "influence" with power. You know our power comes from the people. We're people powered. We can go down and stand before the [county officials] every day and try to influence them, but that's not power. If we're going to stand before anybody, it needs to be our congregations, getting them worked up. . . . Just going down and trying to influence, that's the game that's being played in Washington. . . . It doesn't really bring about substantive changes.

The role of professional expertise was at the center of this disagreement. The "people power" approach to politics didn't get any philosophical disagreement from task force members, but they had a pragmatic both/and approach, and favored turning to other methods when mobilization and confrontation didn't get results.

One of the flash points of the meeting was when Jeremiah said that Brandon shouldn't serve on the Community Benefits Advisory Board because he worked in the for-profit sector, implying that he was too self-interested and profit motivated. Noah said of the incident that Brandon "got kicked in the teeth, and that's no way to treat somebody." While Jeremiah's language in disqualifying Brandon might not have seemed particularly harsh or disrespectful in another context, in this often soft-spoken and affirming faith-based group it was a shocking breach of decorum.

2. Race and Gender Lens: Black and White Men Argue, Women Smooth the Waters

This meeting was half black and half white. The most vehement arguments were among men, sometimes between two black men in the case of Brandon and Jeremiah, and sometimes between Jeremiah and the two most outspoken white men, Noah and Sherman.

Besides the substantive disagreements, there was a clash of male egos. Jeremiah was pulling rank; Noah and Sherman were blustering to get him to back down.

Two women played peacemaking roles. The task force's staff person, Jocelyn, a younger black woman, remained quiet through most of the meeting but spoke up at times to explain each side to the other. She successfully defused one argument by pointing out that a controversial proposal was moot because a date had passed. A white woman, Stacy, placated and praised individual combatants, assertively mediating at some tense moments and suggesting prayers at others.

Whenever conflict heated up, Jeremiah would begin talking in a more African American cadence, using black-preacher-style rhetorical eloquence. This may have been an identity move, code-switching to affiliate himself with people of color affected by the policies under discussion. Or he might have been using an oppressed identity as a form of movement cultural capital. If he was trying to be more persuasive, it was an unsuccessful attempt, since others were skeptical of the motives behind his rhetoric. The accent and cadence of the younger black participants weren't nearly as different from that of the white participants.

The thirty-year age difference between Brandon and Jeremiah put them in different eras of black politics. Jeremiah had roots in the civil rights movement and brought from it a more adversarial form of politics. Brandon took for granted the necessity of seeking all possible allies to the cause, including businesses, whites, and officials.

3. Adding a Class Lens: Class as a Smokescreen for Internal Power Dynamics

This meeting was unusual in how much and how openly participants talked about class. One argument was about how much priority to put on input from directly affected people. Was low-income people's input into policy an ideal to be reached when possible, a helpful accompaniment to sympathetic professionals' input, or the only acceptable form of public input, as Jeremiah asserted?

Immediately after Jeremiah said that Brandon shouldn't be eligible to be on the county's advisory board because of his for-profit job, they had this exchange:

BRANDON: As far as advisory is concerned, if you're building a space shuttle, you're going to need a rocket scientist to advise you.

JEREMIAH: Yeah, yeah, I agree with you. But if you're talking about taking money from the rich and giving it to the poor, you're going to need a poor person there.

BRANDON: Absolutely, and that's why we need to—

STACY: Or at least a Robin Hood. [*group laugh*]

JEREMIAH: And there's no poor people on that list [of slots on the Community Benefits Advisory Board].

BRANDON: There should be; there should be.

Can a professional Robin Hood advocate for the poor in good faith, or can only the poor represent the poor? This is a recurring debate within the Left.

But in this case, the difference between member pressure and professional advocacy was *not* a clear class contrast but was, in fact, an ideological difference covering up a power struggle. Directly affected people were not in the room—or even in the membership, for the most part. The Interfaith Coalition's grassroots membership was primarily middle-class congregation members, including those in Jeremiah's own church, who wouldn't be eligible for any job training the group won. People directly affected by the coalition's poverty issues were *not* the ones to take the annual vote on priorities. Jeremiah's proposal for the task force's next action was a workshop for clergy, who would then bring the issue to their congregations, hardly a bottom-up strategy.

Jeremiah's people-power purism in insisting on foregoing the advisory board opportunity was interpreted by some task force members as a disingenuous, top-down power play to squelch the task force's ability to take initiative while he hypocritically preached bottom-up empowerment.

Everyone at the meeting had at least a four-year college degree except for Brandon; only Jeremiah and Brandon didn't have college-educated homeowner parents. Among the lifelong-professional members, the degree of verbal aggression lined up with their parents' and their own education and occupation. Those with lower-professional (LP) parents mostly remained quiet and/or conciliatory. Sherman, a UMC lawyer, spoke very sharply to Jeremiah, accusing him of destroying the task force's chances for success: "This is the opportunity for the coalition to win an advance, and [*speaking directly to Jeremiah*] I think you're going to lose it for us. And that's frustrating to me." The only member besides Sherman whose parents had graduate degrees, Stacy, made the most assertive and directive attempts at mediation.

It casts a different light on Jeremiah's dig at Brandon's credibility to see them as coming from similar black working-class backgrounds but with Jeremiah having reached more educational and professional heights. When their conflict is recast as one between a straddler high professional with a PhD and a less upwardly mobile person with a vocational associate's degree, then the difference between Jeremiah's adherence to a pure political ideal and Brandon's willingness to compromise can be seen as a class-cultural difference between the more ideological and the more pragmatic.

In talking about Jeremiah disqualifying him as too tied to the private sector, Brandon described his working-class background and referred defensively to the African American tradition of giving back to the community and "lifting as you climb," a tradition that validates an activist role for those with greater educational and professional attainment.

Every task force interviewee focused on Jeremiah's class identity. Noah and Brandon suspected him of being a poseur, someone who played poor to score political points. For example, Noah said, "We're not seeing a multiclass type of coalition. And Jeremiah uses his earthiness, and he is *not*, he's also an expert. . . . I think Jeremiah truly believes that he knows best because he is closer to the class. You know, it's taken at face value."

But Jeremiah did not hide his education or occupational status from an interviewer. He said with self-aware humility, "My father was a working man, you know, a union man. . . . But my life has been a life of privilege. When I agree to look at myself honestly and compare myself to the way the world is, yes, I do live off privilege." In the vehement positions he took, he seemed to have been trying to stay true to the working-class people he came from without pretending to still be working class himself.

Giving low-income people a voice in decisions that affect their lives is an activist ideal much more honored in talk than in action. While it was an ostensible topic at this meeting, in fact none of the alternatives they argued over would have actually meant more low-income involvement. A power struggle among professionals and an ideological disagreement between movement traditions masqueraded as a class conflict.

Two Common Lenses and One Uncommon Lens

Each group spotlighted here carried forward ways of doing things from past movement traditions: from the heyday of the labor movement in the 1930s and 1940s; from the civil rights and student movements of the 1960s; from the "new social movements" of the 1970s and 1980s; from previous community-organizing efforts; or from other traditions that have made up the history of the US Left (Flacks 1988). Some interviewees brought up political ideologies and well-known innovators such as Saul Alinsky or Paulo Freire to explain how their group was run or how their ideal group would operate. Knowing which part of movement history they held as an ideal or as a cautionary tale gives context to their debates over how to operate.

Activists also frequently used the race and gender lens. Decades of hard work on identity politics, while failing to eradicate sexism or racism from the Left, have nevertheless paid off in activists' fluency in using a race and/ or gender lens. The work by feminists of color that began with *This Bridge Called My Back* (Moraga and Anzaldúa 1981) in applying a race and gender critique to social change efforts has continued (Martinez 2000). Online dialogue about intragroup race and racism began early in the Occupy movement (ColorLines 2011; Sen 2011).

While those targeted by racism and/or sexism, in particular women of color, have long taken the lead in challenging social movements (hooks 1981 and 2000; Anzaldúa 1987; Collins 1991; Reed 1999), more recently people in the dominant social roles have joined in (Dyson 1997: chaps. 5 and 6; Kivel 1998 and 2002; Wise 2004; Warren 2010).

As progressive activists, the members of these twenty-five groups tended to be comfortable using a race and/or gender lens informed by this academic and activist work. Interview questions about the race and gender of group members were usually answered easily.

However, a class lens was used much less often. As we will see in the "Missing Class Talk" speech interlude, interview questions about the class makeup of the group sometimes evoked confusion. Many group members made wrong guesses about one another's backgrounds. Vocabulary for class identities was sparse and varied wildly. Virtually nothing was said about what members' class differences might mean for organizational attitudes or behaviors. This vacuum is not surprising given the paucity of attention to class dynamics within social movements.

What could be seen by looking through a class lens? If members' class life stories were known and discussed, what mysteries in activist groups would be cleared up? If class-culture differences were named and understood, what new solutions to voluntary-group troubles would be possible?

It's not that adding a class lens engenders a neat formula for how class-culture differences play out. Note how dissimilar are the class revelations in the five stories. Any simple generalization such as "all working-class people are more X, and all PMC people are more Y" is probably untrue. The class-culture dynamics in social movement organizations are more complex and subtle than that.

To see activist class-culture differences requires comparing many groups. The patterns that appear in these five stories—how people with similar or different class life stories acted similarly or differently—could be idiosyncratic to that group or those personalities and thus of little interest for either socio-logical theory or coalition building. Or they could be class–culture factors that only hold true for a particular combination of race, gender, age, region, and movement tradition. But do some of them perhaps hold true across many social change groups? In this book I attempt to answer that question. Looking through the class lens can add context and complexity to the movement-tradition lens and the race/gender lens. The three lenses are not three alternatives, three competing interpretations of a given situation, but three interwoven strands.

CHAPTER 2

Applying Class Concepts to US Activists

Confusion about class pervades American society, and that confusion distorts progressive movement building. The popular myth that the United States is a classless society is scorned by most on the left, but paradoxically the myth of a classless *movement* lives on. Some activists believe that the very act of sacrificing time and/or money for social change actually removes them from the class system (Carlsson 2008). Class dynamics in the movement are difficult to discuss with people who believe they are nonexistent.

Why does class diversity have such a low profile on the left today? One reason is that it's hard to talk about something without shared vocabulary. In the United States today there are no agreed-on terms for social classes (Metzgar 2003). Both ordinary Americans and academics use widely varied terminology for a varied number of class categories. (See review in Wright 2005.) Authors have broken the class spectrum into two (Fiske and Markus 2012), three (Zweig 2011), four (Breen 2005), seven (Goldthorpe 1980), or twelve (Wright 1985) categories. Any way of slicing the class spectrum is, of course, arbitrary.

To sociologists, "class" usually refers to a cluster of social indicators (such as income, assets, education, occupation, status, etc.), any one of which can be emphasized or deemphasized.[1] A case can be made for giving the most weight to income (Bartels 2006), assets (Conley 1999), power (Aronowitz

what are the classes?

Marx was wrong

2003), workplace autonomy (Wright 1985; Zweig 2011), social status (Breen 2005), or education and other cultural capital (Bourdieu 1984; Lamont and Lareau 1988). The choice of which indicators to emphasize depends on the purpose of the analysis.

Prioritizing Education and Occupation to Spotlight Cultural Capital

In this book I build on the ideas of the French sociologist Pierre Bourdieu. Like Max Weber before him, he tried to explain differences in individuals' life chances, why class inequalities are reproduced from generation to generation. His answer spotlighted "cultural capital," a broad term encompassing formal education, degrees and other credentials, informal knowledge gained from an advantaged background, and manners of speaking and acting (Bourdieu 1984). He also stressed another factor in class reproduction, "social capital": social status and who you know. He termed both of them "capital" because they can be used to gain financial capital (125).

By studying the lifestyles and attitudes of thousands of French people of varied classes, Bourdieu was able to show how each class position generates a certain disposition, a set of attitudes and habitual practices that are carried into every area of life.[2] In this book I investigate whether US activists bring such predictable class predispositions into their social change groups.

Unlike deterministic theories that make individuals seem like robots programmed by society, Bourdieu's theories stress human agency; as we move through our lifetimes, we innovate, we make strategic choices, and we change, but always from the starting place of our class origins,[3] and we are always influenced by the predispositions inculcated in us by our childhood social position, of which we are largely unconscious (Bourdieu 1980).

Because he put cultural capital and social capital on a par with financial capital, Bourdieu's ideas are especially relevant to mixed-class activist groups, where there is often a narrow range of financial resources but vast inequality in education and social networks.

Bourdieu's map of social space (simplified in figure 2.1) distinguishes among types of class privilege. Those above the horizontal axis have more total capital than those below it, but the left-right axis denotes the composition of that capital, whether more financial (in the top right quadrant) or more cultural (in the top left quadrant). Bourdieu's message to his fellow elite French intellectuals and artists was similar to what I'm saying to my fellow professional-middle-class (PMC) activists: the vertical distances between those with less and more total capital are class differences, while the horizontal distances between ourselves

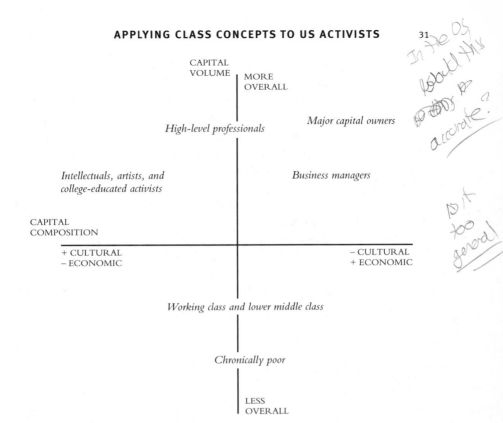

In the US would this be more p̶ro̶p accurate?

Is it too general)

CAPITAL
VOLUME

MORE
OVERALL

High-level professionals   *Major capital owners*

Intellectuals, artists, and   *Business managers*
college-educated activists

CAPITAL
COMPOSITION

+ CULTURAL   – CULTURAL
– ECONOMIC   + ECONOMIC

Working class and lower middle class

Chronically poor

LESS
OVERALL

FIGURE 2.1   Diagram of social space: the volume and composition of capital. Chart adapted from Bourdieu 1984, 128–29, with US class categories in italics.

and business managers are *not* class differences but are distinctions between different types of capital.

The groundbreaking insight found in Bourdieu's most famous book, *Distinction* (1984), is that the class–status hierarchy is perpetuated, among other ways, by differences in tastes. People feel most comfortable with those who share their tastes in food, humor, media, and clothing. Like congregates with like. Those who make the decisions in any field (whether educational, occupational, intellectual, or artistic) resonate with and reward those whose cultural capital is similar to their own. Conscious intention to discriminate by favoring one's own class is not necessary for privilege to be perpetuated. Bourdieu applied this insight to the distribution of intellectual, artistic, and scientific honors, but it is just as relevant to who gains influence and leadership positions within voluntary activist groups.

Ever since *Distinction* was translated into English there has been a debate over how much his concepts apply to the United States. (See review in Holt

1997.) Bourdieu has been accused of overlooking the contexts of time and place, overgeneralizing from a uniquely French cultural perspective (Gartman 1991; Lamont 2000: 181–87; Reed-Danahay 2005). These critics make good points about the vast cultural diversity of the United States and about Americans' widespread lack of reverence, even disdain, for classical high culture. But Holt (1997) looks empirically at US class-culture differences and asserts that while the particulars are different, Bourdieu's fundamental concepts do apply to the United States.

Any generalization about class and taste will be an overgeneralization. Clearly, working-class Americans don't all have the same tastes; college-educated professionals don't all behave similarly; small business owners don't all share the same political opinions; and so on. To make the theory reflect the complicated social reality we see around us, two elements must be added. One is intersectionality with other identities: we have socially constructed race and gender predispositions as well as class predispositions.

The second essential concept to add is Bourdieu's theory of fields, arenas in which people compete for rewards, in which he uses the metaphor of a sports playing field (Bourdieu 1984: chap. 4; Swartz 1997: chap. 6). A movement tradition such as community organizing is an example of a field. Bourdieu conveyed the importance of such contexts with a faux formula that makes no literal mathematical sense (Swartz 1997: 141n) but which neatly ties together the elements that he believed explain human actions: "(Habitus x Capital) + Field = Practice" (Bourdieu 1984: 101). In other words, our habitual behavior comes from our childhood conditioning, the resources available to us, and the conventions of the arenas in which we participate. Humans create and perpetuate the structures of society, including class cultures, by putting our predispositions into practice, as we deploy our various kinds of capital in whatever fields we enter (Bourdieu 1980). It's very hard to see these processes as they unfold; in particular, it's hard for individuals to see their own predispositions or cultural capital.

I share Bourdieu's assumptions that every class life story leaves people with distinct predispositions that play out in social contexts in varied but nevertheless class-influenced ways. For example, attending a four-year residential college has different effects on the worldview of a first-generation college graduate than on the child of two college graduates.

This theoretical underpinning explains why I put the heaviest weight on formal education and occupation in categorizing people by class. Higher education is a central component of cultural and social capital: it changes what people know, who they know, how they talk, and their level of confidence about political participation—all relevant to activist involvement.

It may seem less obvious why occupation is weighted so heavily, since in this book I'm looking at people in their voluntary associations, not their workplaces. But we are shaped by our work experience, especially by the degree of autonomy we have in our work (Wright 1985). For example, the social world, including activism, looks different to people who are supervised at work than it does to people who manage others (Zweig 2011).

With education and occupation weighted most heavily, and with home-ownership and employer status also taken into consideration, one indicator is conspicuously missing: income. Why didn't I categorize survey respondents by income? Income brackets are not social classes. Income fluctuates over a typical life span, so the lowest income brackets include students and other young PMC people whose incomes will later rise, as well as briefly unemployed professionals and PMC seniors whose incomes used to be higher. Such temporarily low-income, high-cultural-capital people sometimes, especially during recessions, outnumber chronically poor people and struggling working-class people in the lowest income quintiles. In addition, household annual income has become more erratic as job security has eroded. *Average* income over an adult's lifespan correlates with education and occupational level much more closely than does income in any given year (Jacobs and Hacker 2008).

Income is an even weaker class indicator among progressive activists, since activism depends on "biographical availability" (McAdam 1988) and thus is more common among people not currently in the labor force such as students and retired people. In addition, many activists make choices to earn less than their maximum possible income; categorizing them only by income disregards their cultural capital.

Race, *What*, and Gender? Intersectionality Analysis and Class

In the American vernacular, race is often substituted for class, with "black" used as a stand-in for poor and "white" used as a stand-in for middle class. While it's true that people of color are disproportionately poor, and well-off people are disproportionately white (Lui et al. 2006), overgeneralization of these correlations into stereotypes renders invisible both white working-class and poor people—the biggest race/class demographic group in the United States—*and* millions of African American, Latino, Native American, and Asian professionals, as well as the few wealthy people of color. Just as a true understanding of class in the United States requires an analysis of institutionalized racism, a true understanding of race requires a class analysis.

The critical race theory first developed by black feminists offers the useful concept of intersectionality: the insight that race, gender, and other identities are not experienced separately but holistically, from an interwoven social standpoint (Collins 1990; Crenshaw, Gotanda, and Peller 1995). But this insight has been applied most vigorously to race and gender, with class as the neglected stepchild. In "race, class, and gender" studies, class often plays the role of a conjunction, like "and" or "but," linking the primary topics of race and gender. See, for example, Rothenberg's anthology *Race, Class, and Gender in the United States* (1995), in which essays on race and gender outnumber explicit class pieces by a factor of more than twenty to one. When class is invoked in "race, class, and gender" studies, it often refers to the negative financial impact of racism or sexism, not to a distinct and equally important aspect of oppression.

Some African American leftists criticize such obscuring of class and reveal classism within black communities (Cohen 1999; hooks 2000; Dyson 2005). As they point out, identity-based movements that don't tackle class issues end up betraying the interests of the least class-privileged members within the identity group. Strolovitch (2007) studied national advocacy organizations that purported to represent one very broad constituency, such as Latinos or women, and found that the issues affecting the multiply disadvantaged subgroups within the constituency, such as low-income lesbians, got the least attention. Instead, the organizations tended to prioritize issues affecting the most advantaged subgroups. If class is not explicitly looked at, the result is often classism, the devaluing of working-class and poor people's views and needs.

In the United States today, most people label themselves with race and gender terms on which there is widespread consensus, making gender and race into self-aware identities, while class is often undefined, making it nothing but a "class on paper" (Swartz 1997: 149–50). Virtually all survey respondents named their race and gender, but most interviewees did not, when asked, provide a straightforward class label for themselves.

Are There Class Cultures in the United States?

Life experiences vary so much within the huge categories "working class" and "professional middle class" that the odds are high against finding much cultural commonality. People in a particular occupation and a particular region may have very similar tastes and opinions, but classes made up of millions of diverse people are defined only by factual similarities, not by much actual shared human experience. In other words, how likely is it that a white male laid-off autoworker in Detroit would talk like, think like, or act like a

Mexican American female migrant farmworker in California, despite sharing the category "working class"?

A number of empirical studies have investigated this question and found
some class-culture correlations. Almost all of them looked for class cultures
in other institutional settings, such as schools, workplaces, political opinion
polling, or social services, not in voluntary groups.

Lamont interviewed PMC (1992) and working-class (2000) men in the
United States and France. She found that US working-class men believed
in creating moral order, protecting, and providing. Working-class men valued straightforwardness and sometimes saw PMC people as phonies; they
looked down on poor people as undisciplined. PMC men valued ambition
and competitiveness on the one hand but conflict avoidance and being a
team player on the other, a contradictory set of values conditioned by their
workplaces.

Lareau (2003) found a difference in child-rearing practices between
middle-class "concerted cultivation" and working-class "accomplishment
of natural growth." One finding from her meticulous research is that PMC
children are constantly quizzed by adults, who ask question after question to
which the adults know the answers. (For example, "What color is the ba-
nana? That's right, yellow! Good girl!") Thus speech is often seen as performance of individual intelligence in PMC culture. Heath's study of language
use (1983), like Lareau's, found that black and white middle-class parents
were very similar in how they talked with children; class differences were
more striking than race differences. Bettie's (2003) ethnography of working-
class and middle-class Anglo and Mexican American girls at a California
high school corroborated these US class distinctions, although she found
more racial differences within classes than Lareau and Heath did.

Bernstein (1971) defined a linguistic class difference in Britain between
the unfortunately named "restricted code" (in which shorthand stock phrases and repetitive slang are substituted for original sentence creation) and the
"elaborated code" (in which ideas are spelled out more in original, multi-
clause sentences). Macaulay (2005) reviewed other empirical studies and disputed some of Bernstein's specific findings; in particular, he found no class
difference in complexity of sentences or thoughts. But he also found that
working-class and PMC people *do* talk differently in many ways; in particular, PMC British people say "I think" more, and they use more adverbs to
qualify or intensify their speech (such as "quite" and "terribly").

Do these language differences exist in the United States? Jensen (2012)
thinks the answer is yes; she corroborates Bernstein's conclusions, finding that
working-class Americans rely more on body language, emotional expression,

and inferences not spelled out, while PMC people tend to communicate information in more explicit terms, while restraining emotional expression.

Jensen's (2012) shorthand for overall class-culture differences is "becoming versus belonging." That is, PMC people tend to see their lives in terms of individual improvement and accomplishments, and working-class people tend to see their lives more in terms of loyalties to extended family, religious affiliation, ethnicity, and/or neighborhood.

Holt (1998) asked Americans with high or low cultural capital about their living room décor. He discovered that different classes may consume the same things, but they consume them with different meanings. For example, a picture of Elvis Presley may be hung on the wall with admiring or ironic intent. Holt's findings are similar to Peterson and Kern's (1996) idea that the American class variation in taste no longer runs along a low-brow to high-brow spectrum but from univore to omnivore; that is, working-class people are more likely to stick to one coherent set of tastes, sometimes ethnically specific, while PMC people are more likely to pride themselves on being cosmopolitan and multicultural, consuming a wide variety of styles. In "Anything but Heavy Metal," Bryson (1996) found that more highly educated people have fewer musical dislikes, and they value tolerance of varied styles; but they tend to dislike musical genres associated with less-educated fans, such as country and rap.

These studies are all of nonactivist settings. The class-culture generalizations made by Lamont, Lareau, Jensen, Holt, and others may or may not apply to activist groups.

Are There Movement Class Cultures?

Movements exist within wider societies and draw on them for cultural resources, but they also develop movement cultures of their own, which differ to varying degrees from mainstream culture (Lofland 1995). Activist groups, like all groups, have group styles, "recurrent patterns of interaction that arise from a group's shared assumptions about what constitutes good or adequate participation in the group setting" (Eliasoph and Lichterman 2003: 737). It can't be presumed a priori that the class culture(s) of any given social movement will be the same as or different from those of the wider social context.

On one hand, many social movement organizations grow out of preexisting community networks. Even intentionally oppositional countercultures are shaped by the class background of those creating them. On the other hand, social movement organizations are by definition trying to change some aspect of society, and often that means making their internal culture different to varying degrees from that of the mainstream. Activists make choices about how much to form a distinct counterculture versus how much to blend in with mainstream norms (Johnston and Klandermans 1995). Too thin an oppositional subculture may mean the social movement organizations will not be cohesive enough to withstand external or internal pressures; too elaborate and too specific a group culture may push potential allies outside the circle of collective identity.

This dialogue among social movement scholars about movement cultures has not often looked at class.[4] Since the 1990s there has been a valuable "cultural turn" in social movement studies, moving away from looking only at material interests and political contexts and more toward the role of emotions and culture in motivating mobilization and demobilization (Johnston and Klandermans 1995; Jasper 1997; Goodwin, Jasper, and Polletta 2001). But only rarely do cultural analyses of social movements talk in terms of *class* cultures. The few books on class-culture differences in social movements are mostly not well known (Stout 1996; Croteau 1995; Rose 2000; Cummings 2003; Leondar-Wright 2005; Ward 2008). The few widely cited exceptions, including Fantasia (1988) and Lichterman (1996), are less explicit in contrasting class cultures. To draw on the literature about class-culture differences in the wider society (Willis 1981; Heath 1983; Bourdieu 1984; Holt 1997; Lamont 1992 and 2000; Lareau 2003; Jensen 2012) requires translation into the realm of social movement organizations, in which class-status markers, valued forms of cultural capital, and expressions of class culture can be very different than in other settings.

But movement culture does relate to class. In US movements over the last forty years, there has been a correlation between more distinct group culture and more class-privileged members; a counterculture is often a distinctly PMC subculture. A somewhat bohemian, green lifestyle has spread among highly educated and prosperous Americans (Brooks 2001), making leftist movement cultures less different from mainstream PMC culture than activists might imagine. Even when class-privileged leaders intend to implement the opposite of a corporate style, tastes in tactics (Jasper 1997) and methods of operating a group may still impart a distinctly non–working-class style.

CHAPTER 3

Four Class Categories of Activists and Their Typical Group Troubles

If I introduced the surveyed activists as 362 unique personalities, or if I clumped them by race or gender, in each case readers would see different aspects of the same people. Instead, I introduce them according to their commonalities within four class categories: lifelong-working-class, lifelong-professional-range, upwardly mobile, and voluntarily downwardly mobile (VDM). This four-way comparison enables me to explore my hypothesis that there are unseen class cultures operating in US movements for social change. In this chapter I create composite class–cultural profiles of these four main class trajectories, describing their typical demographics, cultural tastes, and most common activist troubles.

Categorizing Activists by Class

To compare activist class cultures, first I had to categorize each group member by class. The survey filled out by 362 meeting participants (available online as appendix 1) included questions about their own and their parents' education and housing, how they spend their time, and their parents' main income source. Based on these data I categorized the group members by class background and current class. (Online appendix 2 summarizes the method of assigning activists to class categories.) Table 3.1 breaks out the typical

Table 3.1   Class categories and their education/occupation indicators

Class category	Typical education level	Typical income sources	Some group members' occupations
Chronic poverty	Less than twelfth grade	Public assistance; part-time low-paid work	Housecleaner; farm laborer; single mother on TANF
Working class	High school degree	Steady wage work	Waitress; factory worker; taxi driver
Lower middle class	Two-year college or vocational certification	Skilled trade; blue-collar small-business owner	Administrative assistant; owner of small print shop; licensed practical nurse
Lower professional	BA from non-flagship public college or nonelite private college	Paraprofessional or middle-management salaried job; white-collar small-business owner	Salaried community organizer; kindergarten teacher; registered nurse supervisor
Professional middle class	BA from private or flagship-public university	Professional or managerial salaried job	Clergy; therapist; executive director of local nonprofit
Upper middle class	Academic or professional graduate degree; elite private schools	High-level professional or managerial position	Tenured university professor; lawyer; top manager of national nonprofit

Note: Retired people were categorized according to their former occupations.

income sources and education levels associated with each class category and gives some examples of typical occupations.

Combining information about respondents' current life and their family of origin generated their class trajectories (upward, downward, or lifelong in the same working-class or professional range). For people who have dramatically risen in class since childhood, I use the label "straddler," coined by Lubrano (2004) to denote professionals who grew up working class.[1] Among those who have dramatically fallen in class, I focus only on the more common activist experience of being *voluntarily* downwardly mobile, meaning that activists' life choices have led them to drop far below their parents' professional class level after college, whether they intentionally chose voluntary poverty or not.

For the majority of informants, there wasn't a big difference between their childhood class and their class at the time of the survey; there was a statistically significant correlation between class background and current class.[2] Online table 3.2 shows the percentage of people from each background who were in each class as adults. Just as the data on US class mobility (Hertz 2006) show, while it's common to rise or fall by one notch, it's rare to move to the far other end of the class spectrum.

Profile of Lifelong-Working-Class Activists:
Respectable Worker Bees or Powerhouse Outlaws

The 85 lifelong-working-class informants were demographically similar to the US working class as a whole: disproportionately women (59%), people of color (56%), with some immigrants and Puerto Ricans (16%). The middle-aged or older majority were virtually all parents. Most were encountered in community-needs or labor-outreach groups, though every movement tradition included some of them. (See figure 3.2 online for a breakdown.)

The activists at the lowest end of this category were those whose families had been poor for at least two generations. Most faced multiple forms of marginalization, such as being overburdened single mothers, undocumented immigrants living in the shadows, and seniors and disabled people with insufficient public assistance. For example, a middle-aged single mother with only four years of primary education, Gabriña, had recently come from the Dominican Republic; neither of her parents had a high school degree. She worked part-time cleaning a building at night and was hoping to get a steady unionized job that would raise her pay up to ten dollars an hour.

Much more common than such lifelong-poverty stories were either a rise out of poverty into the stable working class or a fall into poverty from the higher end of the working-class range. While mobility to the top is rare, churning within the bottom class categories has been common in the last half century, and it is becoming more common (Gosselin 2008).

The white working-class men born in the United States from the 1930s to the 1970s, not surprisingly, tended to fall at the high end of this range, lower middle class (LMC) or close to it, in their adult lives, even if they had been born into poverty. Some had also grown up LMC. For example, Devin, a young clerical worker, had taken some courses at a public four-year college but didn't finish the degree; his mother earned a two-year degree and his father a high-school degree; they owned the house where they raised Devin. There's a huge class difference between Devin's life experience and Gabriña's.

This lifelong-working-class range, from impoverished immigrants of color to enfranchised LMC white men, is so broad that it is surprising to find any cultural commonalities at all among them. Yet they did in fact share some similarities in tastes, attitudes, and activist behavior.

A stranger watching the meetings of these activists through a window would have been more successful in guessing which women were life-long working class than in identifying the working-class men, for two reasons. First, weight correlates with class among women in the United

States (Clarke et al. 2008); professional-middle-class (PMC) women tend to be leaner, and working-class women tend to be heavier. A new manifestation of Veblen's conspicuous consumption (1899) is reflected in the bodily signs of past recreation; the visible effects of hundreds of workouts and decades of fresh-food meals are markers of class privilege. Second, while male meeting participants tended to dress alike in jeans and sneakers, working-class women tended to wear much more eye-catching clothes than the mostly plainer-dressing PMC female activists. A few older working-class women dressed up for meetings as if for church; and some young working-class women made an art form of sexy or decorative clothing. Even at a labor-coalition meeting, where many people wore the same union t-shirt, one middle-aged Latina immigrant cinched hers in with a five-inch-wide white leather belt covered with silver rivets.

Brightness of clothing colors alone would have made a good predictor of class. In one welfare-rights meeting, there was a color contrast between two middle-aged white women wearing t-shirts over worn sweatpants: the large woman in the bright-turquoise shirt over pink sweats turned out to be lifelong working class; the bony woman in the white shirt over gray sweats turned out to come from a PMC background. Working-class women of color also tended to wear more and bigger jewelry, in particular large hoop earrings.

Worker Bees, Some Dealing with Disempowerment

Quietly sitting in the background of many meetings were lifelong-working-class activists who saw themselves as worker bees, not expecting to play major or public roles. Some expressed self-doubts and insecurities, seeing themselves as lacking the experience needed for bigger activist roles. In a study of welfare-rights groups, Cummings (2003) found that many poor women held themselves back from formal leadership roles because they didn't want to stick out from their peers; they were more comfortable hanging back together.

While some quiet working-class people were disempowered, other self-confident working-class activists saw meetings as a place to stop in to find out what was going on and get their marching orders. Their listening was active preparation for other roles. In particular, some men in blue-collar occupations seemed to fit this mold: they sat silent during meetings, leading me to imagine them to be disempowered or new to activism; but when I talked with them, some turned out to have good energy for follow-up activities, such as picketing, contacting officials, or making banners. There is sometimes an informal division of labor in which meetings are the turf of the college-educated members. One quintessential example: at the very moment when the mostly white and all college-educated-professional board of Green Homes Green World was discussing their disturbing shortage of board members of color, there were several low-income volunteers of color in the very same building doing hands-on work toward the group's mission.

This turf division wouldn't be problematic if it didn't lead to an underrepresentation of directly affected and marginalized people in making decisions about groups' priorities.

Powerhouse Working-Class Women Leaders

Not all lifelong-working-class activists fell into this predominant pattern of quiet worker bees; others were vocal activists, and a few were powerhouse radical leaders.

Kick-ass working-class women had founded some community-needs groups. Three white women fit this profile most exactly: Dorothea of City Power, Brandy of Grassroots Resistance, and Elaine of Women Safe from Violence.[3] Their differences from PMC leaders suggest that these working-class leaders' shared attitudes and behaviors reflect working-class culture. They all believed that social change would come through grassroots empowerment. With strong, charismatic personalities, they had remained in leadership so long by fighting off challengers.

Six or seven other middle-aged or older lifelong-working-class women also fit this profile of longtime strong leaders; one was African American, one Latina, but otherwise all were white women. No working-class men were observed in such major leadership roles. I don't know whether this is a movement-wide race/gender pattern or whether it's a coincidence due to the small sample size that the powerhouse lifelong-working-class leaders in the study tended to be white women.

The Respectable/Outlaw Spectrum and Rooted or Cosmopolitan Tastes

Some working-class interviewees, in particular those who seemed more disempowered, prided themselves on their propriety and moral uprightness. Others, in particular the most empowered, prided themselves on being outsiders and outlaws, fighting the powers that be.

The archetypes of respectability were certain older African American and Latina Christian women; but a few men, youths, and white people expressed such traditional values as well. Their prior community involvements mostly weren't in political groups but in civic or religious organizations. To them, activism seemed to be part of their upward mobility, allowing them to simultaneously network with well-connected people and to enact their value of helping others, "lifting as we climb." For example, when Brandon, the young black loan administrator with a two-year business degree, was asked about his prior organizational involvements, he listed a black fraternity, the United Way, and the March of Dimes. He joined the more political Workforce Development Task Force at the request of his pastor; this religious path to activism is common among working-class people.

In terms of tastes, the respectable lifelong-working-class survey respondents were not the renowned cosmopolitan omnivores (Peterson and Kern 1996; Bryson 1996). Their most common favorite food was pasta, followed by rice and beans—a sign of the "taste for necessity" (Bourdieu 1984: 374–76). Rooted in their ethnic cultures, many specified their own ethnic dishes as their favorite foods; for example, a Jamaican wrote "ackee and salt fish," a second-generation Polish American wrote "kielbasa," and an African American wrote "greens with ham hocks."

Similarly, their television tastes were a mix of ethnic (BET, Spanish soap operas) and mainstream shows. Compared with other classes, more of them liked crime and hospital dramas, such as *CSI*, *America's Most Wanted*, and especially *Law and Order*. (Just to shake up stereotypes, let me mention that three working-class people listed the History Channel, "nature on PBS," and Bill Moyers.) Unlike anyone in other class categories, several answered the question about favorite TV or radio with station call numbers, for example "1230 AM"—evidence supporting some sociolinguists' theory that working-class language use is more specific, requiring local insider knowledge to understand (Bernstein 1971).

US-born working-class people tended to live in or near their hometown. Putting together their locations with their food and media tastes, the word "rooted" sums up the respectable working-class informants' culture: rooted in their ethnic background, rooted in extended family, and rooted in mainstream popular culture.

The working-class outlaws, fewer in number, tended to be culturally different than the respectable working-class activists. Most were more empowered and experienced activists,[4] and they fell a little higher on the class spectrum, more often LMC. The outlaws combined a pride in personal toughness with more radical ideologies. A few had a working-class identity.

In cultural tastes, the outlaws were much more similar to PMC and VDM activists than to other working-class activists. (And, indeed, some of them may have voluntarily remained working class, defiantly refusing upward mobility.) Their favorite foods didn't necessarily relate to their ethnic back-grounds; four preferred a vegetarian health food (e.g., tofu). A few also had oppositional music tastes that lined up with some PMC and VDM radicals' tastes, such as Tupac Shakur, David Rovics, and Rage Against the Machine. Some didn't watch TV ("corporate crap," wrote one on her survey), while others preferred leftist shows such as *Democracy Now!* and satiric shows such as *The Daily Show* and *The Simpsons.* But these outsider tastes were less com-mon than among PMC-background activists; some working-class outlaws were like other working-class people in preferring mainstream crime dra-mas. Like those in the PMC and VDM categories, the outlaws tended to be uprooted, living far from their hometowns. Most were more culturally similar to college-educated radicals than to the respectable activists of their own class.

Overall, answers to the survey question "Are you religious?" correlated with class: lifelong-working-class people were more likely to be religious than people who were or had been PMC. Catholic was the most frequent denomination, followed by Pentecostal, Baptist, and African Methodist Epis-copal. The strongest religion correlation was with class background:[5] the lower an activist's class background level, the more likely he or she was to say yes to the religion question. This corroborates others' findings on class and religion (Lamont 2000: 40). But within this overall tendency, the working-class outlaws were more likely to say no, they weren't religious.

An example of a religious, respectable working-class activist was Mar-tina, a young African Caribbean immigrant who said her prior organiza-tional involvement was with "the Girl Brigade, it's a group of girls from the church. . . . We go and tell people about Jesus. . . . We try to inspire young girls from the peer pressure . . . so they don't get in trouble."

Within working-class-majority labor and community-needs groups, the most common pattern was that the leaders were not religious, while most rank-and-file members were Christians. Nevertheless, I didn't observe any culture clashes on the touchy topic of belief in Jesus. Community-needs and labor meetings did not include prayers, which was perhaps a sign of defer-ence to leaders.

Ideological Differences but Not Barriers in Working-Class Groups

Instead of ideological common ground, working-class activists tend to be tied to groups by a different set of bonds: personal ties and belief in leaders' trustworthiness. Solidarity, unity, and strength in numbers defined many working-class activists' understandings of how social change happens

(Fantasia 1988; Rose 2000). They seemed to see activism as analogous to a team of sled dogs who get somewhere only by all pulling in the same direction. Thus, solidarity sometimes meant suppressing individual dissent in favor of standing together and backing leaders. Allowing political differences to divide the group was seen as foolish.

I'm so used to categorizing people along the left-right political spectrum that it was startling to see the sense of kinship and affinity between the respectable and outlaw members of community and labor groups. To my eye, these Christians and these atheists or pagans, these respectable community uplifters and these foul-mouthed outlaws, seemed quite different politically—and probably many did disagree on controversial issues such as abortion and gay marriage. Certainly they disagreed on the role of religion in public life. But many of them simply didn't have the habit, so common among PMC activists, of spotlighting ideological differences and polarizing groups over them. It appears that for many lifelong-working-class activists, the salient spectrum ran not from blue to red but from acting *for* the community to acting *against* the community.

Here's a story from a 2008 national political-party convention protest that illustrates this way of dividing friend from foe, this lack of ideological barriers, in working-class communities. On the streets during the protests, I ran into a lifelong-working-class African American activist whom I'd met at a local community-needs group meeting. I asked him what he thought of a local anarchist direct action group. He answered positively, saying that he liked them very much and described some ways that the group had supported his group with concrete aid, such as Food Not Bombs–style free meals at events. Then we came into an intersection where thirty white people were in the street, all with bandanas over their faces. We saw some throw bottles and other objects at cars, and specifically at a white stretch limousine, while others overturned a small dumpster into the street. Without saying a word both of us started backing away from the intersection until we were out of tear gas range, and I turned on my audio recorder to catch whatever happened next. Then he asked me incredulously, "What were they *doin*'? They were throwing stuff at *cars*? . . .Where did they get that from, to throw *that*? Who *was* that?" I showed him a flyer I had taken from a phone pole the day before, in which the direct action group I had asked him about earlier called on protestors to blockade intersections with the goal of preventing delegates from getting into the convention. He groaned a long guttural groan, downward from low to very low pitch, "Ohhhh-ohhhhhhh. They're trying to *block*? Block routes? But that dumpster and all that, that's just . . ." and his voice faded out in astonished disapproval.

To me it was surprising that his earlier positive comments contrasted so much with this negative reaction to seeing property damage in the streets. The flyer calling for street blockades had been stapled by the hundreds on phone polls in his neighborhood. In both convention cities, for several months before the Republican National Convention and the Democratic National Convention, mainstream media had used scare tactics about protestors' alleged dangerous plans, publicizing the realistic possibility of street confrontations as well as politicians' imagined fears of much worse (such as violence against delegates and blowing up buildings, not contemplated by any activist group as far as I know). I don't know whether or not this man had run into any such coverage, which had permeated television, radio, and newspapers to an extent that seemed hard to miss. But it seemed that he hadn't compared various protest groups' political lines with his own beliefs, because he had seen their supportive actions first-hand, and his habitual way of dividing friend from foe was "whose actions are for us and whose actions are against us."[6]

In working-class-majority groups, left-right ideological differences and theological disagreements didn't usually divide groups, and the basis for group membership was personal and pragmatic, not philosophical.

Profile of the Lifelong-Professional Range: Polished Confidence or Self-Effacing Avoidance of Dominance

There are US voluntary groups whose members are prosperous upper professionals in which a lawyer who's the daughter of a doctor wouldn't be uncommon—for example, suburban parent-teacher organizations and charities that hold gala fundraisers—but such mainstream elite groups are not included in this book. By narrowing the focus to activist social change groups, I ended up looking primarily at a more marginal set of PMC people, most of whom brought to groups more subtle and misrecognized class-cultural problems than the upper class's reputed entitlement and snobbery.

All 140 respondents who fell into the lifelong-professional range—from lower-professional (LP) to upper-middle class (UMC)—had been raised by college-educated homeowners in white-collar occupations.[7] But their parents' occupations ranged widely, from small-town newspaper reporter to diplomat, from kindergarten teacher to Ivy League professor. And while a few respondents were enjoying high professional success at the time, as professors, top managers, and lawyers, most were moderately paid community organizers, K-12 teachers, social workers, computer programmers, and the like.

PMC activists' financial situations varied widely as well. A few UMC people revealed a trust fund, inherited wealth, or a vacation home. At the other end of the spectrum, some of the PMC students or recent grads, in particular convention protestors, were currently broke. (I heard that one twenty-five dollar interview fee covered spaghetti and sauce for that night's dinner for six at a group house.) Almost the only universal among these 140 activists was lots of education: an academic four-year program (completed or currently underway) in all cases, and quite often a graduate degree as well. These activists' cultural capital usually far exceeded their financial capital.

Demographically they tended to be US born; they were 86% white or Asian, only 11% black or Latino. About one-third were young adults; most were middle-aged. Six in ten were female.

The theory that the middle class serves the capitalists, assisting them in exploiting the proletariat, would probably not ring true to these activists' life experience, as almost none worked for a large private-sector firm. Their experience of working as a professional or manager was usually for government agencies, universities, hospitals, human services providers, unions, or 501(c)(3) nonprofits. Yet, if one criterion for class domination is organizational control (Wright 1985: 88–93), then these PMC interviewees weren't just higher on a ladder of advantages, they were actually in charge of shaping working-class people's experiences in significant ways (Kivel 2004) by providing their social services, running their classrooms, managing their nonprofit workplaces, leading their religious services, and organizing them into voluntary groups and unions.

The PMC activists tended to have very uprooted lives, thanks to going away to a residential college. The vast majority didn't live anywhere near where they were born, or were born far from where their parents were born, in most cases both. Their tastes were uprooted too; they tended to be cosmopolitan omnivores (Peterson and Kern 1996). Their favorite meals tended to be ethnic food unrelated to their own heritage, in particular Asian cuisines (mostly Indian, Thai, and sushi), followed by Mexican and Italian food. Vegetarian and vegan food were also frequent favorites.

Similarly, in listing their favorite music, some cosmopolitan PMC activists mentioned world music. Many PMC whites loved historical African American greats such as Miles Davis, but very few mentioned any contemporary black artists. PMC musical tastes were very diverse; only Ani DiFranco had more than three fans in the pool of 140 people. Some older white people preferred nostalgic music popular during the anti–Vietnam War movement, such as Bob Dylan, Phil Ochs, or Neil Young.

While working-class and straddler respondents usually specified a TV show in answer to the survey question about favorite television or radio show, PMC respondents were more likely to mention radio, with NPR the most common favorite, *Democracy Now!* next, and the BBC and progressive community stations also mentioned. The television shows with three or more PMC fans were *The Office, Lost,* Bill Moyers on PBS, *The Daily Show,* and the *Colbert Report.* Since the latter three shows cover current events, and since news programs were mentioned most often by this group of respondents, it's clear that lifelong-PMC activists were consuming far greater amounts of news coverage than activists in other class trajectories.

Unsurprisingly, almost half of lifelong-PMC activists were observed in global or local cause groups. Only one in five was observed in a community or labor group.

But no type of group, indeed no single group, lacked lifelong-PMC members. (See online figure 3.3 for a breakdown of where they were observed.) They made up more than a fifth of meeting participants in community-needs groups; almost a third in labor-outreach groups; over a third in anarchist groups; and about two-thirds in staff advocacy, progressive, nonprofit, and militant anti–imperialist groups. As the biggest class category of activists overall, they could be found everywhere.

That Polished Air of Confidence

Some lifelong-PMC activists, in particular those from a UMC or higher-PMC background, spoke with a confident air of authority, commanding the attention of other group members. For example, when Gordon, a lawyer, and Melissa, an executive director, spoke during Green Homes Green World meetings, others tended to turn their heads toward them to listen. Though the two didn't push or argue, much less raise their voices, their opinions usually prevailed.

UMC and higher-PMC activists were more likely to have an "'opinionated' habitus" (Bourdieu 1984: 415) and to speak with "the authorized speech of status-generated competence, a powerful speech which helps to create what it says" (413). While such high levels of self-confidence were mostly found in white men from the top of the professional range, some women and people of color displayed it too.

A number of young activists whose parents both had graduate degrees seemed impressively empowered and knowledgeable, given their brief prior experience. During the convention protest planning, one inexperienced UMC white student, McKayla, frequently negotiated with public officials, sometimes confronting them, sometimes charming them into approving a protest permit.

Some confident white PMC activists fought to win, seeming to accept the use of power to wage an internal struggle. When the interfaith Workforce Development Task Force blew up after its final contentious meeting (described in chapter 1), one reason was that several PMC and UMC white men, including Noah and Sherman, didn't take Jeremiah's cease-and-desist order quietly, but argued vociferously against him, and later went over his head to the Citywide Interfaith Coalition's top leaders. Similarly, Lea, who came from a wealthy family, spoke very sharply at an Action Center meeting about a disagreement with Carrie, and also told Carrie off to her face.

Some confident high-end PMC activists were seen as arrogant and entitled by other interviewees—but fewer than might be expected. One PMC white man, Rufus, was described by some other Labor and Community United members as "difficult," "righteous," and "overbearing." But such criticisms were rare. It wasn't actually confident high-PMC people but unassimilated uprooted straddlers who were most often criticized as domineering by fellow group members.

One interpretation is that confidence isn't necessarily obnoxious if it's displayed without arrogance. Some self-confident high-PMC activists were strikingly popular in their groups. For example, white PMC men Fred and Tony were founders and leaders of groups with large working-class and straddler memberships; members mostly raved about their leadership skills in interviews. Those two and some similar PMC male leaders shared a style of communicating: firm, upbeat, and, most important, radiating respect for others. Compared with the kick-ass working-class women leaders described above, these male PMC leaders related to members less personally, expressing collegial respect rather than affection; they were less likely to swear, criticize, or hug; they were calmer, less heated. They were quite forceful, but coolly so, with no edge of aggression or harshness.

Confident, popular high-PMC and UMC women were praised by other group members for playing conflict-resolution roles during meetings, suggesting compromises, saying soothing things, and explaining the combatants to each other. For example, during the Citywide Interfaith Coalition conflict, white PMC technical expert Stacy said, "I totally understand what you're saying" three times. She assertively told Sherman to back down and show Jeremiah more respect. In interviews, Brandon called her a "peacemaker"; Jeremiah said he felt understood by her and added, "I admire her."

Sometimes people of color from the highest class backgrounds were the most beloved group members. For example, within the contentious group

Easthaver Demands Justice, two smooth-speaking professional members of color seemed to be many people's favorite group members: Mia, a South Asian UMC immigrant, a nurturing conflict mediator as well as an inspiring big picture thinker; and Rodney, an African American in a top management job, who was the calm, humorous voice of reason during disagreements.

It's been said that people like to join a winning team, and all these confident, positive UMC and high-PMC people may have seemed like winners to the interviewees who admired them. And compared with people from other classes, it seemed easier for the confident high-professional activists to talk hopefully about a positive future vision. The people with the easiest lives, less damaged by the class system, may sometimes be the ones to bring the gifts of hope and vision to social movements.

Inconspicuous Workhorses with a Lack of Pizzazz

Not all lifelong-PMC were so confident and polished. Another cluster were self-effacing and ambivalent, or were so understated that they faded into the background or deliberately held themselves back to avoid dominating. Most of these lower-key activists were white people at the lower end of the professional spectrum. Unclear communication characterized these PMC activists' speech in various ways, such as mumbling, low volume, being tentative, contradicting themselves, speaking in a monotone, and complaining so indirectly that it was impossible to tell what was displeasing them.

Most groups included one or more members who fit this profile: a low-key lower-professional (LP) woman, usually white, usually middle-aged, who played a central role in the group, working an unusually large number of hours behind the scenes without being a publicly recognized leader. These women's roles in their groups included being the treasurer, maintaining the database, fund-raising, researching and sharing technical expertise on the group's issue, and teaching group-process skills. Some were employed by the group, sometimes as the one and only employee who played all staff roles, including bookkeeping and managing computer systems. During the convention protests, some white LP women served as street medics or gave legal aid to arrested people. Some were low-key leaders of their groups; some were followers. In any case, their groups were leaning on them. Each of the working-class leaders had one or more of these women quietly backing them up, doing their organizational work.

Most of these female workhorses wore notably drab clothing, usually well-worn jeans with t-shirts or button-down shirts in earth colors, with a little small jewelry or none at all. The few exceptions wore third world craft items or business-casual slacks. Their hair either hung down or was cropped short; except for a few women older than sixty-five, none had chemically styled hair. Contrasting them with most working-class women was like comparing a female and male mallard duck, inconspicuous drab versus vivid colors meant to catch eyes.

Thirty years earlier, these plain personal styles would have clearly been a feminist statement, a refusal to fulfill the feminine mandate to be decorative or sexy; and no doubt some of the middle-aged women first adopted this style during the heyday of second-wave feminism. But in 2007 and 2008 their style didn't seem to be a gender rebellion; none described themselves as feminists. If they had been asked about their clothing, I would guess, based on their other political values, that many of them would probably have talked about rejecting consumerism, avoiding a mainstream corporate image, and not wanting to show off their difference from grassroots group members. In other words, fading into the background was more of a class statement than a gender statement.

These LP white women were also inconspicuous in other ways besides personal style. In fact, many were living quite interesting lives, yet compared with other activists they tended to come across as boring. Many had traveled internationally; many had been arrested for civil disobedience; some were lesbians; some were artists. But they had such dry ways of talking (some polite and feminine, some nerdy and intellectual, some no-nonsense practical) that such life experience wasn't very visible within their groups. I heard one low-key LP woman give a public speech—a cogent radical analysis delivered in a mumbling monotone—and had trouble concentrating on her message. Eliasoph (1998: 43–44) found that her activist informants used plain speech to signal an egalitarian ethic; this may have been the case with these low-key women as well.

A moderate form of voluntary downward mobility, high in education but lower in profession, was common among these low-key workhorse women. This wasn't always a chosen lifestyle: recent college graduates of course tended to be renters with lower-level jobs; and some LPs were no doubt "blocked aspirants" (Gouldner 1979) who had unsuccessfully tried to climb the class ladder. But the evidence reveals an element of choice in many slightly downwardly mobile PMC stories. Given a choice between a better-paying corporate career and lower-paying work that better reflected their values, they had taken the second choice. These income-limiting choices were quite different than the more extreme VDM category profiled in the next section, which included drastic off-the-grid lifestyles as well as sometimes intentional avoidance of professional occupations or financial prosperity. These lifelong-PMC activists had chosen a more modest course of downward mobility. Some did professional work, such as psychological, occupational, or art therapy, part-time to free up time for activism or art; some worked lower-paying jobs meaningful to them. Some nonprofit and union staffers, such as Rodney and Owen, were so elite educated, male, and impressive that a high-professional career would clearly have been an option for them, but their values led them to stay in lower-salaried social change jobs. Others, mostly women, had chosen to work as social workers or teachers; some women were nevertheless prosperous because they were married to professional men.

None of this is new in the social history of US elite classes. Nineteenth- and twentieth-century social roles for PMC and owning-class women as volunteers and human services professionals (Ostrander 1984) continued in a new form in these women's lives. While their PMC great-grandmothers might disapprove of the causes to which they were devoted, they would recognize and approve of making career aspirations secondary to community needs, as many of the great-grandmothers had themselves done in earlier generations (Faderman 1999).

A tiny number of men, transgender people, people of color, and activists from other class trajectories also played this understated, behind-the-scenes role, but by and large these inconspicuous workhorses were PMC white women. I almost missed seeing this race/gender/class-cultural pattern. It's easy to overlook them because of their striking lack of pizzazz. But perhaps the other reason I almost missed them is that I am one of them. Contemplating them as a subcultural cluster made me want to run right out and buy some more colorful clothes, and maybe a motorcycle.

While it's helpful to serve a group by quietly taking care of its organizational matters, lack of pizzazz and avoidance of public leadership also have downsides. As chapter 6 discusses, a predisposition to avoid showiness and to hold back from dominating is sometimes ineffective in empowering others; it can lead to cross-class misunderstanding and can sometimes even strengthen PMC influence in a mixed-class group.

Profile of Straddlers: Pushing Moral Certainty or Feeling Fortunate

Activist groups are full of first-generation college graduates and students, upwardly mobile and straddling the two class experiences of their working-class childhoods and their professional adulthoods (Lubrano 2004; Jensen 2012).

Straddlers were observed in every type of group: they were the most common in labor-outreach groups, where 29 percent of members were straddlers.

They were least common in anarchist groups, where only one survey respondent was a straddler. About one in five or six members of community-needs groups, progressive global or local cause groups, and staff antipoverty advocacy groups were straddlers. (See figure 3.4 online.)

The race and gender makeup of this pool of 53 straddlers was almost exactly the same as in the whole pool of activists (about 70% white and 30% people of color; more women than men). But they tended to be older than the whole pool: over a third were seniors, and over 40 percent were middle-aged; fewer than one-quarter were in their twenties or thirties. Only a few were immigrants themselves, but almost a quarter of them were the children of immigrants.

Straddlers' tastes were much more mainstream than their fellow college graduates in the lifelong-PMC group. Their favorite meals, like working-class activists', were conventional comfort foods from their own ethnic backgrounds, not PMC omnivore tastes: the foods most often mentioned were pasta, ice cream, and turkey. Unlike the white PMC lovers of international food, the straddlers who preferred enchiladas were actually Mexican American.

Similarly, their musical favorites were the mainstream artists most popular among their age bracket and ethnic group: Bob Marley was chosen by a Jamaican immigrant; Frank Sinatra, the Beatles, and Johnny Cash by older white men; two older Chicanos wrote "Mexican"; and an older Irish American wrote "Irish country music." Only a very few chose explicitly radical artists such as Dave Rovics or Rage Against the Machine. About half the straddlers had favorite television shows with massive popular audiences, but with more comedy and upbeat themes than the working-class crime dramas: *Seinfeld*, *Heroes*, *Dancing with the Stars*, and *Top Model*. The other half had news-oriented tastes similar to the PMC favorites (PBS, *Democracy Now!*, NPR, and *The Daily Show*). Similarly, about half were religious and half weren't.

These tastes show much less rejection of the dominant culture than is seen in the PMC or VDM groups and much more straightforward ethnic identities. Perhaps consuming entertainment and food similar to the common fare in their childhood families and communities was a way of staying in touch with their working-class roots.

Straddlers Who Push Moral Certainties in Their Groups

I had an initial hypothesis that straddlers would tend to serve as class-bicultural bridge people, using their mixed-class experience to explain one class to another, and using the cultural capital from their education and professional experience to confidently play mediator roles.

Was I ever wrong! There were only two or three examples, in all the observed meetings and all the interviewees' stories, where a straddler played such a mediating bridge role. By contrast, there were many examples of straddlers playing very strong roles in their groups, pushing a moral certainty that they linked with their working-class backgrounds. True believers in some set of values, many were at the center of their groups' conflicts. Some tried to be the conscience of their group, persistently calling on the group to be true to its principles, sometimes gently and sometimes vehemently. A few were seen by other members as obnoxious, haranguing ideologues.

The story in chapter 1 in which Jeremiah scolded the Workforce Development Task Force for not following the Citywide Interfaith Coalition's community organizing method is a good example of a straddler with moral certainty pushing a group to adhere to his values. The more pragmatic people who pushed back were all nonstraddlers. Jeremiah was no longer working-class, but he saw his "people power" advocacy as a way to stay true to his community of origin. What other members saw as an obnoxious, bullying power play he saw as remembering where he came from.

Some straddlers spoke with awareness of how their working-class roots, and sometimes their ethnic identities as well, led them to identify with the currently working-class members of their groups and to be their fierce defenders. Hannah, a young Latina organizer, referred to her class and ethnic roots in describing her reactions to Rufus, a domineering white PMC man: "I'll be honest, I'm a harsh critic [of Rufus] because . . . I think as a Latina . . . 'Who *is* this white man trying to run this African American organization?'. . . I *am* protective of Latinos. I *am* protective of African Americans and low-class. And who am I to speak? Because . . . my parents were working people."

How assertively straddlers pushed their moral certainty was associated with two aspects of their life stories: how unassimilated or assimilated into PMC culture they were, and how uprooted from their families and childhood communities.

By "straddler" Lubrano means established professionals like himself, people who have come very far from their working-class roots and now fit into their new professional/managerial class milieu. But some working-class people get college degrees (in particular as nonresidential older students, at public colleges, and/or in vocational fields) and yet remain fairly unassimilated into PMC culture. Such unassimilated straddlers continue to have some aspects of a working-class life after gaining a four-year degree, such as renting in a working-class neighborhood, working a working-class job, and/or keeping their working-class friends and cultural tastes.

Culturally, such borderline straddlers were similar in some ways to lifelong-working-class people: some spoke with the accents of their childhood neighborhoods; many lacked interest in group-process debates; for some, their involvements had come through one-on-one relationships or through issues personally affecting them and their families. They seemed to keep many working-class strengths while gaining through higher education the additional confidence and skills to play stronger activist roles. One such example was Laverne, a black woman who had steadily gotten more involved with community groups since going to vocational public college in middle age. Higher education combined with enduring connections to working-class communities sometimes produced activists with the best of both worlds. But in other cases the resulting mix of class cultures was problematic. Sometimes straddlers had lost the rootedness that stabilizes and constrains many lifelong-working-class activists; they were not just *unassimilated* straddlers but *uprooted* straddlers, with no accountability to neighborhood, workplace, or extended family. In their families' class journeys, these activists may be the Moses generation, those who have left the land of bondage but won't live to enter the Promised Land.

Some of these uprooted, unassimilated straddlers had gained typical PMC faults, such as ideological rigidity and impersonality, without losing typical working-class faults, such as a quick mistrust trigger and interpreting disagreements in personal terms. Harsh critique plus thin skin adds up to a syndrome best described by the playground taunt "you can dish it out, but you can't take it." As a result, as chapter 9 illustrates, the uprooted and unassimilated straddlers were the class trajectory most likely to be identified as problematic hotheads by other group members. With neither working-class roots to stabilize them nor the smooth confidence of lifelong-PMC cultural capital, they risked being seen, fairly or unfairly, as the loose cannons of the Left.

In the story in chapter 1 about Dirk's overbearing and allegedly deceptive behavior, he exemplifies this pattern of borderline straddlers who play the role of problematic hotheads in activist groups. He had completed four years of nonresidential public college but had only held working-class jobs, and he lived far from his family, making him both unassimilated and uprooted.

Other straddlers were also criticized for extreme misbehavior. For example, Carrie threatened to call the police on fellow activists and Tye threatened to kick someone's ass. Such unassimilated straddlers were going beyond the usual, accepted ways of waging conflict in working-class communities and in progressive groups; they pushed their sense of moral certainty in a way that fellow activists saw as problematic. Straddler strengths—class-bicultural perspectives, working-class anger amplified with new words and new confidence from PMC cultural capital—sometimes seemed wasted if expressed in excessively antagonistic ways.

All straddlers have to make sense of the contrasting class environments they encounter, but the meanings they draw from the straddler experience vary. Some of the most intense conflicts within groups had a pair of uprooted, unassimilated straddlers at the center of the storm, each pushing a different way of being true to working-class people or values. An example from an explosive national political convention protest-planning intergroup conflict illustrates how varied straddlers' moral certainties can be. Two young men each invoked loyalty to their working-class roots to explain their decisions about which convention protest group to join, but in diametrically opposite ways.

Porter, a white man in the first generation of his family to go to college, was relatively assimilated into PMC culture, but as an uprooted straddler living far from his family, he shared with less assimilated straddlers the trait of pushing moral certainty within groups. He was one of three founders of The People's Convention to push most insistently for a stronger nonviolence pledge during convention protests. To Porter, nonviolence was a class issue. He was critical of radical groups that verbally or physically attacked police, US troops, or veterans. To him, "unconditional nonviolence" meant respecting working people who were just doing their jobs. He practiced what he preached: during protest events, I watched Porter walk up to cops, offer to share his water, and say things like, "How are you doing with this heat, officer?" and "Thank you for watching out for us." Needless to say, this was quite different than how some other protesters talked to the police.

Contrast Porter's way of framing his hybrid class identity with that of Emilio, another young upwardly mobile college student, actually the son of straddlers. Emilio prided himself on both keeping the toughness he learned on the streets of his poor urban neighborhood *and* learning new ways as an adult activist in Stand Up Fight Back (SUFB), a militant convention protest group: "You know I didn't have the best childhood. . . . I grew up around people who . . . were quick to fight. They were quick to be very primitive. . . . And me, trying to evolve as a human being . . . trying to say 'No, we can't be quick to fight'. . . [but] my primitive instinct is to say we need to kick this kid's ass. . . . Unfortunately my anger can get the best of me."

Emilio had a strong outlaw identity, but as a college graduate, he was both more self-righteous and more threatening than the typical lifelong-working-class outlaw. Like other unassimilated straddlers, he held on to some working-class cultural traits. To explain his activism, he referred to family members and friends wounded in Iraq, a moral shock affecting people he knew personally, akin to how lifelong-working-class activists tended to describe their activist origins. Like many working-class interviewees, he revered his group's founders and loyally rejected all criticism of them. His perspective on the intergroup conflicts was that the stakes were so life-and-death serious that it was foolish to get hung up on unimportant ideological distinctions, a common working-class view. His understanding of how change happens fit the working-class unity frame: "I don't even understand how people want to divide. I mean we have power in numbers. The only thing I see that matters is a mass show of participation."

Growing up, he was taught a masculine warrior ethos from soldiers in his family, but he had reinterpreted it to reflect his family's shift from the working class to the professional middle class: "I'm not going to follow blindly anymore. . . . If anything, I'm giving the orders." True to the PMC personalist mode (Lichterman 1996), his ultimate loyalty was to his own ideals. He drew ideological lines in the sand; for example, he regarded groups with nonviolence pledges as liberal sellouts.

Emilio's way of defining a hybrid class identity was very different than Porter's: a transformed warrior ethic of disciplined aggression rather than pushing for respect for workers and being the conscience of the group; insistence on unity and loyalty rather than a commitment to civility during disagreements.

Others in their groups guessed that Emilio grew up poor and that Porter was middle class, probably because of their ethnic difference. But Porter actually came from a lower rung on the class ladder than Emilio, whose father became a lawyer and a homeowner during Emilio's adolescence. Porter, as a white man with a gentle manner, could pass more easily for lifelong PMC, but in fact he was raised by hourly wage earners with high school diplomas. Their contrasts show how relying on assumptions about race and class, instead of facts, can muddy the class dynamics of a situation.

Smiling at Good Fortune: Rooted and/or Assimilated Straddlers

The uprooted, unassimilated straddlers pushing their certainties in helpful and unhelpful ways made up only about four-tenths of all straddlers. They stand out because of their forceful roles, not their numbers. The other straddlers, the majority, were either more deeply rooted in working-class communities or more assimilated into professional life, or both.

Some straddlers, in particular people of color, still lived where they grew up, and several organizers were doing outreach to working-class people matching their own ethnicity—the most rooted straddlers. Others had achieved high professional status as professors, lawyers, local politicians, or executive directors, or middling professional status as teachers, social workers, or nonprofit managers; some of these full-time employed professionals—the most assimilated straddlers—now lived and socialized with PMC suburbanites. A few fit both categories, both rooted and assimilated, such as Katrina, a Latina executive director who worked and owned a home in a mostly low-income neighborhood where people of her national heritage were the majority.

Comparing these rooted and/or assimilated straddlers with the lifelong-PMC activists in similar occupations, there's a difference in emotional tone. These straddlers seem more contented with their lives and their activism. Like the loyal working-class worker bees, they appeared to have little desire to make waves inside their groups. They criticized their own groups much less often than did uprooted, unassimilated straddlers or lifelong-PMC and VDM activists. Perhaps because they perceived their careers to be going well, they didn't seem as ego invested in their voluntary groups as did many other activists. Or perhaps cross-class experience sometimes imparts resilience. My composite impression of these contented straddlers, who were disproportionately US-born Latinos, is a lot of big relaxed smiles. Their personalities ranged from jovial jokesters to serene spiritual women to curious leftist intellectuals, but the commonality was a happy affect.

My interpretation of this upbeat affect is that some straddlers regard themselves as lucky. In a visceral way unknown to people from professional backgrounds, straddlers with satisfying and/or well-paid work feel fortunate to have escaped their childhood circumstances. They think they dodged a bullet, and it shows. When I interviewed a Latina social worker, Shirley, at her small single-family home on a tree-lined street and asked how she liked living there, she said, "It's what I dreamed about as a little girl, looking out the window at the projects—so I got my dream!"

It's not surprising that a well-paid lawyer or professor from a working-class background would exude a glow of gratitude, but even some straddlers with insecure nonprofit jobs described themselves as fortunate. Hannah, a Latina straddler employed as an organizer with Labor and Community United, said of her position, "I'm secure for at least two years. Two, three years . . . so this is a semipermanent thing. . . . I like [my job]."

In a chapter titled "Duality: The Never-Ending Struggle with Identity," Lubrano interrupts his tales of straddlers torn between two worlds, feeling at home nowhere, to say, "You'll find among the limbo set people who are *totally at ease*, despite the duality. When I meet such a man, I linger in his presence, hoping to glean a secret or two. . . . Self-possessed and centered, they easily handle the dichotomy of their past and present circumstances. For them, it just happens. For the rest of us, however, duality is hard work." In this investigation, a subset of straddlers also seemed to feel at home and at peace.

Profile of Voluntarily Downwardly Mobile Activists

Some college-educated respondents had made choices that drastically lowered their occupational level. Some were living in voluntary deep poverty, squatting, deliberately remaining unemployed, lowering their carbon footprint, and/or avoiding spending money in the capitalist economy. Others were organizers getting only stipends or poverty-level wages from activist groups. Some lived in collective houses or apartments and worked part-time at restaurants or copy shops, freeing up time for activism. Before the August/ September 2008 convention protests, some who usually fit into the latter category had left their part-time jobs and collective homes to volunteer full time for the summer in the convention cities, temporarily falling into the voluntary deep poverty category. These voluntarily downwardly mobile (VDM) activists varied as to whether poverty was an intentional class destination or an unintended side effect of choices made for other reasons.

Most VDM people, 82 percent, were encountered in anarchist groups. But, as chapter 4 shows, anarchists were not all VDM; most fell into other class trajectories. And as we have seen, many modestly VDM activists had managed to attain homeownership and stable white-collar jobs that qualified them for the PMC category. With those groups subtracted, only 22 survey respondents out of the whole pool of 362 fit the strict definition of VDM— in the professional range in childhood but working-class range now—18 in anarchist groups and 4 in other groups.[8]

But while their numbers were relatively small, voluntarily poor members were iconic within anarchist groups. For example, living off the grid to minimize one's carbon footprint and learning do-it-yourself (DIY) skills were prefigurative ideals mentioned both by those who were and by those who weren't practicing them to the degree of becoming VDM.

The element of choice takes the VDM trajectory out of any definition of a "class" as an outcome of economic and social-stratification forces. And while the other three broad trajectory categories (lifelong working class, straddler, and lifelong PMC) were diverse by gender, age, and to varying extents race, the VDM cluster was more homogeneous: two-thirds male, 91 percent white, and almost three-quarters in their twenties. All grew up in the United States. Thus, to be more precise, the VDM activists form not a class trajectory category but a race/age/class/lifestyle/ideology cluster. Yet their privileged class backgrounds are a crucial component of their profile; a well-off child is more likely to become a VDM adult. As Lamont puts it,

"People [who] have had more 'formative security', i.e. they or their families had a strong market position during their growing-up years are, therefore, less concerned with materialist values and with economic rationality" (1992: 152).VDM activists were even more consistently uprooted than the PMC activists. Very few were born in the same metropolitan areas where their parents were born, and very few lived near where they themselves were born.

The VDM lifestyle is often presumed to be a youthful phase, and indeed some of the convention protestors were voluntarily homeless and unemployed only for that one season of direct action planning. But for most, downward mobility had been a fairly long-term state, lasting for several years, up to a decade. If the economy allows it, some of them may eventually find ways to become only moderately downwardly mobile. They may attain by middle age the stable housing and the employment compatible with their values that the PMC moderately downwardly mobile people had found; in some cases these may be similar life stories glimpsed at two different stages. Or perhaps some of these VDM activists will be working in middle management at Sprint or city hall in ten years. However, there's historical precedent for never selling out by getting a mainstream job. "It's just a phase" is a patronizing assumption.

The Bonds of VDM Subcultural Style

The VDM survey respondents were tightly homogeneous, with shared styles, tastes, and opinions—a true subculture (Hall and Jefferson 1975; Hebdige 1979; Adilkno 1990). Olivia from the Parecon Collective called it "the whole DIY scene."

The personal style that marks the antiauthoritarian subculture—dreadlocks on white people, worn-out black clothes, multiple piercings, and patches with torn edges and slogans or A's in a circle—was common but not universal among them. Some would have blended in among the casual plain-styled PMC progressives in their jeans, t-shirts, and sneakers. A common pattern was to dress in eye-catching anarchist garb during direct actions but to wear plain casual used clothes at meetings.

The style elements that were permanently part of one's body, such as tat-toos and dreadlocks, served to distinguish the long-term, fully committed subculture members from newcomers and weekend activists, just as long hair signified immersion in the sixties counterculture. By the end of two weeks at the convention protests, I found myself relying on dreadlocks as a subcultural sign. For example, when I couldn't figure out which bus stop was nearest to a Convergence Center (protestors' headquarters), I just got off when the white people with dreadlocks got off. Unlike bandanas and black clothing, which can be easily put on and off, these permanent markers served as a rough safeguard against disguised infiltrators. Though the activist-turned-FBI-informant Brandon Darby and some Earth First! infiltrators blended into radical groups over many years, the shorter-term police spies I saw in convention protest groups were shorthaired, unpierced people who looked more like cops than anarchists. (The police plant Canton, profiled in chapter 1, didn't even bother to put on dark-colored clothing, which was just foolish.)

All the VDM survey respondents answered "no" to "Are you religious?" except for one Taoist and some pagans. Their most common favorite musical genre was radical punk (such as Mischief Brew and Bad Religion). Otherwise, their music tastes, mostly explicitly radical, were spread across genres and artists, ranging from hip-hop (bambu) to folk (Pete Seeger) to Afro-Latin (Orishas).

In answer to the question about favorite television or radio show, pirate radio, *Democracy Now!* and anti-TV answers such as "I don't indulge" outnumbered NPR and PBS. Tellingly, the one and only apolitical mainstream-hit TV show mentioned, *Project Runway*, was the favorite of the one and only African American VDM person, who was also the only one to list a meat dish as her favorite meal. Most white VDM activists, as in the lifelong-professional range, preferred ethnic food from ethnicities not their own (especially Thai, sushi, and Indian) or vegan dishes.

Compared with the wider variety in the other class-trajectory categories, these preferences show a very narrow range of tastes, reflecting cohesive values pervading many areas of life, including food, music, clothing, lifestyle, and activist practices. This homology of style suggests that atheism and anti-TV attitudes express meanings similar to black clothing and vegan food. These tastes drew a circle of connection among those inside it; but they also sometimes drew a circle of exclusion for those outside it and alienated by it.

Class, Tastes, and Militancy in the Four Class Trajectories

The picture painted by the above class profiles is oversimplified, of course. There were exceptions to every generalization. But defining these seven activist types within four class trajectories gives a useful class-culture orientation:

1. Respectable, relatively disempowered working-class worker bees
2. Powerhouse working-class outlaws
3. Uprooted, unassimilated straddlers pushing moral certainty
4. Contented straddlers not making waves
5. Polished, confident higher-PMC and UMC people
6. Inconspicuous LP workhorses avoiding dominance
7. Homogeneous VDM people in the DIY anarchist subculture

Though clothing styles and preferences in food, music, and radio and television programs may not seem to have much to do with strengthening social change groups, the taste distinctions among these four broad class-trajectory categories (see figure 3.1 below and table 3.3 online) can sometimes be obstacles to coalition building, especially if not recognized as class cultures.

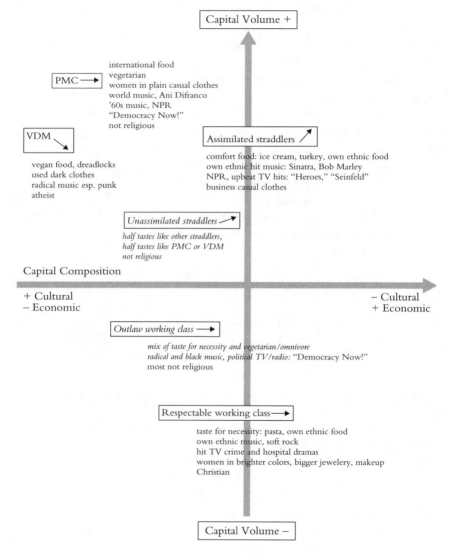

FIGURE 3.1 Activists' tastes in the social space of volume and composition of capital. *Note*: small arrows indicate class trajectory: upward, downward, or lifelong in one class. Italics indicate mixed tastes.

Militancy Is Not a Class-Culture Trait

Militant or moderate political beliefs did not line up with class. There are some folk theories on the left about which class tends to be more radical and which more reformist, but none of them appear to be true. Radicals may claim that poor people are the ones who really understand what's wrong with the system and who will take action because they have skin in the game while privileged people are too invested in the status quo to accept structural critiques. Moderate liberals, on the other hand, may claim that privileged intellectual ultraleftists don't understand the bread-and-butter concerns of working-class people, who need a bigger piece of the existing pie and can't risk the little they have on dangerous tactics for utopian goals.

But the reality is that within every class category of activists there are radical and moderate strains. Among my informants, the respectable working-class activists, the contented straddlers, and the confident, polished upper-PMC activists tended to be more moderate, closer to liberal reformist in their political philosophy. The empowered outlaw working-class activists, the uprooted unassimilated straddlers, the dominance-avoiding LPs, and the VDM activists tended to be more radical. But there were counterexamples to all these generalizations.

In the US population as a whole there *are* some class/politics correlations. Working-class people tend to be more socially conservative and economically liberal (Frank 2004; Bageant 2008). But among left-of-center social change activists, such as members of these twenty-five groups, the most radical or most moderate person in a group may come from any class.

The typically working-class focus on implementation details should not be presumed to be less idealistic than the ideological orientation more often injected by PMC and VDM activists. A wonderful example of a working-class-majority group injecting its political values into its operations happened when the office manager of City Power came to a board meeting with a proposal to switch banks because a notorious conservative politician was part owner of their current bank. Several members expressed horror at the idea of supporting that politician with their banking business; no one dissented from the proposal to switch to a community-based bank. Their political idealism was expressed through a nitty-gritty operational decision.

Most groups I studied had attracted people with roughly similar views on controversial issues. Similar political beliefs were associated not with a shared class but with a shared movement tradition.

CHAPTER 4

Movement Traditions and Their Class-Cultural Troubles

Going into various activist groups can feel like entering different worlds. How people talk and dress is different; how meetings are run and decisions are made is different; what people laugh at is different; how they wage conflicts is different.

Social movement organizations have classed and raced roots in the earlier generations of activists who created their movement tradition and in the past political and economic environments that shaped those earlier generations. These roots formed the group styles inherited by today's social movement organizations.

In the last chapter I introduced the 362 survey respondents by their class trajectories; now I introduce the groups' movement traditions. The twenty-five groups I looked at fell into four broad traditions: grassroots community organizing; professional antipoverty advocacy; the labor movement; and social change groups working on both global and local causes (further divided into three ideological tendencies: progressive/nonprofit, anarchist, and militant anti-imperialist).

Both class background and current class were strongly associated with movement tradition.[1] However, every group was class diverse to some extent. Thus, movement tradition can't be used as a stand-in for class cultures, except in the case of voluntarily downwardly mobile (VDM) anarchists. (For details, see table 4.1 below and online table 4.3 and online figures 4.1–4.7.)

Table 4.1   Movement tradition percentages within each class category

Class	Community needs (%)	Labor outreach (%)	Antipoverty staff advocacy	Progressive global/ local (%)	Militant global/ local (%)	Anarchist global/ local (%)	Total number
Working-class range	**35**	23	6	15	1	19	85
Straddlers (upwardly mobile)	19	**27**	9	**40**	4	2	53
Professional range	9	11	14	**49**	4	15	140
Voluntarily downwardly mobile	9	0	0	9	0	**82**	22

Note: Total number = 300. Most frequent movement traditions are in bold. Because of rounding, percentages across each row may not add up to 100%.

Within each movement tradition, interviewees raised a fairly consistent set of worries and criticisms, and distinctive troubles cropped up repeatedly at meetings. In each case the typical troubles were related to the predominant class culture of the group.

Community-Needs Groups in the Community-Organizing Tradition

Six groups fought for very basic unmet needs, usually for *local* poor people, but sometimes with a wider geographic scope. All used variations of the methods of the community-organizing tradition pioneered by Saul Alinsky (1971) and still taught by the Midwest Academy (Bobo et al. 2001). There are four key elements of this methodology:

1. Recruitment through one-on-one outreach, such as knocking on doors
2. Empowerment through victories on small, winnable campaigns
3. Leadership development through giving inexperienced recruits a slowly escalating series of tasks and roles
4. People-power tactics of packing hearing rooms and confronting officials

The goal of community organizing is not just winning reforms but also developing disempowered people into the empowered, committed members referred to (sometimes euphemistically) as "leaders."

The best-known networks in this tradition are the Industrial Areas Foundation and the now disbanded Association of Community Organizations for Reform Now (ACORN) (Warren 2001; Atlas 2010).[2] But more common than local affiliates of such large, staffed national networks are small, local freestanding community groups (McCarthy 2005: 195–99), such as five of the six groups studied here. Three of them, with a mostly female membership, traced their roots directly to the National Welfare Rights Organization in the 1970s (Abramovitz 2000; Kornbluh 2007) and to efforts to protect the safety net from welfare cutbacks in the mid-1990s.

Five of the six groups provided some form of direct help for members in need, such as individual advocacy with welfare offices, food giveaways, eviction resistance, or help with court appearances. But more of their work focused on winnable campaigns for specific reforms, such as reversing a budget cut, getting a law passed, or filing for a court order against a slumlord. While all six groups did educational work as well, it usually played a secondary role to mutual aid and reform campaigns. Their funding came from individual donations, fund-raising events, and in three cases foundation grants or government contracts. Their staff size ranged from zero to three.

Nearly Absent Poor Activists and Disempowered Working-Class Activists

These six groups especially welcomed low-income grassroots people directly affected by the group's issue, such as violence survivors, people facing foreclosure or eviction, or welfare recipients. All six were impressively mixed race, though most leaders were white. And each group was successful in including some low-income and otherwise marginalized people.

However, the reality was usually less grassroots than public portrayals implied. The active membership also included students, professional advocates, and VDM people from professional backgrounds. Two of the six groups were founded by professionals not personally affected by the problem; two had mixed-class founding groups; only two were founded by working-class people who had been affected by their groups' issues.

At these groups' meetings, fewer than 10 percent of attendees were currently living in poverty; about half were working class or lower middle class. By class background, one-fifth came from poverty backgrounds, and about 40 percent came from working-class or lower-middle-class (LMC) backgrounds. Almost half of all members either were or had been in the professional range. About two-thirds were in a different category now than in childhood; these groups seemed to be gathering spots for class-mobile people, more so than for poor people.

The spokespeople who publicly represented the cause tended to come from higher class backgrounds than the grassroots members. Professional women of color in particular seemed able to use stereotyped assumptions about their race and gender to speak for the poor, without in fact being poor. It was rare to see a lifelong-poor person in a public or leadership role. The central trouble for these grassroots community groups was how seldom leadership development actually happened, how few lifelong-poor people actually became empowered. Three groups asked recipients of direct aid to pledge to help others after their crisis situation stabilized; but only a small percent came through on that promise.

All these groups were adept at overcoming the "invisible walls" (Stout 1996) of transportation, child care, translation, and the like. Four regularly served free meals with their meetings; two paid stipends to some members. Clearly, the logistical nightmares of poverty were not the only barriers keeping poor people out. It is time-consuming to form the intensive, long-term relationships that result in the transformation of very disempowered people into formidable leaders; and paid staff members are usually too expensive, given limited funding, to deploy in such a labor-intensive role. And not everyone has the knack of empowering others. The result was a mismatch between intentions to raise poor people's voices and the reality.

The Downsides of Personal Ties: Turnover and Overreliance on Leaders

In community-needs groups, personal bonds were the main glue that held people together—or didn't. The downside of personal loyalty to leaders combined with disempowerment can be quitting when trust is eroded. Overreliance on personal bonds of trust makes recruiting hard and retention even harder, leading to a rotating door of poor and working-class people joining and disappearing.

Most long-term community groups were missing earlier cohorts of members who had quit in mistrust and rancor. For example, Grassroots Resistance had recently lost some members who became critical of the leadership. While quitting in disgust happens in all kinds of groups, in working-class-majority groups loss of disaffected members seemed to happen more regularly. The history of most long-term community groups includes rift after rift, schism after schism.

Since these groups' moral authority with government officials and funders came largely from having people personally affected by the problems as active members, whenever those numbers fell, it was a major problem, not just politically, but for the organization's very survival. Small numbers also precluded the use of the mass confrontation tactics favored by many activists in the community-organizing tradition. Losing previously active people was a serious form of trouble for these groups.

The weakness of groups based on personal loyalty is revealed by the fact that of the six long-standing community groups, there had been *zero* transitions from the founders to new leaders. Not just Elaine, Dorothea, and Brandy, but also Fred of Neighbors United, a pair of leaders of Safety Net for All, and two Low-Income Women Rising founders had each been in continuous leadership positions for twelve to thirty-five years. These eight leaders were aging (born in the 1940s or 1950s, except for one born in the 1960s); they wouldn't be leading these groups forever. By contrast, a number of successful founder transitions had happened in the long-term activist groups in the other movement traditions. Since the longtime members who had stayed active were those loyal to these particular leaders, and since these powerhouse leaders had rare combinations of needed strengths, it is hard to imagine a transition to new leadership after the current leaders are gone.

Many community-needs groups without such long-term, dedicated, and trustworthy leadership had arisen and folded while these older groups plugged on, creating cohesion through bonds between the founding leaders and the core group. They were only as strong as those relationships. Since any given leader can only sustain a limited number of one-on-one relationships, this basis for group cohesion serves to keep groups small. And building a group on pre-existing social ties tends to reinforce the racial and class segregation of the wider society.

Trusting bonds are central to all social movement groups, but the necessity for such individual relationships of trust seems to be a defining characteristic of working-class-majority community groups in particular. Some pairs of individuals will always become estranged, but a healthy group should be able to survive those broken personal bonds. The Alinsky community-organizing tradition has a number of mechanisms to prevent such overdependence on founding leaders, including the Industrial Areas Foundation's regular rotation of lead organizers among regions (Warren 2001). But as McCarthy (2005) found in a national study of social movement groups, most local grassroots groups addressing community needs are not part of networks with such rules but are freestanding local organizations. They are on their own in figuring out solutions to their troubles.

The Labor Movement Tradition

Three of the twenty-five groups were labor-outreach groups rooted in the labor movement tradition. One was a successful unionization drive with meetings attended by potential members from multiple worksites. The second was a multiunion body attended by members and staff of many unions in one geographical area. The third was a labor-initiated coalition, whose member groups included not only unions but also community groups and social services agencies giving support to worker-justice campaigns.

Such coalitions with nonunions have become much more common since John Sweeney became president of the AFL-CIO in 1995 and reversed decades of labor movement insularity (Lichtenstein 2002: 255–69). Labor federations and central labor councils used to do political work almost entirely with their member unions, but they have increasingly collaborated with faith-based organizations on living-wage campaigns (Pollin and Luce 1998), with immigrant organizations, with workers' centers (Fine 2006), and with students, environmentalists (Mayer 2008), and other progressive groups. Jobs with Justice is the best-known national network of local community-labor coalitions.[3] To what extent unions' internal culture has changed to facilitate such alliances with other groups, or how many culture clashes continue to happen, is an open question.

Unions are almost the only organizations in the left-of-center political scene in the United States to have a large, steady funding stream from membership dues. These three labor-outreach groups each had only one or two staff dedicated entirely to the group, but they had many union resources to draw on for administrative, lobbying, and communications functions. Despite setbacks from weak and unenforced labor laws and a steadily shrinking unionization rate (Lichtenstein 2002: chap. 6), unions and labor-sponsored groups remain the wealthiest and most independent political force on the US left. Confusion about cross-class alliance building is often caused by the contrast between such large-budget organizations with working-class members and small-budget organizations with professional-middle-class (PMC) members.

Labor activists base today's organizing on the historical exemplar of the early labor movement of the 1930s and 1940s (Lichtenstein 2002: chaps. 1–3). But today's labor movement is very different from those years of industrial union growth. Looking at the membership of these three groups, they included both "old labor" (mostly white, middle-aged men doing relatively high-paid jobs in manufacturing and skilled trades in shrinking unions in shrinking industries) and "new labor" (mostly immigrants and women of color doing low-paid service work in growing unions in growing fields).

At labor-outreach meetings, the majority of participants came from working-class or poor backgrounds. But only four in ten had been lifelong in the working-class range; almost 30 percent were straddlers, the highest proportion of straddlers in any movement tradition. These straddlers were not only teachers and other unionized professionals but also allies from non-labor groups. Involvement in a coalition convened by unions may appeal to activists from working-class backgrounds as a way of staying true to their roots.

The average current class of the labor groups was pulled down by some very low-paid, scantily educated workers recruited to their first meeting by the Local 21 Organizing Committee. Most longtime union members in labor-outreach groups were part of the labor aristocracy, stably employed homeowners, some of whom had taken some college courses or earned a public college two- or four-year degree.

Compared with rank-and-file union members, experienced labor activists disproportionately had leftist politics and experience with other social movement groups. Many staff and elected leaders didn't rise from the rank and file but were moderately downwardly mobile PMC people who joined the labor movement out of political conviction (Early 2009: 149–52).

Power from Above

Top-down command-and-control authority was found only among union staff. Some union members and staff expressed frustration with hierarchical decisions by union management. They chafed at the limits placed on the decision-making power of rank-and-file members, low-level staff, and community partners. Workers praised staffers Owen of Local 21 and Tony of the Tri-City Labor Alliance for respecting the members and empowering them, as if that were a surprise.

Around the United States, some autocratic labor leaders have taken advantage of working-class disempowerment and a tendency to rely on strong leadership. Workers' struggles for internal democracy, such as Teamsters for Democratic Union and breakaway Service Employees International Union (SEIU) locals, are outnumbered by situations where corrupt or simply out-of-touch union officials have faced little resistance (Lichtenstein 2002: 257–60; Early 2011). Contrasting models of directive versus participatory leadership, which seem fairly irrelevant within most all-volunteer social change groups, are still hotly debated inside the labor movement.

Small Turnouts Weaken Solidarity

A united front of solidarity, all for one and one for all, makes sense to people rooted in stable working-class communities, with their norms of mutual aid and closing ranks against outside threats. Given this reliance on mass solidarity, small turnouts were not just disappointing but sometimes left organizers at a loss for other tactics. Inactive members were regarded as free riders, benefiting from the hard work of the active few.

Sometimes absence was given a class interpretation by union interviewees: the absence from meetings of the relatively prosperous homeowners in the labor aristocracy and of professional allies was interpreted as middle-class complacency and lack of solidarity; conversely, the absence of low-wage service workers was seen as evidence of the hardships in their lives. Labor interviewees defined small numbers as their most serious trouble. The question they most wanted answered was "Where is everybody?"

Staff Antipoverty Coalitions in the Professional-Advocacy Tradition

Three coalitions brought together professionals who, in their day jobs, responded to a single thorny, intractable problem facing local low-income people, such as poor schools, lack of health care, joblessness, or unaffordable housing. These coalitions' goals were to share information about the problem and to collaborate on joint activities that their individual organizations couldn't do alone, such as lobby days and educational forums. Such joint efforts, aimed at generating the clout needed to reform policies and win state funding, can be found in most major metropolitan areas and in most human services fields. Besides professional associations of legal aid lawyers, social workers, and the like, there are few permanent national federations of such local or state groups. In the 1990s I directed a federation at the state level, the Massachusetts Human Services Coalition.

The advocacy coalitions in this book took more risks than do more mainstream, respectable multiagency groups, such as the United Way or mayor's commissions on community problems. They pushed government agencies and elected officials harder and proposed more expensive reforms or more community input than those respectable groups would advocate. Less formal and more political than trade associations, advocacy coalitions are able to be nimble in responding to budget cuts or community crises (Meredith 2001). Individual professionals and agencies can let the coalition make risky criticisms of state and local governments and advocate deeper change while protecting their separate reputations.

A few members reported being assigned to represent their agencies to the coalition, but most participants had volunteered to join. Some were able to count the time spent on the coalition as work hours for their employer, while others volunteered their time. Members included social workers, public health educators, legal aid lawyers, teachers, clergy, low-level government officials and politicians, and staff researchers, organizers, and lobbyists from advocacy organizations. The top leaders of these three mixed-race, mixed-gender groups were professionals of color. While the Workforce Development Task Force was part of a bigger interfaith coalition with multiple staff, the other two each had only one paid staff person.

Tenuous Ties among Competitors

The central trouble reported by members of these coalitions was turf wars among member groups. Because coalition members included large staffed organizations such as social services agencies, dependent on public and foundation funding, the financial stakes were higher than in other movement traditions. Direct competitors for the same funding sometimes met at coalition meetings, which made collaboration a dicey matter. The Brontown Affordable Housing Consortium had recently reconstituted itself after a rift between groups that accused each other of being territorial and undercutting other members' funding. Inner City Advocates was tiny during the observation period, and much whiter than it had been before the African American director had stepped on the toes of a number of black community leaders working on the same issue.

At other times the competition was subtler, over community prestige or over whose frame would be used in the coalition's communications and joint projects. The coalition's choices of messages and program activities could make or break a member's reputation with government officials and private funders. The Workforce Development Task Force actually disbanded after the power struggle described in chapter 1. Such fierce clashes were rare; more often, the polite indirectness and weak conflict-resolution skills learned from lower-professional (LP) childhoods gave most members of these coalitions inadequate resources for openly dealing with competing interests.

Individual members' career advancement might get a boost from the coalition's joint activities; but a controversial coalition involvement might jeopardize future job opportunities. They had the contradictory allegiances (Wright 1985) of the so-called new class of not-for-profit employees (Gouldner 1979): allegiances to the people whose needs they served, to their organizations, to their individual careers, to the coalition itself, and to a vision of a fairer society that motivated them to attend meetings and take political risks.

A few interviewees saw it as a problem that none of the people affected by the issue attended any of the meetings observed. Except for a few interns and community organizers, class diversity in these groups came primarily from people's differing class backgrounds; these groups had 17 percent straddlers and another 17 percent who had risen within the working-class range, amounting to less than 35 percent coming from working-class backgrounds. Involvement in such coalitions may have appealed to these straddlers and working-class antipoverty workers as a way to give back to their communities of origin while working in a job in human services. However, the mean, mode, and median current class of participants at staff antipoverty coalitions was PMC. As this class composition would predict, the modes of dealing with territorial conflicts within these coalitions varied from dominance by overconfident upper-middle-class (UMC) and PMC members to fights started by unassimilated-straddler conflict-wagers to indirect politeness by lower-professional (LP) conflict-avoiders.

Global/Local Cause Groups in Three Social Change Traditions

Thirteen social change groups were multi-issue, making the connections between varied injustices. Thus their missions tended to require more words to explain, and more abstract words, than the labor-outreach, advocacy-coalition, and community-needs groups' missions.

Twelve of these thirteen global/local cause groups, including all the ad hoc convention protest groups, were all-volunteer groups with no paid staff. Their fund-raising tended to rely on requests for individual donations and on grassroots benefit events. Again, confusion about class dynamics arises when PMC-majority voluntary groups have vastly less funding than dues-funded unions and grant-funded community-based organizations.

These groups tended to have a less racially diverse membership than those in the other three movement traditions. Three were entirely white. Only three of the thirteen groups had achieved the cherished diversity goal of a substantial contingent of active members of color. A bit of class diversity was present in several of these groups, but all thirteen groups had mean and median class backgrounds in the professional range.

The Personalist Pitfall

The most frequent trouble reported by interviewees from these thirteen global/local cause groups was rancor, factionalization, and difficulty getting people from different political tendencies to work together. As chapter 5 shows, this trouble stems from the class life story most common in these groups: radicalized in college, individually choosing an issue or ideology to give primary loyalty to, then carrying this individual commitment into an organization—the kind of self-directed political identity that Lichterman (1996) calls "personalist" and Rose (2000: 16) calls "internally controlled."

To some PMC activists with such inner-driven political loyalties, struggling with other activists over the political line or over which group process best reflected the group's values could seem as valuable as external political struggle. Historically, this movement tradition has included many groups that blew up after a short lifespan over ideological or group-process differences, such as the Student Nonviolent Coordinating Committee (Polletta 2002), the Black Panthers and SDS (Breines 1989), the Clamshell Alliance (Epstein 1991), and early feminist groups (Strobel 1995). In almost every case, the fiercest combatants were college-educated activists, many from professional families. Organizing inner-directed PMC activists is like herding cats.

Jasper (1997) calls this tradition "post-citizenship movements" (7). Compared with groups working to get a piece of the pie for a pre-existing social identity, such as women or African Americans, these groups have to do more internal work in order to create a collective identity, more often identifying with a particular tactic (87) or subcultural symbol (159)—a setup for internal focus and arguments.

To describe these thirteen groups as one movement tradition is tricky, since they strongly disagreed on ideology and historical exemplars. The phrase "social change" was used by all of them to summarize their vision of a more just world; they all prided themselves on thinking globally but acting both locally and globally; and all saw themselves as building a multi-issue radical movement. But they agreed on little else. There were three main ideological strands.

The Progressive and Nonprofit Traditions

Most of these groups had their roots in the "new social movements" that arose in the 1970s and 1980s, the mostly white PMC feminist, environmental, antinuclear power, and antimilitarism groups that stressed egalitarian process and direct action tactics (Epstein 1991; Breines 1989; Jasper 1997). Well-known examples of this movement tradition in 2007–8 were the antiwar groups United for Peace and Justice and Code Pink, Bill McKibben's climate change network, and School of the Americas Watch.[4]

While anarchist and militant anti-imperialist activists sometimes referred to this movement tradition as "liberal," many college-educated activists within the tradition considered that word to be an insult, connoting a wishy-washy tendency to compromise with the powers that be. They tended to prefer "progressive," a word they share with Democratic Party liberals to their right on the political spectrum. Whether or not they were pacifists, these activists were comfortable making a nonviolence pledge for all direct action. Some saw themselves continuing the nonviolent civil disobedience tradition begun by the civil rights and antiwar movements of the 1960s.

The ad hoc convention protest groups in this tradition, such as The People's Convention, had their most recent roots in the globalization movement's mass protests at the meetings of international bodies and at the 2000 and 2004 political conventions. In the rare, iconic moment of multimovement convergence at the World Trade Organization protests in Seattle in 1999, this movement tradition was found in the Direct Action Network's disciplined blockade, which successfully shut down the WTO meeting site for a day, and in the march with labor on the permitted route, not with the untargeted property destruction in downtown Seattle.

Group members born in the 1940s, 1950s, and 1960s—baby boomers, more or less—tended to be the carriers of this tradition. They were majority white, mostly college educated, and majority female. While all class trajectories showed up in these groups, each group's average was in the professional range. Less than one-third of the participants in these groups came from working-class, poor, or LMC backgrounds, and fewer than one in six were in those classes as adults.

The Internal Eye, with Nonprofit versus Social Change Process Differences

Many progressive global/local activists kept one eye focused on the internal workings of the group at all times. Interviewees variously reported their groups' worst troubles as too much or too little time spent discussing internal process, too many bureaucratic rules or too much internal chaos, too much domination by a few people or too extreme antileadership attitudes. Most of the passionate advocates of consensus decision making or majority rule were found in the progressive global/local groups. Prefigurative norms of embodying a more just society in how the group operated collided with impatient desires for efficiency in reaching external social change goals.

Some of the sharpest conflicts over organizational structure and group process arose between the nonprofit group style and the "new social movement" group style—two movement traditions that I combine in this section because they were so often found in the same coalitions, the same voluntary groups, and sometimes within the same person. Nonprofit 501(c)(3) organizations with boards, executive directors, and offices were a major influence on how the more informal voluntary groups operated. Because I am spotlighting voluntary groups with regular membership meetings, staff-run nonprofits are underrepresented here as compared with their strong presence in the US Left overall. National progressive nonprofits with local chapters active during the study period included the National Organization for Women (NOW) and the Sierra Club. Among the progressive groups in this study, only Green Homes Green World was a staffed 501(c)(3) nonprofit; but so were many member groups within coalitions such as Peace and Justice Now, the Convention Protest Coalition, and The People's Convention.

Two examples of voluntary group norms drawn from this nonprofit tradition are quorums and strategic plans with goals and objectives. While such nonprofit norms were familiar to most of these activists, the new social movement tradition of volunteer-led, single-issue nonviolent-action campaigns was home base to more of them. Arguments over consensus versus majority-rule decision making sometimes erupted between activists with these two different sets of experience. Often, but not always, the nonprofit mode lined up with more moderate, liberal political values, while the progressive social change mode lined up with more radical political ideology.

Diversity Angst

The progressive and nonprofit global/local cause groups faced a contradiction between their professed antiracist values and their weak membership diversity. All these groups were founded by white college-educated people, except for Immigrants United, which was founded mostly by college-educated nonimmigrants of color. But their diversity problem stemmed not just from having white PMC founders (some diverse community and labor groups had those too) but from being founded by activists with personalist commitments to stick to a particular issue, tactic, group process, or political line, which, unsurprisingly, tended to appeal primarily to other white PMC people. Many members wanted racial diversity, but they wanted even more to hold on to some white-culture-derived feature of the current group.

Individual members disagreed about whether or not disproportionate whiteness meant the group was a failure. To some, lack of racial diversity was an intolerable violation of their political values.

The Militant Anti-Imperialist Tradition

The militant anti-imperialist tradition is under-represented in this study compared with its presence in the US movement today. Only the ad hoc convention protest group Stand Up Fight Back had a Far Left ideology and a focus on imperialism by the United States and its allies.

SUFB was an unstaffed ad hoc convention protest group that raised money through concerts and individual donations. The membership was disproportionately male, middle-aged, white, and PMC. But there were a few members of color and some class diversity (a handful of working-class people and 12% straddlers; the founders and leaders were disproportionately straddlers). This limited diversity was not seen as a particular problem. Though the group claimed to represent poor communities of color, according to the leaders' political values, a privileged group could be in solidarity with oppressed communities without including them as members as long as they consulted leaders of color for political advice and remained accountable to them.

SUFB's conflict with The People's Convention reflects a key ideological split in the movement today, most visible in the rift in the mid-decade anti-war movement between the Act Now to Stop War and End Racism (ANSWER) Coalition (founded by the Workers World Party) and United for Peace and Justice (UFPJ).[5] If SUFB had not been part of a major movement strand of the twenty-first-century Left, exemplified by ANSWER, I might have dropped the group from the study as an outlier.

The signature issue of the disagreement between these two movement traditions has been Palestine. To oversimplify, militant anti-imperialist activists emphasized this Middle East issue more strongly than others did and criticized only Israeli and not Palestinian leaders; on the other hand, if progressive and nonprofit groups talked about the Middle East at all in 2007–8, the war in Iraq was their primary issue, and most strove to sound even-handed by criticizing both Israeli and Palestinian leaders and in affirming a two-state solution. This issue continues to be so hotly contentious that it's rare for college-educated people with opposing views to remain in the same social justice organization unless the topic is completely avoided.

In terms of rhetorical style and political vision, the ANSWER/UFPJ split roughly parallels the differences between the civil rights and black power movements (Brown 1992; Harding 1983). Some SUFB members and other militant leftist interviewees praised black nationalists and other male heroes of color from the 1960s, such as leaders of third world national liberation fronts. Arguments over nonviolence continue virtually unchanged from those movement divisions of forty years ago.

The Missing Base

This militant anti-imperialist movement tradition today faces the conundrum that most working-class and poor people of color, whom they vocally champion, don't hold radical-leftist frames on any social issues, including their own oppression. In the late 1960s, some public expressions of rage had a galvanizing, mobilizing force (Cluster 1979; Gould 2009): the militant rhetoric of the Black Panthers, American Indian Movement, and other such groups lit a spark at the grassroots level. But those who have tried to do the same since have found a much less favorable political environment. Look, for example, at the tragic story of MOVE in Philadelphia: militants were shot, firebombed, killed, and jailed in 1978 and 1985 without ever winning broad support in the African American community that the group intended to mobilize.[6] The ANSWER Coalition has had more success in building a militant anti-imperialist organization, largely through mobilizing experienced college-educated activists and by avoiding the violent rhetoric and tactics that have marginalized some other militant groups.

The militant anti-imperialist tradition was a vocal minority within the convention protests. SUFB shrank over the months before the DNC, keeping close alliances only with one anarchist group and two militant groups of color. SUFB's political position lost credibility in some interviewees' eyes when they claimed a mass base they couldn't produce.

Rancorous Conflicts

The harsh language and heated emotions that these activists directed at political elites were sometimes turned against movement rivals and internal dissenters as well, which intensified the intramovement conflict before the Democratic National Convention (a case unpacked in detail in chapter 9). Interviewees from Stand Up Fight Back, including Emilio (profiled in chapter 3), all agreed that their greatest problem was that other groups insisted on separate organizational identities and refused to subsume themselves into SUFB; they expected all compromises to be made by others.

Extreme breaches of shared values happened in all types of groups, but by celebrating outlaw status and eschewing remedies such as civility codes, this militant anti-imperialist group left itself with the fewest resources to rein in its own hotheads. This tradition has strengths, such as courage and persistence, but its angry emotion norms and antiprocess bias can leave groups without much capacity for conflict resolution.

The Anarchist Tradition

Three of the convention protest groups as well as the Parecon Collective were explicitly anarchist, although all welcomed nonanarchist members. In addition, some activists born in the 1980s brought anarchist ideas and the do-it-yourself subculture into other groups.

In today's anarchist ideology, all forms of authority—from the US military to multinational corporations to local cops to leaders of nonanarchist progressive groups to individual activists who talk too much at a meeting—are seen as manifestations of the same system of domination that is the root of all injustice (Bookchin 1982). The masked street confrontations for which this subculture is renowned, including property damage and physical resistance to police control, are intended to express wide-ranging resistance to authority.

Most anarchist groups choose to remain independent, affiliating only loosely with national or international networks such as the Anarchist Black Cross Federation.[7] The best-known network of groups in this movement tradition is Food Not Bombs,[8] whose volunteers cook and serve vegan meals to homeless people and others in many US cities. Critical Mass,[9] which takes over city streets with swarms of bicycles, is another national network in this tradition.

The anarchist movement tradition seemed to have two cultural strands: punk and pagan. Punk grew from alienated working-class British youths' imitation in the 1970s of Jamaican and other West Indian styles, using chains and ripped clothes to project a menacing asceticism (Hebdige 1979: 65–66, 87). This style spread across the Atlantic with punk music, such as the Sex Pistols and the Clash, and morphed into today's hard-edged urban anti-authoritarian VDM scene (O'Connor 2008).

The pagan subcultural strain of anarchism grew out of cultural feminism, wiccan spirituality, and back-to-the-land subcultures of the 1970s (Starhawk 1979, 1988; Binkley 2007). Some wings of the feminist and antinuclear movements, as well as the 1980s movements against military intervention in Central America and for lesbian and gay rights, incorporated pagan rituals into meetings and direct action (Jasper 1997: chap. 8).

In Leach's (2009) terms, the punk-derived strain of anarchism emphasized "oppositional autonomy" (confrontations with political authorities) and the pagan-derived strain emphasized "constructivist autonomy" (creating alternatives that prefigured a noncoercive society). The punk and pagan subcultures are not mutually exclusive; some individual activists seemed influenced by both.

The three anarchist ad hoc convention protest groups were very low budget, relying on individual donations and fund-raising events, as well as on the unpaid work of VDM members. But not all anarchist groups were penniless; the Parecon Collective supported its educational efforts through a worker-run co-op.

The commonly held image of the prototypical anarchist as a young, white, college-educated male from a privileged background was roughly true of the mode in these groups but was complicated by the presence of a few middle-aged people and some lifelong-working-class people (over one-quarter of all members). Two-thirds of members of anarchist groups came from the professional range of backgrounds. Their mean class background was the highest of any movement tradition, with 22 percent coming from UMC backgrounds. But most were not current professionals: more were VDM or students and other young adults who had yet to hold professional jobs.

Mistrust and Troubles with Community Building

The most frequent complaint made by members of anarchist groups was mistrust. Suspecting (often correctly) that infiltrators paid by the government were present at meetings, anarchists in direct action groups withheld trust from anyone who hadn't been vouched for by a trusted comrade. Besides fear of infiltration, there was mistrust about inadequate courage for street battles, mistrust about egoistic opportunism, and mistrust about domination within groups, particularly sexist male domination.

In anarchist groups, a stranger coming to a meeting aroused suspicion. Trust was built instead during street confrontations—a relatively rare opportunity to watch how someone acted, not readily available when there was a need to check out any given newcomer—or through intensive experiences of living together or playing in bands, experiences shared only by a small core group. Only in a few cities during a few years has a large "scene" of anti-authoritarians provided a social context for anarchist political action (Leach and Haunss 2009).

The organizational tone that resulted from mistrust was often strangely cold, quiet, and cliquey. Given that trust was especially needed for some of these groups' high-risk tactics, the weak foundation for building a sense of community with new recruits was a big problem within this movement tradition.

Missing Strategy Components

The lack of pragmatism that is a risk of any ideologically driven activism seemed most pronounced in the four anarchist groups. Between the broadest goals of overturning neoliberal capitalism, patriarchy, and all other oppressions and the most immediate goal of blocking a certain street, anarchist interviewees tended to articulate few intermediate goals. Identifying midrange reform goals, or even acknowledging authorities enough to negotiate with them, sometimes seemed a betrayal of the dream of a horizontal society, as it did to some in the Occupy movement in 2012. The entire strategic vocabulary used by other groups to talk about public education, media framing, and pressuring politicians was rejected, leaving a large, muddy hole.

There were exceptions to this anarchist avoidance of intermediate strategies. I participated in a well-planned anarchist march to the offices of all the major polluters who funded the supposedly environmentally friendly Democratic National Convention. When we handed out flyers about each corporation's violations, some bystanders seemed shocked to learn of convention sponsors' environmental violations; thus we met the goal of exposing the hypocrisy of the self-proclaimed "greenest convention ever." But this was an exception to an overall vagueness of purpose.

Some off-the-grid lifestyle proponents naively envisioned a simple additive process whereby a sustainable economy would pop into existence when enough individuals changed their habits, without pushback by corporations or other entrenched powers. Meadow put this strategy into words most clearly. Looking no older than twenty-five though in her late thirties and energetically upbeat, Meadow was a good advertisement for the healthy effects of an off-the-grid lifestyle; and her low carbon footprint no doubt had some direct positive effect on the planet. But she revealed the limitations of individual VDM lifestyle choices as a movement strategy when she expressed intense frustration over how few Americans were willing to drop out of the capitalist economy:

> There aren't bike tribes going from garden to garden; it's not happening. Because I've experienced that, I grieve. . . . I feel like a foreigner; I don't feel I belong in American culture. I'm a visionary; I see how things could be different and I'm acting towards that vision. That's very unusual in this country. Most people are resigned. [People say to me,] 'I'm glad you have those ideals, but we're never going to have that in this country.' [They say,] 'Wouldn't it be great if we grew our own food and stopped this environmental catastrophe from happening? But it's never going to happen'—hopelessness!

The protest action Meadow was organizing had few takers, presumably in part because it included physical rigors. Her story reveals weaknesses in the strategy of being an exemplar of a different mode of life in hopes that lifestyle choices will eventually add up to a mass withdrawal from mainstream institutions.

Some of the anarchists' current and historical exemplars, such as the Zapatistas in Chiapas, Mexico, and the Spanish anarchists of the early twentieth

Table 4.2   Class percentages within each movement tradition

Movement tradition	Working-class range (%)	Straddlers (upwardly mobile) (%)	Professional-middle-class range (%)	Voluntarily downwardly mobile (%)	Total number
Community needs	**56**	18	22	4	54
Labor outreach	**41**	29	31	0	49
Antipoverty advocacy	17	17	**65**	0	29
Progressive/ nonprofit global/ local	12	20	**65**	2	104
Militant global/ local	12	25	62	0	8
Anarchist global/ local	29	2	**37**	32	56

Note: Total number = 300. Most common class trajectories in each movement tradition are in bold. Because of rounding, percentages across each row may not add up to 100%.

century, existed in such different political times and places as to provide little concrete guidance to twenty-first-century US anarchism. The anarchist interviewees were looking farther into the past and farther into a utopian future for their model of activism than were those from the other movement traditions.

The Interplay of Classes and Movement Traditions

The chapters that follow examine the class-cultural troubles of each movement tradition and each class category profiled in this chapter: low turnout and high turnover; disempowerment and entitled domination; over-reliance on leaders and antileadership attitudes; excessive ideological barriers and too much internal focus; clashing approaches to antiracism; mistrust, rancor, and intramovement attacks; self-effacing and indirect communication; and weak conflict-resolution and community-building mechanisms.

Class figures into such group problems in two ways. First, a group is most likely to run into the troubles associated with the class conditioning of its founders and the majority of its members, the individual predispositions they bring into the group. Second, a group is also likely to run into the troubles particular to its movement tradition, with its class-specific historical roots. The interaction of these two sets of classed influences affects each group's style and its resources for problem solving.

As we have seen, every group was class diverse, and many members were class incongruous with their group's movement tradition, such as lifelong–UMC labor leaders. (See Table 4.2 for class breakdowns within each movement tradition.) When movement tradition norms contradict core members' class predispositions there's no neat formula for which one prevails. Individual personalities, political contexts, and race and gender dynamics also complicate the picture.

Each class culture and each classed movement history has its own distinct strengths, as the coming chapters show. The challenge of building a stronger and more unified movement for progressive social change is not just to find common ground to bridge differences but also to tap the resources within all class cultures to find new solutions to group troubles.

PART II

Activist Class Cultures and Solving Group Troubles

CHAPTER 5

Where Is Everybody?

Approaches to Recruitment and Group Cohesion

"Is Marc coming?" "Isadora told me she'd be late." "I *know* Eddie is coming." The early arrivals at some meetings started out chatting cheerfully, but as the minutes passed and most chairs remained empty such comments about who was missing gradually took over the conversation.

The first challenge in building any social movement organization is to get people in the door, literally and figuratively. Too few new people joining and too few members showing up to meetings: these are the most common and most basic of activist group troubles. This chapter looks at how group members approached turnout problems and finds that their attempted solutions lined up with their class trajectory.

Activists talked about two components of improving turnout. First, the need for new people and the best ways to recruit them were perennial topics in meetings and interviews. Beliefs about what worked to recruit varied by class. Second, a voluntary group must also have at least a rudimentary sense of collective identity, a sense of "we." Collective identity is a dynamic work in progress, not a settled fact—a verb, not a noun (Melucci 1995). To continue to exist, a voluntary group must have enough camaraderie to keep people coming back to meetings and events. Understandings of what bonds people together also varied by class.

Why would recruitment and group-building approaches differ by class? In this chapter I argue that activists' distinct classed paths into activism explain their varied approaches to recruiting new members and building group cohesion. To summarize this argument: working-class activists, most of whom were recruited into activism through pre-existing networks to work on issues that affected them personally, turned more often to immediate incentives to recruit others. They used food, mutual aid, services to individuals, and teasing and self-deprecating humor to strengthen camaraderie. By contrast, professional-middle-class (PMC) people, most of whom first made commitments to activism via individual conversion to progressive ideas and then joined ideologically compatible groups as a second step, tended to rely on agreement with the group's political ideas to draw in new people, often overlooking working-class community-building practices. Voluntarily downwardly mobile (VDM) activists were even more likely to have joined a group through ideological affinity, as well as through attraction to a distinct subculture. Even more than other college-educated activists, some majority-VDM groups omitted food, humor, individual relationships with new recruits, cheers, and even greetings as means of developing group cohesion. But as the most distinct movement subculture, majority-VDM anarchist groups had their own unique ways of strengthening identity with the group. Activists' own experience of getting involved shaped their practices of getting others involved. The participants' paths to activism and their beliefs about recruiting others were probed in interviews and were often revealed during meetings as well. The question "How did you first get involved?" was asked of more than 50 of the interviewees, and it was also asked by several meeting facilitators during introductory go-arounds. Meeting participants came to activism by three well-trodden paths. First, their friends, family, or colleagues invited them to join a group (Klandermans 1997; Somma 2009). Second, they were shocked by something awful in the community or the world (Teske 1997), and they then found similarly concerned people with whom to work on that one issue (Han 2009). Third, some had a job or religious affiliation that involved attending a coalition meeting, which then became a voluntary passion. These three common answers (invited, shocked, or extending from another role) were just as likely to be heard from people of all classes, races, age brackets, and in some cases genders. (Women disproportionately mentioned being recruited by a friend.) But in terms of *who* invited them to get involved with *what* issue, there were some class-distinct patterns, described in the three following class profiles, that reveal how the very meaning of activism varied in different class communities.

Activists' beliefs about recruitment methods were also uncovered in both interviews and meetings. Most interviewees were asked, "What would it take to make this into a bigger group?" and "Who else can you picture at these meetings, and what would persuade them to come?" In addition, at several meetings with low turnout, the gripe sessions about low turnout included revealing discussions of how to get more people to attend in the future. Very different ways of thinking about recruitment emerged from these interviews and discussions. Two cases of low-turnout meetings in particular, profiled in the next section, illustrate a striking contrast in activist class cultures.

Straddlers, with their hybrid working-class/PMC life experience, did not have a distinct set of group-building beliefs and practices; but working-class, PMC, and VDM activists each had a very distinct class-cultural approach to turnout problems. Three class-profile sections, following two illustrative meeting stories, unpack the logic of these classes' approaches to recruitment and building group cohesion.

Class Contrast between Two Low-Turnout Meetings

The classed approaches to recruitment and group building can be illustrated by comparing two cases. At both these meetings more than half the elected board members didn't show up: first, at a meeting of the all-PMC Green Homes Green World (GHGW); and second, at the same small working-class-majority meeting of the Local 21 Organizing Committee profiled in chapter 1, where rank-and-file members clashed with the LP organizer Lynette.

These two meetings offer a race contrast as well as class contrast: the Local 21 rank-and-file elected board members were all black, with only white organizer Lynette and one other white activist present; GHGW board members were mostly white, with just one Latina.

In both meetings, some members came late, so there was a prolonged informal time for small "Where is everybody?" discussions. The most obvious difference between GHGW's and Local 21's discussions was the issue of selective incentives (Gamson 1990: 69–70). Much of Local 21's discussion focused on what incentives would get new people in the door. The lifelong-working-class black rank-and-file leaders couldn't believe that other workers would ignore a campaign that would so clearly benefit them, possibly within a year if their unionization campaign succeeded. They wearily discussed how to get people to show up for shorter-term gratification, such as skills training or a free zoo trip for their kids. By contrast, material self-interest never came up at GHGW, whose members were presumed to have enough interest in the issue and enjoyment of the group's activities to stay involved.

Food, the most immediate kind of incentive, was handled very differently in the two groups. Though the GHGW meeting started at 6 p.m., no food was provided. (One member brought a bag dinner from home, another a take-out sandwich.) In the discussion of low board member turnout and recruitment, food was never mentioned. By contrast, the Local 21 meeting provided food for everyone. The quality of the food was discussed, sometimes jokingly, as the reason for the board absences. Those who preferred Chinese food pretended the pizza was the reason for the low turnout.

This emphasis on quality of food and entertainment continued in the argument, described in chapter 1, over whether or not a party with hot dogs and no alcohol in a public park would draw in new people, with all the black working-class members vehemently arguing that it would not. Marion said, "If [the party] ain't on a boat, can't get them to [show up]. . . . Bring your family, have a zoo day or something." The proposed hot dogs were seen as a step down from the pizza served at regular meetings. The members couldn't believe that white LP organizer Lynette didn't understand that a workplace skill-certification training that would enable people to earn immediate higher wages would be the biggest draw, giving workers a tangible taste of the benefits unionization would bring.

By contrast, during GHGW's long discussion about prospective board members, what the individuals would gain by joining the board was not mentioned. Potential board members were considered because of their affiliation with the mission and usually ruled out because they would be too busy with other commitments. In her interview, board member Melissa said those who "share the ethic" tended to join Green Homes Green World. No one suggested recruiting their own relatives, which some Local 21 members had done. When asked what their family and friends thought of their involvement in the group, GHGW interviewees mentioned only supportive reactions, except for one from a right-wing Republican relative who disagreed ideologically. But Martina of Local 21 answered, "Well, they say it's a waste of time because we're not getting any benefits from it."

Both groups laughed a lot, releasing the frustration about no-shows, but their type of humor was different. The joking comments about tardiness in particular exemplified class differences in sense of humor. As the "Humor and Laughter" class speech interlude following this chapter shows, working-class-majority groups more often elicited laughter with teasing and fake bad behavior, while PMC-majority groups laughed at wordplay and cultural references. Lynette's faux scolding of latecomers was one of many fake-bad comments that elicited laughter:

ALONZO: Man, these Pepsis are hot!
MARION [sarcastically]: You didn't really expect us to get ice, didja? . . .
LYNETTE: The pizza was hot for the people who came on time!
MARTINA: Oooh! [group laughter]

Since GHGW board members sincerely wanted to recruit more people of color and low-income people to their board, the obscurity of some humorous references could pose a problem in making recruits with less formal education feel welcome:

> MELISSA: I was saying that the only way to start on time is if we really start the meetings on time. [*Calling into hallway:*] Perry, where are you?
> PERRY [*from hallway*]: I'm right here.
> MAYA: We're subverting the tardiness paradigm. You should join us. [*group laughter*]
> MELISSA: My God, that's great. Can I put that in the minutes? [*laughter*]

Not as obscure as Maya's academic postmodern reference but still perhaps difficult for a politically inexperienced member to follow was this exchange about a vendor whose acronym, NEDO, was pronounced similarly to the acronym for the North American Treaty Organization:

> MELISSA: NEDO? We're paying NATO? It sounds so wrong. [*group laughter*]
> GORDON: Dick Cheney doesn't surveille us if we make a regular contribution.

Gordon of GHGW also used a certain fake formality, imitating a legal document or a textbook to sound funny, that was heard only from white and black men from upper-middle-class (UMC) backgrounds. For example, he sidestepped a question from the staff director by pretending to dictate for the minutes: "Board expresses its sense of appreciation for being informed of these impending changes, but defers to it being an executive director's function." As a lawyer, Gordon mixed managerial technicalities with a characteristically PMC sense of absurdity in word play:

> MAYA: We're adjourned.
> MELISSA: We can't vote to adjourn though. [*group laughter*]
> GORDON: Right, we don't have a quorum, so we have to stay here until somebody gets here. Of course, we didn't have a quorum to convene, so maybe we were never really here at all. [*group laughter*]

On the other hand, Local 21 members filled in the premeeting time of waiting for more people to show up mostly with teasing and banter, a very different flavor of humor. Marion seemed to be pretending to be at a singles party, Alonzo mock-accused her of drinking, and Will used an exaggerated mock insult:

MARION [*in fake flirtatious voice*]: Hi–i! [*giggles*]

ALONZO: Marion, did you have a beer before you here?

MARION [*to Alonzo*]: I didn't know for sure you were a Scorpio, but
     your eyebrows—

WILL: You should have looked at his tail! [*big laugh from Marion*]

The emotional tone of the two meetings' "Where is everybody?" discussions was also very different. Local 21 rank-and-file members expressed anger at the no-shows in their tone of voice, body language, and ad hominem
criticisms, including exaggerated antagonism to the point of mock threats
of violence. For example, Alonzo said, "I remember Martina call somebody
[who said] 'Don't call me no more.' Probably if Martina was right in front of
her, she'd have knocked her out! [*Marion laughs*]." When Local 21 members
were united in frustration at Lynette, they made eye contact, tag-teamed each
other in teasing her, and used expressive body language (the women slumping
and leaning into each other, Alonzo pacing around the room, putting on his
hat and pretending to walk out).

By contrast, in the relatively formal nonprofit GHGW, low turnout was
calmly discussed as a procedural problem, a lack of a quorum. At a white
high-professional's suggestion, all agenda items requiring a vote were post-
poned. The proposed solutions to low turnout were more procedural than
in other groups, such as polling absent members about the best night of
the week for future meetings. All GHGW members stayed upright in their
chairs, with no dramatic body language. If they were angry at the no-shows,
it was impossible to tell.

Why did these two groups react so differently to a poorly attended meeting? The answer is that activism itself means two very different things to
lifelong-working-class and college-educated people, and these different definitions lead to different approaches to recruitment and building group cohesion. The roots of these differences are revealed in activists' autobiographical
statements about how they came to the group or the movement.

Working-Class Paths to Activism and
Resulting Group Culture Traits

Because working-class activists were often recruited by people with whom
they already shared circumstances (neighborhood, family, workplace, or a
common problem); because they had more often been offered selective incentives that benefited them individually; and because they usually drew no
clear contrast between activism and other less-political community involvements, they tended to define activism as helping people and providing mutual aid for one another's day-to-day needs.

People from working-class backgrounds (both currently working-class and straddlers) tended to describe not only how the group's issue affected them personally (as Han [2009] also found) but also how the group's work benefited particular individuals in need. Altruistic motives of helping others and "giving back to the community" were incorporated into working-class accounts of their activist life stories, not in opposition to wanting to improve their own family's lot, but woven together, often in the same sentence or paragraph.

> ELSIE: I go all around the world fighting for better health care, not just for myself, but for the millions of people that don't have medical and the seniors and the children that can't get insurance.

Working-class activists talked about children and grandchildren much more frequently than did PMC and VDM activists. Sometimes younger generations were invoked as the motivation for activism, its intended beneficiaries (cf. Eliasoph 1998: chap. 3 and 246–48). When Nicole was asked why she got involved in activism, she answered: "My personal reason is I have a three-year-old grandson. . . . I want to see things be better for him. . . . My family leaves it up to me to do all this community work. . . . I wanna change things." Similarly, when asked what people in her group had in common, one working-class Latina in a staff advocacy group said, "I think that the people who are at the table really, really care about kids."

Working-class people used the word "kid" more than *seven* times per ten thousand words spoken, a very high incidence. This working-class rate is more than twice as frequent as professional-middle-class (PMC) interviewees and all college-educated interviewees, and more than three times as frequent as voluntarily downwardly mobile (VDM) interviewees.[1] Similar ratios were found for the less-common words "child" and "grandchild."[2] Straddlers talked about children less often than lifelong-working-class interviewees but more often than PMC and VDM interviewees.

In addition to children and families, relationships among activists were also central in working-class involvement stories. In answering "How did you first get involved?" many lifelong-working-class and straddler activists referred to a trusted leader who had recruited and/or mentored them or a politician or other public figure who had inspired them. As a result, they tended to emphasize such one-on-one relationships with leaders when they talked about drawing in new people.

Members of most working-class-majority groups in the study shared a situation, such as an occupation or workplace, a neighborhood, or being a welfare recipient. This partially explains why working-class and straddler interviewees talked about activist groups in terms of linked fate and shared benefits. But even when it wasn't literally true that everyone in the group was affected by a problem, people from working-class backgrounds made a rhetorical point of tying everyone's self-interest together. For example, in explaining why Women Safe from Violence attracted both survivors and those who hadn't faced violence, Nadine said, "No one is actually immune from [violence]; a whole spectrum of different people have been brutalized." To rally support for a health-related bill that would affect one member union in particular, a Tri-City Labor Alliance member made the point that "we're all patients." Common threats and common needs were invoked both rhetorically and literally in working-class narratives and recruitment efforts.

Not Political Ideas but Personal Impact

In a strangely strong correlation, agreement with the group's ideology or political ideals was mentioned as a recruiting tool by a group member from a working-class background only once: at a meeting, one straddler talked about creating a moral shock by publishing horrific "My Lai type" images of the Iraq war. All lifelong-working-class interviewees and all other straddlers, when asked what works to recruit, *entirely omitted* political ideas from their answers. More broadly, activists from working-class backgrounds only rarely mentioned political agreement in meetings and interviews. A bigger sample of thousands of working-class activists would no doubt find at least a few who stressed using their group's underlying political ideas to recruit like-minded people. But clearly ideology as a recruitment tool was much less often emphasized by working-class activists than by PMC activists.

Instead, personal impact was key for people from working-class backgrounds. As seen in the Local 21 example, working-class activists stressed what benefits the new recruit would get in the short term: immediate help with their problems, a chance for money or job advancement, or a realistic short-term plan to win a campaign benefiting their families. This was true even if interviewees were now college-educated straddlers and even if they were in antiwar or environmental groups; but personal impact was most heavily stressed by lifelong-working-class activists in labor or community-needs groups.

Working-class activists tended to be very skeptical that simply education or information would motivate nonactivists to become active. Nicole said, "I think that a lot of the people don't wanna get involved . . . until it actually happens to them, or . . . if it hits them in a personal way, then you'll see them react and they wanna make a change."

Even straddlers working on issues that didn't affect them imagined that others would be drawn in by a personal connection with the issue, as Jeremiah suggested:

[Someone] was saying "we can't get students involved in these issues." And one of the things I was suggesting is that maybe we got the wrong issues . . . maybe if we stop trying to organize students around issues of the '60s, you know, and look at issues of 2008, maybe we can organize it. And he said, "Like what?". . . If you throw out students loans . . . you're gonna get a lot of takers, people are gonna come to you and say "What about this student loan thing?"

Even advocacy campaigns for longer-term policy change were sometimes framed in terms of personal unmet needs in order to attract new recruits. For example, Dorothea said that the City Power staff would soon be going to the welfare office to recruit for a grassroots lobbying campaign against a budget cut by "flyering and saying stuff like, 'Come to this meeting and tell us why you need more money on your welfare check.'" With issues that were difficult to personalize, such as climate change, some activists, disproportionately from working-class backgrounds, found self-interest angles, such as saving on energy bills.

When working-class activists focused on self-interest and personal benefits, instead of on political ideals, as the key to recruitment, was that a realistic or unrealistic assessment of their constituencies? In a study of the pro-life movement, which has many working-class adherents, Munson (2008) found that agreement with the movement's antiabortion positions did not always precede joining a pro-life group but in fact often came second; he concludes that most social movement scholars overemphasize the role of ideas and political beliefs in mobilization (5). Eliasoph (1998) heard activists and community volunteers attribute self-interested motives to potential recruits (83, 186); they avoided idealistic discourse, even though they themselves had public-spirited motivations. She explains this contradiction by tracing a long history of highlighting individualism and "the language of self-interest" in US public discourse (253).

Similarly, it was obvious that the working-class activists in my study were familiar with altruistic self-sacrifice as part of involvement in social change groups. They themselves gave many unpaid hours, and most did unpleasant tasks for little glory. For example, Bette, a core member of WomenSafe, spent day after day for many years in courtrooms, monitoring for judicial misconduct; a less inherently rewarding task can scarcely be imagined. But when they talked about getting new people in the door initially, even the most altruistic working-class activists focused on others' individual incentives. As one labor outreach activist put it, "We think it's important to increase community participation . . . but people say, 'What's in it for me?' It's a real challenge."

A number of the community-needs groups had had bigger memberships in past years, for example during the welfare reform fight of the mid-1990s; and a decade later, some had made very few changes in their messages and goals despite a new political context. The shrunken size of some working-class-majority groups may have stemmed from their habit of only rarely discussing which issues and frames would attract more new recruits.

Working-Class Definitions of Activism as Helping and Mutual Aid

Helping people was the very definition of activism in some working-class communities. Because they themselves or someone they knew had gotten concrete assistance from their group, interviewees from working-class backgrounds described their groups' goals as helping people, while those from professional backgrounds virtually never did. For example, a low-income African American, Courtney, said the goal of City Power was "to help and empower people . . . help them help their selves." White straddler Estelle of Safety Net for All said the group "began to help poor women find out how to get the benefits they needed, how to work their way through the welfare system." In their interviews, working-class activists used the word "help" (and its variations such as "helping") more often than interviewees of other classes, 1.3 times as often as PMC activists, 1.5 times as often as straddlers, and 1.8 times as often as VDM activists.[3] Most commonly, they included the word "help" when describing the goal of their group.

In talking about community-needs groups, it may seem tautological to say that the group met community needs. Of course members of these groups were more likely to talk about helping people in need, since their members and constituency included people personally affected by pressing problems. But individuals' own class trajectories predicted whether they talked about helping people more reliably than did their movement tradition. The PMC members of community-needs groups didn't mention helping individuals. For example, Alexis, a lifelong-professional Latina in a mostly low-income antipoverty group, said her reason for joining was "contributing to ending what's going on right now with poverty in America," which framed the group's assistance to impoverished individuals as an abstract, generalized cause. I suspect that "helping" would seem to many PMC activists too patronizing, too condescending a role for someone as advantaged as themselves to play.

Conversely, working-class members of advocacy and global-cause groups did tend to frame their groups' goals as helping individuals, even when other group members didn't. For example, in the lower-professional-majority group

Brontown Affordable Housing Consortium, whose mission was mostly policy advocacy, one of the few members from a working-class background, Michael, a young white straddler, was also one of the few to omit references to policy change from his answer about the goals of the group and to stress instead how the consortium enables member agencies to better help people in their urban community: "It allows all of those organizations . . . to tell what they're doing . . . what's going on so that everybody can get together to decide who can help who . . . what would best help [low-income people] in [Brontown]."

To emphasize the virtues of their groups, working-class activists tended to tell stories about particular individuals who had been helped. For example, older white working-class welfare-rights organizer Toni said, "One of the participants in one of [our] workshops did get help through Safety Net for All. He came out of prison, he got married, had a family, couldn't get a job, couldn't get an apartment. Through information that we provided, he was able to get an apartment and turn his life around, so that's good."

At a meeting of the diverse but majority-white-PMC group Easthaver Demands Justice, there was an introductory go-around about members' other community involvements. PMC members mostly talked about their environmental and antimilitarism causes using general terms, but African American straddler Laverne focused more on her other community groups' impact on individuals in need. She seamlessly linked opposition to the Iraq war to support for one particular traumatized veteran; and she described bank-reform advocacy in terms of preventing one particular woman's foreclosure. Her brief check-in mentioned far more specific individuals in need than did any PMC-background member's check-in.

Working-class activists seemed to use a zoom lens on the impact of activism, focusing closely on a small number of known human beings, in contrast with PMC activists' wide-angle lens. For example, note how Rhonda starts with her labor-community coalition's general issues but then zooms in on vivid images of family life: "That's why we push things like living wage . . . anything in the labor movement that we feel can empower the black community, we take it to them. . . . We want families to work one job so that they have someone at home to be with their children the rest of the hours. We don't want them working two or three jobs; then the home is neglected."

The three experienced white working-class founders of community groups, Dorothea, Elaine, and Brandy, all described well-tested methods of recruiting by first providing services to people in crisis, then asking for payback in the form of volunteer hours, drawing them in to activism through direct individual assistance. Brandy said, "We developed a system . . . where we help people with food, clothing, housing, utilities, getting their kids back, whatever it is. It's a commitment to giving back to this movement. People have to give time."

Dorothea talked ambivalently about the costs and benefits of direct service, which City Power had alternated doing and not doing over the years:

> We couldn't do services and organize at the same time. . . . I would be asking different folks, "If you had to describe City Power, what would you [say we] do?" And they would say, "Oh, you help people." And it's like, "Oops!" Well, not that we don't, but . . . when that became the primary definition . . . something's off track here. . . . I actually have very mixed feelings about leaving [behind] some of the kinds of services and advocacy that we did before, like having clothes to give away and a food pantry. It did, in the end, really divert us from the more political . . . stuff, and we just had to give it all up. . . they came in for food, and came back as a volunteer. . . the Black Panthers did it.

For these experienced working-class leaders, direct services were a means to an end, with strategic pros and cons. But to most less-experienced working-class-background activists there was not a meaningful distinction between providing services to individuals and advocating or agitating for policy change. Combining services with organizing was usually taken for granted, and direct aid to individuals was presumed to draw recipients in and bond them with the group.

All community involvements that helped someone were part of the same broad category for many working-class activists. A Neighbors United member, middle-aged Latino Gil, mentioned both activist and nonactivist groups in a go-around about community involvements: "The reason why I got involved with this is the first thing I believe in [the goal]. As far as my participation in the community, I'm involved with kids in Little League, basketball, football, and just to make it a better place for everyone."

For many working-class informants, as with Gil, activism was just one form of giving back to the community and helping others. Brandon referred to his parents' immigrant roots in his explanation of his community involvement:

> INTERVIEWER: Okay, where does your interest in social justice come from?
>
> BRANDON: Our parents never reached anywhere and closed the door behind them. Being from the Caribbean, we've always had family come up, sometimes family would live with us for a while. You always had to reach back and you always had to give back.

It is surprising to find that this sense of obligation to community service was as common among working-class whites and Latinos as among black activists. African Americans have often been observed to have a sense of linked fate across class lines (Shelton and Wilson 2006; O'Brien 2008). "Lifting as we climb," the slogan of the National Council of Negro Women, has historically been a black ethic of race solidarity and community uplift. Many black people have been taught to give back to the community once they achieve any above-average educational or occupational advantage. Thus it might be predicted that references to giving back to the community would have been heard primarily from black activists—which was disproportionately true, but *only* among straddlers and lifelong-working-class black activists. Black interviewees from PMC or UMC backgrounds did not use similar "giving back" language—they had learned different ways of talking about their political ideals—nor did they report doing any apolitical community assistance. It appears that the African American ethic of giving back to the community, in its traditional form and rhetoric, may usually persist for only one generation after leaving the working class.

Conversely, several white and Latino working-class activists did use the linked fate frame for community involvement. For example, lower-middle-class (LMC) white Martha said, "You have to give back to the community. If I were a singer, I'd sing for free. I'm a [health care worker], so I give to [health care access]." The *class* association with a helping ethic seemed stronger than the *race* association.

Mutual aid among members was common in all working-class-majority groups, both formally as part of the mission and informally through one-on-one connections between members. While the term "direct services" implies a giver and a receiver, mutual aid means any member can give and any member can be a recipient. Unions and community groups' missions often included defending members against attack. WomenSafe founder Elaine said members "look out for each other's back"; and the group's mission included protecting members as well as others from violence.

Unlike the one-way definition of solidarity common among white PMC activists, who usually presume themselves to be the givers of solidarity support and less-privileged people to be the receivers, the word "solidarity" for working-class activists usually meant an exchange of aid in times of need, with an expectation that any member might be the next to need help, based on the norms in many working-class extended families (Gerstel 2011; Jensen 2012). The symmetrical language of mutuality seemed central to working-class-background activist talk. For example, Slim described the mission of the Tri-City Labor Alliance as "anything in solidarity with any of the locals."

In low-income groups and unions, commitment to the group was often equated with members' commitment to one another, because solving members' problems was the goal of the group. The words "protect" and "protection" came up in descriptions of such groups' missions. A member of Grassroots Resistance said, "It makes me feel so much more protected that somebody out there is looking out for me. There isn't anybody else going to look out for us." Union staffer Gary said at a meeting, "Protect as many as you can the best you can—that's what unions are all about," and other Tri-City Labor Alliance members responded en masse by calling out "Right" and "Yeah."

Informal mutual aid mentioned within working-class-majority and straddler-majority groups included visits to sick members, setting up e-mail accounts for less computer-literate members, doing members' hair, pet sitting, driving to rescue a stranded member with a dead car, offering home hospitality, and lots of child care. Women were more likely to give such personal assistance to one another, but some men offered it as well. Working-class-majority groups were more likely to recognize milestones such as birthdays, births, weddings, and deaths with cards or by attending individuals' life-cycle events. Only one PMC-majority group was observed doing a group card, for a graduation.

One template for working-class-majority activist groups was the family. In working-class calls for solidarity and mutual aid, analogies to sibling relationships were sometimes used. For example, one community-needs group had "sisters" in its slogan; and some old-time union activists called members "brothers and sisters." Working-class-majority groups were also much more likely to include actual relatives, so references to family were not only figurative. Almost every labor-outreach group, community-needs group, and working-class-majority group had one or more family cluster: siblings, parent/child combinations, spouses, in-laws, and in a few cases cousins or more distant relatives. Leaders in particular drew their family members into their groups. Even those relatives who weren't part of the group were often invited to open events or participated in a loose social network around the activists.

There is a downside to this working-class norm of mutual aid and family-style small-group culture: if fellow activists are expected to be as close as family, involved in one another's lives, then groups must remain small or the expected intimacy is lost. The skill of collaborating with large numbers of near strangers can become rusty if all prior activist experience has been with brothers and sisters in a small, intimate group.

Offer Immediate Incentives—in Other Words, Feed People!

The most common and easily arranged form of immediate incentive for meeting attendance is food. Food was mentioned as a recruiting tool far more often by lifelong-working-class people than by those in any other class category. They had a pragmatic sense that the quality of entertainment and refreshments mattered to recruits. "Snacks are so important," said Myra, a working-class Latina in a professional-majority advocacy coalition. In fact, in many cases food and entertainment were the first things working-class-background interviewees mentioned when asked how to get new people to join, as a member of Neighbors United explained:

> INTERVIEWER: What would it take to get other people? Like, what would persuade the not already active to come to this?
>
> DEVIN: Well, I think you need some kinda entertainment. . . . You can bring a friend and say, "We're gonna go get some food, listen to some music, ya know, hear [a Neighbors United leader] speak, and you can tell me what you think of her."

Food was offered to everyone at *all* working-class-majority groups and *all* groups in the community-organizing tradition. Sometimes the organization paid for pizza or another type of takeout; sometimes leaders or hosts cooked; sometimes members brought store-bought or home-cooked food to share.

Gender also played a role: male-run straddler-majority groups didn't provide food, but straddler-majority groups mostly run by women did. Cooking was a special role of some women of color and white working-class-background women. For example, Pamela, a white straddler, made lasagna for the Neighbors United meeting and welcomed latecomers with "Have you eaten?" But a few regular cooks and food providers were male, as were some of the working-class interviewees who emphasized food as a recruitment tool. Class, even more than gender, was associated with mentioning or providing food.

Not surprisingly, the groups that tended to have preplanned social events were those with the highest budgets, such as staffed nonprofits and unions. The Tri-City Labor Alliance had lots of what Slim called "perks," such as trips to ball games and a holiday party with free food and drink. Low-budget groups, such as ad hoc convention protest groups, socialized only informally, if at all. Part of the class correlation with food stems from this difference in size of budget; the all-volunteer groups with no institutional funding tended to have PMC or VDM members. While labor-based groups had the largest budgets, even the lowest-budget grassroots community-needs groups offered more food and other selective incentives than the global/local cause groups did.

Is it just common sense that because the constituencies of community groups and labor groups have financial hardships, recruits would be more responsive to selective incentives? Are the motivations of a movement's beneficiaries inherently different than the motivations of other activists (Myers 2008: 168, 183)? Is this perhaps just a pragmatic matter, not a class-culture difference? Apparently not: straddlers and working-class members of global/local cause and advocacy groups with mostly middle-class constituencies, such as Jeremiah and Laverne, also stressed self-interest factors and immediate incentives, while PMC members of low-income groups didn't. The pattern matched informants' class backgrounds more closely than groups' movement tradition or constituencies.

Person-to-Person Relationship Building

When working-class people talked about outreach, they were more likely than PMC people to stress developing relationships between key leaders and new recruits. Similarly, while the time-honored method of asking new people to take on small roles was mentioned by all classes except the VDM, people from working-class backgrounds were more likely to say that distributing tasks was the leader's role.

One-on-one relationships with empowering leaders seem central to working-class understandings of recruitment. Some working-class women described the strong role that particular leaders played in empowering them. Straddler Hannah, from the other side of the relationship, described how she gradually built her relationship with rank-and-file union member Aaron, got him involved in Labor and Community United, and worked with him to gradually take on bigger roles.

Putting together these four themes heard in working-class descriptions of paths to activism and approaches to recruitment—being personally affected by the issue, mutual aid and giving back to the community, sharing food and entertainment, and one-on-one bonds with leaders—the overarching theme is *connection*. Activism is rarely a solo path for working-class-background people who have been conditioned to live a more interdependent life (Fiske and Markus 2012: 2).

The fact that well-off straddlers also often described their activist paths in these same connected ways is evidence that this approach is not simply a matter of necessity but a class-cultural understanding, a predisposition formed by a working-class childhood and family.

Professional-Middle-Class Paths to Activism and Group-Culture Traits

Because people from PMC backgrounds tended to enter activism through an individual decision about their political values, which predate involvement in any particular group, and because their groups tended to be collections of strangers brought together by such individual political passions, more of them expected ideas and ideological agreement to bond the group together—and indeed, political beliefs were the strongest bond in some PMC-majority-background groups. (Chapter 9 includes stories of PMC-majority groups that fractured or in which members became hostile to each other over ideological conflicts, which was not observed in any working-class-majority groups.)

Many lifelong-PMC and VDM people's accounts of how they became activists included moments of private decision, along the lines of "I was reading a lot of Howard Zinn, and I started looking for a progressive group to get involved with." For example, when asked how she got involved with Green Homes Green World, Bethany said, "I had recently moved to [this city], and I was wanting to, you know, get connected to progressive work around town." The private dimension of such commitments is why Lichterman (1996) calls the typical PMC activist identity "personalist." When Teske (1997: 51–56) finds that activists on both the right and the left had three themes in their stories of how they became politically involved—a personal crisis, a moral discovery, and a lifelong commitment—he seems to be describing the formation of a personalist activist identity most commonly held by college-educated activists.

Because of their idea-based path to activism, many PMC activists emphasize ideology in their approach to recruiting. They tend to overlook the importance of short-term pleasures at meetings: they laugh and tease less, and usually they don't serve food. PMC activists have fewer unmet basic needs, so mutual aid doesn't often occur to them as a means of building group cohesion. While many working-class activists mentioned the name of a mentor, leader, or role model who invited them to join or inspired their activism, the PMC or VDM interviewees never once mentioned a known mentor in their own activist stories, only invitations from peer friends. Some did mention authors they had read, but the emphasis was on the ideas, not on the person as a role model.

Given their own paths to activism, it's not surprising that some activists from PMC backgrounds said that the key to recruiting new people is the right issues or ideas. Five PMC interviewees talked about the value of working on multiple issues, because each issue attracts different people. Picking the wrong issue is a recipe for failure, others said.

Opinions varied on how ideas and issues would draw new people in. Some activists from PMC backgrounds felt that horrific information would jolt people into action—the moral shock theory (Jasper 1997). Others said that new recruits would match the group's ideology or agree with its with political stance. Some pointed out that each possible focus has its own constituency, an "issue public" (Han 2009, citing Converse 1964), and so the choice of issues affects who becomes interested. For recruiting PMC-background people, this approach seems realistic, since so many PMC interviewees did refer to the group's ideas or issue in their autobiographical explanations of how they became involved.

Unlike the activists Eliasoph (1998) observed, who talked politics backstage but switched to a self-interested "I'm just a mom who wants to keep my family safe" rhetoric in the public sphere, these college-educated activists presumed that potential recruits would be attracted, not repelled, by broad political ideas. Perhaps the difference is that Eliasoph analyzed "front stage" communications with the media and I analyzed "backstage" interviews and meeting discussions (Goffman 1959). Or perhaps what she calls "momism" (183–85) holds sway in certain movements, such as antitoxics groups, more than others, such as the antiwar issue most prominent for my PMC-majority groups.

Some global/local and advocacy groups included spouses and unmarried romantic pairs, but no siblings, parent/child combinations, or other relatives were observed in those PMC-majority movement traditions. Only one set of PMC relatives was seen in any group, a family cluster in Neighbors United. Since most PMC activists had joined their groups as solo individuals, it probably wouldn't occur to them to invite their relatives to join. While working-class activists were more likely to have nearby relatives to recruit, PMC activists tended to live far from their families of origin, making family recruitment infeasible.

Absence of Working-Class Recruitment Incentives

In another strangely strong class correlation, when activists were asked how they came to get involved in their group, being personally affected was *never once* mentioned by a PMC-background interviewee. This must be a statistical fluke; if thousands of PMC-background activists were asked how they first got involved, at least a few of them would no doubt mention how the group's issue affected them personally. But, clearly, personal impact is a more common theme among working-class-background activists. As a result, methods of recruitment involving selective incentives only for members—empirically shown to correlate with the success of social movement organizations (Gamson 1990: 69–70)—were rarely emphasized by lifelong-PMC interviewees.

The working-class emphasis on mutual aid was also missing in PMC accounts of activism. There was one exception, when Sheila babysat the kids of fellow City Power member Ranelle; otherwise, it was unheard of for a lifelong-PMC activist to offer such personal assistance to another group member other than a romantic partner or spouse.

Most striking of all, not one lifelong-PMC interviewee mentioned food in answer to the question about recruitment. Most PMC-majority groups didn't have food at their meetings; the few that did were the most racially diverse urban groups. Perhaps they imagined that their potential constituents were not poor or hungry and thus wouldn't be lured by food; if so, they should learn from the luxurious junkets offered to high-earning doctors by pharmaceutical companies. Trade shows and professional seminars that serve shrimp, caviar, and champagne are evidence that all classes respond to food incentives. The same argument can be made for entertainment; more professional conventions are held in Orlando and Las Vegas than in Omaha.

It's not necessarily a problem not to serve food, particularly in more-advantaged class and race settings where it's not expected. Some foodless meetings had great turnouts. But in four situations where PMC-majority groups were plagued by poor turnout, even though their frustration-filled "Where is everybody?" discussions included brainstorms of possible recruitment methods, no one mentioned food.

The absence of the most common working-class recruitment methods—stressing the personal impact of the issue, offering selective incentives and immediate gratifications, family-style mutual aid, and developing one-on-one relationships with leaders—seems to be a symptom of the class segregation of PMC activists. If they had had more exposure to working-class activists, these additional recruitment tools might have occurred to them.

Special Problems of Community Building in Majority-VDM Anarchist Groups

Voluntarily downwardly mobile anarchists sometimes defined themselves as the opposite of PMC progressive activists: more radical, more committed to "being the change," more opposed to hierarchy within activist groups, and less beholden to mainstream employers and consumer culture. But, in fact, anarchists who were VDM from professional or UMC backgrounds tended to have the PMC personalist traits to an even greater degree.

Shared ideology was usually the centerpiece of their collective identity. Most decided which group to join based on deeply held political values, and they expected others to affiliate on similar grounds. Some drew sharp ideological boundaries:

> GAIL: The anarchists are suspicious of the motives of the [local branch of a national socialist party], and this is based on the fact that they know that the socialists have double-crossed anarchists back to the Bolshevik Revolution and don't trust the socialist agenda, don't trust them because the socialists are statist and believe in the power of the state.

Because these individuals usually affiliated with groups based on agreement with anarchist ideals, and because some rejected not just authoritarian coercion but sometimes even the seductions of persuasion and incentives, they sometimes found themselves with a very narrow repertoire of acceptable recruitment and group-building practices.

However, the VDM anarchist groups also had advantages in group building: they had the most distinct movement culture; they shared the clearest ideological affinity; and they intentionally created the need for mutual aid among people living off the grid or thrown together during direct actions. But these advantages didn't outweigh their distinct weaknesses.

Even more than PMC-majority groups, they tended to offer no selective incentives. As we will see, some even opposed recruiting on principle, to the point of not greeting new people at meetings and in other ways keeping their internal group culture unenthusiastic. As mentioned earlier, mistrust of possible infiltrators exacerbated an already chilly meeting culture, leaving VDM anarchist groups with a serious recruitment problem. Their most vibrant activities took place on the streets or in private gatherings such as parties and squats. But new people interested in plugging in to the scene were sometimes unable to find those gatherings, which had unpublicized locations, and were more likely to be able to find anarchist meetings, which didn't tend to give a good impression of this subculture.

The Conundrum of How Antirecruitment Groups Can Recruit

When I walked into a meeting of my third anarchist group, and for the third time no one greeted me, I knew I'd found a subcultural pattern worth investigating. As I watched others arrive, the core members mostly didn't greet them either. In no other kind of group was "Hello" omitted. What was going on? I started asking every anarchist interviewee about greetings and the warmth or coldness shown to newcomers.

I discovered among some young white anarchists a deliberate, values-based avoidance of any explicit community-building effort, and sometimes even an intention not to recruit new people. Some saw the resulting coldness as a problem. For example, Dallas said, "I'm remembering my first Action Center (AC) meeting, 'Isn't anyone going to say hi to me?'" Gail, a LP nonanarchist and thus somewhat of an outsider within the majority-VDM-anarchist Action Center, said, "The attitude of the meetings is not very warm and welcoming towards newcomers at all. . . . That funny silence, and that funny coldness or reserve—while they say they're all about community; it makes it really hard to feel that there is much of any community at all. It's not a warm community."

Mistrust of Infiltrators

One reason for the chilliness was the presumption that strangers might be spies. Newcomers were often met with initial suspicion and had to prove themselves trustworthy. VDM white man Dallas said, "When new people come, [I feel a] twinge of suspicion, wondering their motives." Virtually every interviewee in militant and anarchist protest groups brought up worries about government infiltration. Experienced anarchists modulated the conversation depending on who was present. A white VDM man in a convention protest group, Brodie, said, "Gauge trust by who's there and have the conversation you can have based on who's in the room." Some experienced anarchists were angry when inexperienced participants asked about confidential matters in open meetings.

This mistrust not only chilled the organizational culture within anarchist groups, it sometimes shredded the bonds between individuals. Whether this fear and mistrust was excessive and harmful was an active debate within this movement tradition.

> ZORRO: Anarchists don't do coalition building [because we have] trust issues, because there's so much repression, it makes it hard for us to organize. . . . A lot of the Green Scare people that were locked up, you know, that happened because of the snitches and informants. . . . We don't work in a very close, intense way with people if we don't know them well. . . . We also have this critique: Are we being too paranoid? Should we loosen up a little bit to be able to coordinate

and talk to each other more or is it completely necessary? . . . We
laugh at ourselves, okay, we're the paranoid crew. . . . Anarchists are
so hunted that we sometimes lie to each other to keep each other
and ourselves safe.

Most common precautions against surveillance didn't interfere with
group bonding: banning photography and recording, wearing masks during street actions, and keeping no confidential information on computer
hard drives. Tactical details went unmentioned at open meetings. But other
measures did come between people. Newcomers had to wait until trusted
associates vouched for them before information would be shared or before
they were allowed into certain subgroups and roles. Using pseudonyms, not
giving out contact information, making sure the addresses of convergence
spaces and meetings didn't appear on the internet, and changing times and
places at the last minute were all practices that put up barriers that kept even
innocent new people out. It seems to me that actual government repression
may be doing less damage to this movement than the self-inflicted harm of
mistrustful "security culture."

But security fears can't explain all the anarchist chilliness toward new people. The Parecon Collective was an alternative business, not a direct action
group, and members expressed no concern about government repression, yet
interpersonal coldness happened there too.

> OLIVIA: [One man] has been in the collective for like maybe ten years . . .
> and he's really hard to talk to . . . he will not say hello to me. He'll
> come down[stairs], and he'll be like, "Hey, what's up," and I'm like,
> "I've been here for like two hours and you haven't said hello."

What could explain this interpersonal chilliness? Are young white PMC-
background men weak in interpersonal sensitivity attracted to certain cold
anarchist groups, or do the group cultures of these groups cause people to
turn off their social empathy and warmth? Gail and Dallas of the Action
Center had the first interpretation, that their group was attracting people
with weak social skills. Gail said, "The desire for connection I think is
there. . . . They don't know how, I think. I really put that down to youth."
Dallas included some self-analysis when asked why there were no greetings as
people arrived: "We're just waiting for business [to start]. . . . I self-identify
as a misfit, not 100 percent socially comfortable. I feel as though the people
in the group are similar in that way."

I was disturbed to hear that Dallas saw all attempts to recruit new members
as too manipulative: "We're not a recruiting organization. I want people to

associate with us because they feel similar. We don't want to evangelize! . . .
All these forces that want to convince [you]: religion, politics—someone's always pushing something! . . . [We don't want] fake smiles [*fake overenthusiastic
voice:*] 'Oh, hi, we're really glad you're here!'"

Dallas was not the only VDM interviewee or the only anarchist to express
ambivalence or negativity about the very idea of recruiting. To find the
same attitude in the Parecon Collective, where fears of surveillance were less
salient and where most members were LP or PMC, not VDM, emphasizes
that it is a specifically anarchist subcultural trait:

> INTERVIEWER: Have you tried recruiting at all? Do you talk to family
> and friends who are not part of [Parecon] about it, and how do they
> react? Have you tried to persuade anybody, and how did they react?
> RUPERT: Not really. . . . I don't want anyone to perceive that I'm
> pushing it on them, and furthermore, you know, I'm not interested
> in someone doing something they don't actually want to be doing.

The entire approach to recruitment and mobilization of the community-
organizing-movement tradition—appeals to self-interest, one-on-one outreach,
and invitations to play small roles—seemed foreign to VDM anarchists. Even
those who didn't oppose recruitment on principle didn't mention any of
those methods. The political philosophy itself was expected to be the agent
of recruitment. For example, a founder of Autonomous Zone, Brian, said,
"A group should come together under a common political goal, because
we're all anarchists." Similarly, Meadow answered a question about her group's
ground rules and membership criteria by stating that ideological agreements
would take care of all that: "In contrast to sitting down and writing a set of
bylaws, instead, use the cause of the group to make the group attractive to the
right kind of people and they [will] take on responsibilities. . . . People are
only going to join who know what the cause is, if they believe in it. That's
the screen." Collective identity was sometimes based on nothing more than
affiliation with anarchism:

> ZORRO: I can't even speak to who "we" are because Autonomous
> Zone only exists in this [convention] context. So when I say "we,"
> it's a temporary, suspended group of anarchists who have all traveled
> here and are working together.

It seems that ideological agreement alone was supposed to be the main
glue keeping anarchist groups together. Despite the rapid growth of the anarchist movement tradition in the 1990s and early 2000s and its role in the
Occupy movement, this seems to me a fragile bond.

Chanting as Coercion: A Story of Contact across Subcultures

One story exemplifies the VDM anarchist rejection of explicitly revving up group cohesion. Several months before the conventions, the Convention Protest Coalition had a multigroup gathering for everyone and anyone who wanted to protest. Over two hundred people gathered in an auditorium for plenary sessions led by a series of upbeat activists, mostly women of color. In particular, Janelle, a middle-aged African American wearing a spangle-covered electric-blue jacket, led a call-and-response to get the crowd chanting. She mostly used familiar leftist rally chants ("What do we want?" "End the war!" "When do we want it?" "Now!"), but she also improvised requests for responses. Later a Latino speaker called out, "How's everybody doing?" and then asked again more loudly when the first crowd response was too soft. Another cheerleader called out each organization and every state represented at the gathering, yelling, "Let's hear it for—." Clearly the goal was to get everyone pumped up and yelling in unison, a familiar group-bonding technique in the labor and community-organizing-movement traditions, particularly in African American groups, as well as in nonactivist settings such as sporting events and self-help seminars.

At the next meeting of the anarchist Action Center several members mocked those coalition plenaries, and especially the mass chanting. After a meeting break, Dirk gathered people's attention by chanting sarcastically, "Three Word Chant! Three Word Chant! Three Word Chant!" He was making fun of the group-building efforts that he associated with those he called "communists" and "liberals," who seemed to him the top-down opposite of anarchists. During a discussion of the conference, Dirk said, "They had the usual rhythmless chants." In his interview, Dallas explained this disapproval of chants: "I see chants as empty, as a feel-good artificial [thing]. . . . Personal autonomy means not forcing yourself, not forcing anyone else."

But another dimension to the story reveals what the antichanting anarchists were overlooking. At the Action Center meeting, members expressed surprise that the AC and other anarchist groups were not attacked or marginalized during the conference, even though they knew that many participants disagreed with their "diversity of tactics" approach (disruptive street protests without an explicit nonviolence commitment). One of the concrete outcomes of the coalition gathering was to get everyone's agreement on a statement that included a commitment not to say anything negative in public about other convention protestors. AC members cynically expected to hear objections to including them and other anarchists under the umbrella of this unity pledge, and they also expected it to be violated before the conference was over. They were surprised that this didn't happen.

I see a connection between their opposition to unison chanting and their surprise at the strength of the unity pledge. During the big coalition conference, a collective identity, a sense of "we," was created and reinforced among the varied convention protest groups, some of them rivals or even previously hostile. The plenary chanting and cheering was a powerful ingredient in how that alchemy happened. Since most AC members regarded it as manipulative groupthink, they were at a loss to account for its effects in cementing the coalition unity that included them.

Mock chanting to signify antiritual attitudes seemed so idiosyncratic that I assumed I wouldn't encounter it again after hearing it at that one Action Center meeting; but then I heard something very similar at a Parecon Collective meeting, an anarchist setting where there were no notable tensions with nonanarchist groups:

> RUPERT: Should we bring it in for the Parecon Cheer? [*Olivia laughs sharply at his sarcasm*]
> TAYLOR: How does the cheer go?
> RUPERT: I dunno—[*sarcastically*] "Camaraderie!"
> TAYLOR: Gimme a "P". Gimme a "A"—

Similarly, Zorro said of a call-and-response chant at an Autonomous Zone meeting, "Fucking cheers, and that's bad facilitation."

Zorro took it upon herself to explain to me the values underlying punk-anarchist opposition to explicit community-building efforts. After a spokescouncil at which pagans led a guided meditation (during which she and her friends didn't close their eyes as instructed), she told me, "I hate that religious shit. Keep it organic; don't force it."

To Zorro, Dirk, and some other punk-influenced anarchists, "natural" and "organic" were the opposite of authoritarian. Their threshold for what seemed too coercive was very low. Whole-group cheers, rituals, exercises, and even invitations to get involved seemed like brainwashing, impinging on individual conscience.

Pagan-influenced anarchists who favored more explicit efforts at group building were sometimes clever at dodging the opposition of more punk protestors, acknowledging the antiritual faction and attempting to bridge culturally to them. To open a spokes council with a ritual, Sage said, "I'd like to ask your permission to raise up energy in the room. If that's not your cup of tea, it's okay to tolerate it. In the pagan [affinity group], this is how we express solidarity." Nevertheless, many people kept their eyes open and rolling during the song and ritual that followed.

The recent literature about emotions and social movements (Goodwin, Jasper, and Polletta 2001; Gould 2009) has shown how emotional arousal related to public identities (Han 2009: 96) can lead to political involvement. Social movement groups often succeed in recruiting when they touch emotional chords in potential recruits. The cool atmosphere at some anarchist meetings may prevent this emotional reaction.

Subcultural Style, Music, and DIY Re-Creation of Mutual Aid

The young white anarchist subculture, despite its problems with mistrust and opposition to recruitment and explicit community building, also had some strengths in building a sense of cohesion. Their movement culture, described in chapter 4, with styles of clothing, cloth patches, hair, lingo, and other subcultural markers, made their group identities more distinct than those of nonanarchist groups.

The most powerful social movement organizations tend to have a three-part identity: with the group, with its wider movement, and with a social location (such as "women" or "workers") (Gamson 1991). The anarchist groups had the strongest movement identity of any movement tradition I studied, rivaled only by the labor identity in certain unions. On Lofland's (1995) spectrum of degrees of movement culture, from easily blending into the mainstream to highly distinct, this subculture had the greatest degree of movement culture.

As a participant in the convention protest marches, I often couldn't distinguish protestors from passersby in crowded city streets, because bystanders dressed so similarly to many marchers; but I could always distinguish the boundary of the anarchists' actions by their bandanas, black clothes, and flags on tall poles. Anarchist direct action participants seemed to have a strong sense of cohesion during street actions.

In addition, for some majority-VDM anarchist groups, voluntary poverty was part of a prefigurative effort to create a more collective, sustainable economy in miniature, so they had a similar mutual aid ethic as that observed in working-class community groups. By their principled disconnect from the mainstream economy, off-the-grid activists artificially created needs for interdependence. Without credit cards, and in some cases without jobs, homes, or health insurance, some young convention protestors relied on Food Not Bombs or similar groups to feed them, and found housing by couch surfing with other activists. Local squatters oriented out-of-town protestors on where and how to stay safely in abandoned buildings. Street medics took care of minor medical needs. Like the Occupy Wall Street–inspired encampments around the globe, the convergence centers set up for every major globalization protest in the 1990s, and every political convention since at least 1996, were places not only for meetings but for basic needs such as sleeping, bathrooms, first aid, internet connection, and food and water. These free and shared goods and services were seen as prefiguring an alternative economy.

But this mutual aid during direct action campaigns didn't usually extend to meetings. There was shared food (gleanings from a dumpster-diving expedition) at only one of the observed anarchist meetings. At one meeting, several individuals went out to buy their own slices of pizza and brought them back to eat; probably a whole shared pizza would have cost less than the slices.

Playing in bands together, whether punk bands or political brass street bands (like those that gather for the annual Honk! festival in Somerville, Massachusetts),[4] is another way of building a sense of subcultural identity. The hilarity at the Honk! festival has given me a completely different impression of the DIY anarchist subculture than I got by going to four groups' chilly, low-affect meetings.

Historically, some anarchist movements, such as the Spanish anarchists and the Wobblies in the 1930s, had substantially or primarily working-class memberships. It's an interesting thought experiment to imagine how anarchist groups would be different if the same were true today. It's difficult to imagine the same lack of greetings, low affect, and refusal to pump up group spirit in any working-class-majority group today. The avoidance of explicit group building seen in the four anarchist groups was not only a matter of ideology, age, personality type, race, and gender, but was also influenced by the class-cultural predispositions of members from PMC and UMC backgrounds.

If so many VDM activists didn't reject identity with their privileged class backgrounds, their PMC class-cultural traits, such as an overemphasis on ideology and an underemphasis on relationship building between core and new members, might have less power to weaken the anarchist movement. Class cultures denied always cast a longer shadow.

Are Class Culture Differences in Group Building a Problem?

To some extent, each activist class culture emphasizes the recruitment mode that is most effective for its class constituency. Currently working-class and poor people may in fact be most likely to be drawn in through short-term incentives, and once in the door, they may form attachments to groups through one-on-one relationships, mutual aid, and laughter-filled meetings that build camaraderie. Progressive-leaning college-educated people may be best re-cruited by cutting-edge ideas. Young VDM people with antiauthoritarian leanings may be best attracted by subcultural markers of rebellion and anar-chist ideology. Perhaps these are just class-culture *differences*, not class-culture *clashes*?

The problem with each group happily continuing its habitual recruitment and group-building practices was that all the groups were too small to reach their goals. Most participants wished for new members and better turnout. Some wished for more cross-class alliances with other groups. In addition, some groups had a goal of being more racially diverse. Growth and diversity depend on understanding what appeals to people of other classes.

Class Speech Differences I

Humor and Laughter

In the last chapter we saw how two groups coped with low turnouts using humor and laughter. Whole-group laughter was heard during almost every meeting, but at different rates of frequency depending on class.[1] Working-class-majority groups laughed an average of once every 8.75 minutes.[2] Professional-middle-class-majority (PMC) groups laughed an average of once every 15.71 minutes.[3] Voluntarily-downwardly-mobile-majority (VDM) groups seem to have laughed even less.[4]

Group sense of humor—what tended to make everyone laugh in meetings—also varied quite a bit by the groups' majority class. No meeting included any actual jokes with punch lines. Instead, humor was woven into conversations. Laughing about individuals' foibles, both self-deprecating humor and teasing others, was much more common in working-class-majority groups than in PMC-majority groups.[5] Laughing at word play and cultural references tended to happen in PMC-majority groups.

Teasing was often part of a back-and-forth in which people joshed each other. Some teasers knew the targets of their teasing well. In a Brontown Affordable Housing Consortium meeting, for example, members needed no explanation as to why Charlotte wouldn't actually be baking for the bake sale:

CHARLOTTE: I am bringing really good desserts. [*group laughter*]
DARLA: She is such a good faker!
CHARLOTTE: I bake really well at the stores. [*group laughter*]

TABLE 1.1 Mean rates per hour of three types of humor in meetings by class background

	Working-class-background-majority meetings	PMC-back ground-majority meetings	Ratio between rates
Number of meetings	8	10	
Individual foibles	3.2	1.2	**2.73**
Fake bad behavior	3.2	1.3	**2.54**
Word play and cultural references	0.44	1.28	**0.35**

Note: Untranscribed and very mixed-class meetings are excluded from table. Working-class-background includes straddlers; PMC-background includes VDM. Straddler-majority groups tended to have a similar humor pattern to lifelong-working-class-majority groups.

A related form of humor, fake bad behavior, was the most common source of laughter in all class categories, but working-class-majority meetings laughed about it more often than PMC-majority meetings. Only rarely was a specific individual mock insulted, and never a new or marginalized person. Usually it was the group itself that was targeted. For example, note the general focus of this quick retort from a working-class white man in a City Power meeting:

RANELLE: How about a talent show?
DARIUS: I don't know anybody with any talent. [*group laughter*]

Pointing out something problematic about the group's functioning (shorthanded here as snafu—"situation normal, all fucked up"—to reflect the typically irreverent tone) was a common cause for laughter in all meetings, with no class correlation.[6] Snafu comments that don't sound like jokes nevertheless evoked lots of laughter: "We could read the minutes if I hadn't left them home."

These three types of humor—self-deprecating and teasing, fake bad behavior, and snafu—have in common negativity about the group and its members. Such negative barbs accounted for 62 percent of all laughter-eliciting speech at working-class-majority meetings, compared with only 45 percent at PMC-majority meetings. Such negative humor was heard most often in labor-outreach and community-needs groups.

Humor scholars Robinson and Smith-Lovin (2001) categorize humor in task groups as "differentiating humor" versus "cohesion-building humor." They find that differentiating humor, including directed jokes at one's own expense, is used more by higher-status members of the group, such as men and frequent participators (146), and that it has the effect of reducing group cohesion:

"Differentiating humor calls attention to the separate group members, as when a speaker jokes about him- or herself, or when a speaker teases another group member, or subset of other group members. These types of jokes may be more likely to be used in hierarchy building. At any rate, they break down the sense that 'we're all in this together' and point out distinctions among group members" (142).

My findings contradict Robinson's and Smith-Lovin's in two ways. First, I found an association between differentiating humor and lower class status, not higher. Is class different than gender? Perhaps, or perhaps the groups we observed were different. Their task groups were ad hoc groups of southern undergraduates in the 1980s, which probably included few people steeped in the working-class negative-humor style I observed. Second, differentiating humor *did* build cohesion in these working-class-majority groups. Successful groups whose members were clearly enjoying one another's company tended to have lots of laughter, mostly at negative comments about self, others, and the group.

How did negative comments build group cohesion? First, they seemed to signal familiarity, the closeness required to abandon polite formality (Hay 2000: 720). Members and leaders demonstrated publicly that their bond was too strong to be broken by negative comments that might cause offense if said by an outsider. Many scholars have noted the prevalence of teasing among working-class people as verbal play (Heath 1983; Miller 1986; Norrick 2010: 233). Bourdieu describes French peasant humor this way: "Ritual mockery or insults which are neutralized by their very excess and which, presupposing a great familiarity, both in the knowledge they use and the freedom with which they use it, are in fact tokens of attention or affection, ways of building up while seeming to run down, of accepting while seeming to condemn" (1984: 183).

Second, teasing and self-deprecating comments played a role in preventing free riders from avoiding meetings and shirking group tasks. Many negative humorous comments referred to slacking off. Meetings are often boring, and members of voluntary groups often feel tempted to show up late, leave early, or not come at all. By joking about wishing the meeting would end, these individual temptations are transformed from a private stress to a shared experience, something everyone feels, thus building the sense of "we." Note the opening joke of guest speaker Reggie, a labor leader unaffiliated with Tri-City Labor Alliance who wanted TLA's support but knew his presentation would prolong the meeting:

TONY: Thanks for coming.
REGGIE: Thank you for having me. What a great night; it's ninety degrees outside; everybody probably wants to be somewhere else. [*group laughter*]

While direct criticism might weaken group cohesion, a joking tone followed by laughter allowed absences and undone tasks to be sanctioned more lightly. Teasing others about what they had failed to do chivvied members along; it was a gentle form of social sanction for slacking off (Hay 2000: 719, 723–24). For example, at the small Safety Net for All meeting, to which several members didn't show up, there was this exchange between two working-class women:

TONI: I just wanted to ask the minute taker if she would put down the people who are absent as "absent" on that list. We haven't been doing that.

LIDIA: So why do I have to do that?

TONI: When I see my name as absent . . . on a meeting that I'm supposed to be at, I always feel guilty. [*group laughter*]

LIDIA: So is that what it is, to make them feel guilty?

TONI: No, to let them know we were thinking of them! [*group laughter*]

A teasing reference to a shortfall in effort, and the laughter it evoked, served to ease the potentially tense moment (Hay 2000: 735–36). As Peggy Miller writes, "To tease is to convert a dispute into a mock dispute" (1986: 209).

These positive functions of differentiating comments also worked for PMC activists, but more of them, especially older white women, seemed to be constrained by a cultural prohibition on teasing. Robinson and Smith-Lovin (2001) found that women used self-directed humor less often than men; only high-status members can afford to joke at their own expense, they hypothesized (146). In my experience, this gender difference is prevalent only in the professional middle class.

While leading workshops on classism in the mid-2000s, I discovered a teasing taboo for some PMC women (especially middle-aged and older white women in the helping professions) that contrasts with some working-class people's comfort with teasing. The national nonprofit organization Class Action offers a workshop called "Promoting Respectful Communication: Responding to Verbal Classism," in which one participant reads a real-life classist comment and another has to respond instantly; the group then formulates general principles for what works with people who make classist comments. I led this exercise at three social worker conferences, and in those mostly PMC and female settings, I observed that professional women tended to favor polite modes of changing the minds of classist commenters, never discussing teasing or open anger unless the facilitator brought them up.

But one such workshop included blue-collar maintenance men. An Italian American man, Antonio, tried this retort to a classist comment: "Cut it out, that makes you sound like an asshole." A subset of the group laughed, including some other working-class men; but others didn't laugh. A lively disagreement broke out, with several professional women insisting that insults always alienate the listener; Antonio and another blue-collar man insisted that sometimes that's exactly what does work. "But not teasing! Teasing is never okay," cried out one white woman in a distressed tone. She seemed to think of teasing as cruel tormenting of the marginalized, what bullies do. I don't think this is what Antonio was advocating; I think he was imagining a relationship of sufficient familiarity that an exaggerated put-down would work to chasten offenders without making them feel mistreated. To pull this off successfully requires some specific class-cultural competence.

Teasing and other banter has been documented as an African American test of in-group knowledge and cultural competence (Kochman 1981; Miller 1986). I suspect that there's a similar class-cultural boundary between working-class and PMC Americans of all races about teasing and being teased.

Unique to working-class-background women of color was a form of body language that bonded them as they laughed together: making eye contact and moving upper bodies toward and away from each other. For example, in a Neighbors United meeting, when Fred barked at an overtalker, "Doug, be quiet!," Gil said, "Ooh, smack down!," and three working-class and straddler women of color caught eyes, then shrieked and laughed as they rocked their bodies forward, then back, in sync. The meeting then moved forward with noticeably less tension. An almost identical pattern of eye contact, body language, and laughter was observed among the black women at the small Local 21 meeting profiled in chapters 1 and 5.

Another form of humor, though not very frequent in any group, usually occurred at PMC-majority meetings: word play and cultural references. Laughter at such references happened three times as often in PMC-majority meetings as in working-class-majority meetings.[7] Most examples of word play that elicited laughter in PMC-majority groups were brief puns and neologisms. For example, the pretraining before the training could be "kindertraining"; instead of retiring, someone was "re-wiring." Most cultural references that were met with laughter in PMC-majority groups were brief allusions with political content, such as "It's another 'Good job, Brownie!' " (referring to President Bush's praise of the official who botched the Hurricane Katrina response). Most laughter-evoking cultural references seemed to be easily understood by all group members, as when the interfaith group jokingly alluded to the Bible and Saul Alinsky.

More problematic were cultural references not understood by working-class or otherwise marginalized members. In a mixed-class meeting of East-haver Demands Justice, an upper-middle-class (UMC) member referred to the hand sewing that Irene was doing with a literary reference to Dickens and the French Revolution that some members didn't understand, including at least two working-class members:

> IRENE: I'm always sewing.
>
> MIA: Irene is our Madame Defarge. She's deciding who's going to get guillotined.
>
> MAN: We wish! [*laughter*]
>
> SEVERAL PEOPLE: What? What?
>
> [*Overlapping speech and laughter as others answer with explanations about the French Revolution,* Tale of Two Cities]

As we saw in chapter 5, the board members of Green Homes Green World were troubled by poor turnout and the difficulty of recruiting volunteers of color to serve on the board. No doubt there were many causes of these recruitment troubles, but the kind of humor enjoyed by the all-PMC board members, such as the "subverting the tardiness paradigm" comment, probably didn't help.

Laughter and humor helped create and demonstrate a sense of familiarity at activist meetings; they were key building blocks of group cohesion. Yet humor culture clashes, such as unfamiliar cultural references and the PMC women's teasing taboo, sometimes cause problems for mixed-class groups.

CHAPTER 6

Activating the Inactive

Leadership and Group-Process Solutions That Backfire

A dozen people sat in a circle without speaking. They were having a meeting, but long silences dragged on as they all waited for someone to say something. What was going on? Action Against Empire (AAE) had a big problem with unequal participation, and at this meeting the group's informal leaders were holding back their own participation in hopes that someone else would step up.

Usually the same three members not only did most of the talking at AAE meetings but they also did most of the tasks between meetings. Two of them, Alton and Ira, found themselves in the uncomfortable position of holding antihierarchy values and yet being treated as the informal leaders of their group. These two men, one a white lower professional (LP), the other an Asian American college student from a mixed-class background, returned time and again to this dilemma in their interviews, criticizing themselves for failing to put their ideals into practice. They had two approaches to equalizing participation: holding themselves back from overparticipation, and introducing group processes designed to draw out the less-active people. At the AAE meeting I observed, neither approach worked: more than half the members were silent except for initial introductions and saying yes or no to proposed dates.

Many voluntary groups face this problem of too many passive members and too few active ones. And as we will see, many college-educated activists tried the same two strategies that Alton and Ira tried in AAE, only to find them insufficient, or sometimes even backfiring. A third approach, trust-worthy leaders championing member interests, suggested almost entirely by working-class activists, was not a panacea either, but it did add some methods of mobilizing the inactive that were missing from the first two strategies. The leaders who used it won members' trust through beneficial action and then played strong roles in developing inactive members' involvement.

Dimensions of Disempowerment and Class

The essence of movement mobilization is transforming people from passive to active, from being unwilling to speak up to being outspoken. Until that transformation happens, newcomers and socially marginalized people, as well as simply shy people, can find activism intimidating; they may struggle to find their voice and their sense of inner power.

Ten interviewees put their experience of disempowerment into words, making insecure statements including the following:

- "I'm not that smart to do that."
- "I have a fear of getting up in front of people and talking, and I'm still sort of nervous about that."
- "I never want to be in charge. . . . I'm just a helper in the background."
- "I don't know if it's really my place . . . maybe because I don't really have too much knowledge of it like they do."

Nine of the ten people who put their disempowerment into words were women. Racially, they were diverse in proportion with the whole pool. In terms of class, half had lived lifelong in the working-class range; none were lifelong professional-middle-class (PMC). It seems that disempowerment is experienced, or at least verbalized, most strongly by less-class-privileged women, as Cummings (2003) also found. The triple threat of being female or transgender, working-class, and new to activism was associated with the most passivity and silence.

How do marginalized people become and remain disempowered? When Gaventa (1982) investigated why poor people in an Appalachian valley didn't rebel against the exploitive coal companies, corrupt politicians, and inattentive union locals that impoverished them, he turned to Lukes's (1974) dimensions of power to define three kinds of powerlessness: a straightforward lack of resources and clout; barriers to participation in decision-making arenas, along with discouragement due to anticipated defeat; and susceptibility to myths and ideologies that block critical consciousness (21). The quiescence in the Appalachian valley was caused by the interrelationship of these three kinds of powerlessness (256), and no doubt the same mix inhibits working-class activism throughout the United States today.

In another revealing study, Croteau (1995) interviewed working-class nonactivists about why they didn't get involved in middle-class-led social movements. His findings show that it is *not* primarily disagreement with the cause, lack of knowledge, lack of time, or logistical obstacles that keep working-class people from becoming activists. The main reason for their lack of involvement, Croteau found, is "the absence of efficacy" (chap. 5), a sense that activism wouldn't do any good. Sometimes this discouragement reflects a realistic understanding of how little regard politicians have for input from people like themselves. But sometimes disempowerment is learned helplessness, carried over from experiences of oppression, which prevents effective political action.

In interviews, core members of virtually every group expressed concern about quiet inactive members and how to get them to speak up and take on more roles. This seems to be one of the most universal social change group troubles.

Approaches to Inactive Members and Leadership

Because concepts of leadership were very closely tied to preferred solutions to the problem of inactive members, approaches to activating the inactive showed up most clearly in response to a question asked in fifty-one interviews, "Who are the leaders of your group?"

To both activists and social movement scholars, successful leadership usually means fostering member empowerment (Morris 1984; Polletta 2002). Movement how-to manuals emphasize this activating function of leadership (Kahn 1991; Bobo, Kendall, and Max 2001). These manuals talk about leadership very differently than the most widely known leadership typologies, which contrast dichotomous types: directive versus participative modes (Likert 1961; Heller 1973) or task-oriented versus people-oriented leadership (Bales 1950; Shartle 1956; Hersey and Blanchard 1977). The task/relationship dichotomy is not a controversy that polarizes today's activists. Almost universally, interviewees valued both.

Command-and-control leadership is not an option for social movement organizations, as members are free to choose their own level of participation. Only three of the fifty-one interviewees who were asked about leadership (all of them respectable African American Christians from working-class backgrounds) presumed that leaders make a plan and tell the members what to do. The other 48 expressed the goal of getting members to participate more actively in decision making. But there were class differences in what they thought leaders should do to advance that goal.

Classed Strategies of Activation Tied to Concepts of Leadership

Three strategies for increasing active involvement, each with a different underlying concept of leadership, were promoted primarily by activists fitting a certain class profile:

1. Holding back from domination. Underlying this strategy is a concept of leader as dominator, best serving member involvement by self-monitoring, allowing others room for autonomous action. This strategy was advocated and practiced most often by voluntarily downwardly mobile (VDM) and lower-professional (LP) activists.
2. Facilitating stylized group processes. Underlying this strategy is a concept of leader as manager, best serving member involvement by designing and running processes that require everyone to speak, for the concerted cultivation of equal participation. This strategy was advocated and practiced most often by PMC and assimilated-straddler activists.
3. Trustworthy championing of member interests. Underlying this strategy is a concept of leader as trusted protector, best serving member involvement by strong chairing and fostering mutual loyalty with concrete aid, leading to the accomplishment of natural involvement. This strategy was advocated most often by working-class activists, and practiced most often by class-diverse leaders of working-class-majority groups.

Not only did these approaches come primarily from distinct class trajectories, but the dissenters who raised concerns about each approach also typically came from a different class than the proponents. The rationales for and against each strategy had roots in activists' class cultures.

Strategy 1. Holding Back to Avoid Domination: Allowing Autonomous Action

This strategy required more dominant group members to hold back and deliberately speak less, to make space for quiet members to speak up.

The interviewees who advocated holding back were mostly young, white members of the groups in the anarchist traditions. In ten of the fifteen interviews with members of anarchist groups, this strategy for increasing quiet members' vocal participation was advocated. Half the interviewees who advocated holding back were younger than twenty-eight; half were male, and half were female; nine were white, and one was Asian American.

For example, in the Action Against Empire meeting described at the beginning of this chapter, this was Alton and Ira's main response to the vastly unequal participation within the group. They left long pauses. But it didn't work; the quiet people remained quiet. Even when they held back, Ira and Alton were by far the most vocal members. In his interview, Ira expressed guilt about this imbalance and said that he should have been "stepping back and not taking up so much space." However, whenever he and Alton did sit silently for a few minutes, they fruitlessly waited for the facilitator or someone else to speak up, which casts doubt on the effectiveness of using only this strategy. Analyzing the silences in the meeting in light of Ira's self-described intention to hold back, we can see that he and Alton were intentionally performing a nondominating, egalitarian role (Goffman 1959). But in other members' eyes, this performance didn't work to remove them from the leadership of the group.

The mostly VDM or LP advocates of the holding back strategy tended to answer the question "Who are the leaders of your group?" with a negative judgment of the very concept of leadership, or else they answered, "We are all leaders." Some referred to race and/or gender domination, suggesting that men and/or whites should try to speak less. Twenty or thirty years earlier, such negative definitions of leadership would have been associated with radical feminism (Taylor and Whittier 1995: 169), but in 2007–8, antileadership was primarily an anarchist ideal.

Leon, a VDM white convention protestor, was the only holding back advocate to include class as a basis of domination: "I hate the word 'leaders.' I see it come up over and over, informal hierarchies. The people who've been here for a year and a half are more comfortable in their voice. . . . It's hard for new people or nonwhite or non–middle-class people to incorporate themselves. People self-select; those who can, dive in."

Three college-educated men in two antihierarchy groups displayed a telling behavior. While chatting before the meeting, they spoke at an average volume, with typical male cadence; but as soon as they stepped into a facilitation or presenter role, they spoke at a much softer volume. Sometimes their sentences ended with an upward lilt like a question, the way some deferential young women speak, but men rarely do. For example, "For the agenda? we could start with this issue from last time? that we didn't finish?"

In answer to a question about why he spoke in that lilting way, Ira's self-aware response explained the ambivalent, self-doubting, seesawing quality characteristic of LP's speech:

Alton and I, we're both men, and I think relative to other people in the meeting, we take up a lot of space. And especially when there's female facilitators, we don't do a good job of like stepping back . . . one side of my brain is trying to be like hyperconscious and somewhat overcompensate for trying to recognize when I should be speaking up, when I shouldn't be speaking up, who's speaking up, who is not. . . . I guess associating like softer voice, not being so imposing, either in the volume of my voice or my body language. . . . It's more of an effort to put ideas out there, not impose them.

Rupert, the young white man from an upper-middle-class (UMC) background in the Parecon Collective, also answered a question about this phenomenon by describing being torn between assertiveness and holding back:

INTERVIEWER: I noticed Julius, before the meeting started, he was chatting, say [*loudly*] this was the volume of his voice—–but when he was in the facilitator role, his voice was really soft, and he had those little tentative things where it goes up [*lilting tone*] at the end of the sentences. What do you think is going on there?

RUPERT: I think he is conscientious about being authoritarian in a group setting and perhaps overcompensating or would rather err on the side of being tentative instead of being authoritarian.

INTERVIEWER: Like a firm voice might sound like making too much of his facilitator authority?

RUPERT: Right. Going from facilitator to "discussion leader"—you know, you can't draw the line that says this is where you go from being a good facilitator to *pushing* the conversation along. . . . I think I tend to be more authoritarian. It's a balance of being conscious that I'm a guy, and I shouldn't be taking up all the air time [or] pushing the conversation where I want it to go—and balancing that with like [*louder, frustrated tone:*] "We're not talking about what we're supposed to be talking about here!"

These white men were prefiguratively trying to embody their goal of a world with no top-down authority by refusing to act in a dominating way themselves. Like VDM lifestyle choices, holding back appears to be not a class-culture strategy only; it could better be described as a norm typical of a particular age/race/class/gender/ideology intersection.

The association of the holding back strategy with a VDM class trajectory is strengthened by observing who dissented from it: primarily non-VDM people in majority-VDM groups. Its most articulate critic was Gail, the middle-aged white LP nonanarchist in the primarily VDM, anarchist Action Center. Her critique echoed the classic article "The Tyranny of Structurelessness" by Jo Freeman (1972). She described the unintended negative consequences of the antileadership stance common in young anarchist groups more generally: "We're talking about the very micro, micro things about the anarchist culture, the young people culture. There's . . . a real unwillingness to speak out and take leadership or be assertive about one's point of view. . . . I identify it as being about power. I identify it being about leadership and the reluctance to take leadership."

Within the Parecon Collective, Olivia, the one lifelong-poor member, was the only one to express skepticism about avoidance of leadership. Instead, she proposed stronger and more conventional facilitation and simple majority-rule voting to draw in new and marginal people; she didn't propose to solve the problem of underparticipation by holding back, nor by innovative group process, though she had been exposed to both those leadership strategies in the Parecon meetings. Both she and Gail pointed out how the holding back strategy backfired, how VDM activists' discomfort with power ended up reinforcing the power of core members.

Strategy 2. Facilitating Stylized-Group-Process Techniques: Managing Concerted Cultivation of Equal Participation

In answer to questions about their groups' leaders and about their ideal group, 12 interviewees brought up three to six specific group-process techniques, often advocating them as ways to get quieter members to talk more.

Most of these techniques required each meeting participant to speak, for example by answering a particular question. Often they required certain people to speak in some stylized way (for example, just one person per small group reporting back only on the points everyone agreed on). Recent examples of stylized speech processes were seen in the Occupy movement's general assembly "mic check" ritual (a call-and-response sometimes used even when actual amplification was available) and hand signals during decision making.

The most frequently suggested process was go-arounds (each person taking a turn speaking without any response). Go-arounds had various purposes: evaluations of the meeting; opinion gathering during decision making; and to open the meeting, something more elaborate than the ubiquitous introductions, such as personal check-ins or a playful question (e.g., "If you were a tree, what kind of tree would you be?"). For example, Ira said, "The go-around-the-circle thing is something I like 'cause everyone has a chance. . . .

I think it makes the situation more comfortable. So if I'm facilitating, I like to ask if we can go around the circle."

Many interviewees suggested group-process techniques to solve other problems as well, such as conflict resolution. Some advocated a structured sequence of steps in consensus decision making. Several spoke in favor of facilitation training to teach the group's processes.

The 12 interviewees who advocated stylized group processes were diverse in gender, age, and race. This strategy seemed to predominate in one move-ment tradition: seven of the twelve were in global/local cause groups. But class background was their biggest commonality: eleven of the twelve came from privileged class backgrounds, higher than the overall pool of interview-ees and higher than the median for their groups. Four were lifelong PMC. Seven were VDM; of these seven, four grew up PMC and three were raised UMC or owning class—very privileged class backgrounds.

The only lifelong-working-class person who advocated multiple stylized-group-process techniques was also the most ambivalent about them. Doro-thea, the founder of City Power, told a story about identity caucuses with both positive and negative outcomes. She also answered a question about how her ideal meeting would begin with a nuanced statement containing both upsides and downsides of process techniques: "Sometimes City Power has started meetings with check-ins, and that's been interesting, but if some-body's in a personal crisis, that can totally divert the whole meeting . . . I like it when agendas are put together collectively and where anyone who's interested in learning the skills of facilitation and leadership can do so. Not everybody is. Some people would really prefer to be the doers, but most people are interested." The eleven more class-privileged interviewees favor-ing this strategy tended to have far fewer qualms than Dorothea about styl-ized processes as a means of increasing active involvement.

A few PMC interviewees with high-level nonprofit jobs emphasized the sophisticated skills required to run a good meeting. For example, a profes-sional union staffer wished members got more training in parliamentary procedure. And an African American top manager in a national nonprofit said that his views differed from other members':

INTERVIEWER: If you were in charge of the next meeting, what would you do to make it go better?

RODNEY: I would try and set the context, like what is it that has got-ten us to this point, what decisions do we need to make. . . . I'm a trained facilitator. I've run trainings before, so I kind of come at this with a very, very specific almost technical lens.

Blake, a white nonprofit staffer, moderately VDM from a UMC background, was an exemplar of this leadership style. While facilitating one Easthaver Demands Justice meeting, he was observed using four stylized processes: a personal check-in with a specific question to answer; breaking into pairs and reporting back on what the *other* person said; a goal-setting process with a sequence of several steps; and writing key points on big paper under prewritten headings that sorted member input into categories. He frequently cut off those whose words did not fit into the current process step and redirected them to another part of the agenda when their point would be appropriate. He blended the managerial orientation of his early PMC conditioning and elite education with the countercultural process style of his movement tradition. Clearly, facility with creating and leading such group processes is part of the PMC cultural capital needed for leadership roles in the nonprofit sector and in many global/local cause groups.

This association between PMC culture and the stylized-process leadership strategy is strengthened by examining who dissented from it. When Blake facilitated the EDJ meeting in such a stylized way, not everyone cooperated, and not everyone approved. The dissenters and noncooperators were all people who grew up working class or poor. Interviews with two dissenting EDJ members, one a white male and the other an African American female, illuminate how stylized group process might not fit with working-class cultural conditioning. Mack called for a more spontaneous, natural way of building group participation. From a working-class background and retired from a unionized skilled trade, he was a fairly unassimilated straddler, class culturally different than most EDJ members and also a blunt curmudgeon in personality. His disagreement with EDJ's process is worth quoting at length, because he elaborated sentiments that were signaled less directly by other working-class-background informants:

> I don't happen to believe that these organizational tricks. . . . I come out of the union movement, but . . . this writing things on a paper and putting them all up, I don't happen to think that any of that is very useful. I mean people feel like they're doing something, but then the process becomes an end to itself, and I don't think it contributes anything of substance. I have a pretty extreme view of this stuff . . . and bridle at being put through that stuff. . . . People who come out of a certain tradition, in a sort of nonprofit world in what's called community organizing, tend to love that stuff. . . . I feel that that practice, although it tries to present itself as being very democratic, and it really strives for everyone to participate, but the reality is if a small number

of people develop a very complex agenda and really control what happens, my view is that, in fact that's *less* democratic than something that's more spontaneous.

Another EDJ process noncooperator, Laverne, was one of three middle-aged or older black interviewees from working-class backgrounds who were notably disinterested in organizational questions. A veteran of many grassroots campaigns in her urban, mostly black neighborhood, Laverne answered questions about group process with brief, vague, passionless answers, but she became passionate when discussing her past community activities. She proudly invoked black leaders' names as she described the wonderful things groups had accomplished under their direction. She said about one group, "Oh my goodness, they kept us hopping! [Well-known black male leader] was a very good teacher!" After repeatedly probing for group-process opinions and finding none, the interviewer asked her directly:

INTERVIEWER: Some people I talked to, they're super opinionated about the process and how decisions get made, you know, the structure and how the meetings get run. But I get the feeling that that's not something you care that much about.
LAVERNE: Well, you mean in running the meeting?
INTERVIEWER: Some people are really opinionated about how decisions get made, by a vote or who's facilitating and how that's done . . . what about you?
LAVERNE: Well, as long I'm able to take part in the meetings, I'm not really too upset about who's facilitating the meeting. As long as it comes to a good conclusion.
INTERVIEWER: You don't care how you get there.
LAVERNE: Exactly. As long as it's not too drastic.

Within this mixed-class group, both meeting behavior and opinions about group process roughly lined up with class, in particular with class background.

THE ROOTS AND PURPOSES OF THE STYLIZED-GROUP-PROCESS STRATEGY

These stylized processes have come into US social movements from numerous sources: social work (Benjamin, Bessant, and Watts 1997), Quaker tradition (Butler 1981), the second-wave feminist movement (Iannello 1992; Ferree and Martin 1995), organizational-development consulting (Lakey et al. 1996), and diversity training (Adams and Lee 2007). During the prefigurative movements of the 1970s and 1980s (Breines 1989), Movement for a New Society (Cornell 2011), the War Resisters League, the Highlander Center, and the National Coalition Building Institute trained activists in these techniques.[1] Training for Change continues to teach them today.[2] Meetings that use these methods can be formal, with many preset agreements on process steps, or spontaneous, with innovative processes coined on the spot. But in any case, their creative and interactive process style contrasts with the simpler, more businesslike meeting procedures taught by labor educators and the Midwest Academy's community-organizing school (Bobo, Kendall, and Max 2001).

In the 1990s, the anarchist direct action wing of the anti-corporate-globalization movement kept some processes from these earlier traditions, dropped others, and added new ones, as did the Occupy movement. The anarchist-influenced groups in this study were the most likely to use hand signals during decision making and to use consensus decision-making methods with a preset sequence of steps.

The rationale for more elaborate group processes is often expressed in terms of cultivating the empowerment of less-empowered members. For example, the social workers who wrote *Making Groups Work* (Benjamin, Bessant, and Watts 1997) wrote that a facilitator's role includes "increas[ing] the competence and confidence of group members" (89) and leading "structured exercises" that foster "experiential learning in groups" so that the "group can see its dynamics" by encouraging members to "take a slight risk, experiment or try something out" (131). These authors put stylized group processes into the context of a long process of increasing agency and skills, akin to Freire's (1970) *conscientização,* critical consciousness raising that gradually expands the capacity to act. In Polletta's (2002) formulation of the three benefits of participatory democracy—solidary, developmental, and innovative—these stylized-process advocates stress the developmental aspect.

But to other proponents, stylized processes are intended to instantly equalize power by creating identical spaces for each voice. Iannello (1992), for example, says that anarchist-feminist practices of consensus decision making, rotating roles, and other alternative structures by themselves prevent domination and create shared leadership (42–43). Sociocracy is another method in which egalitarian processes are expected to produce an equality of power (Buck and Villines 2007). The short-term outcome of equal turns to speak is sometimes stressed over the more realistic developmental goal of slow skill building over time.

Resonances of an Earlier Movement Era: A Personal Reminiscence

I'm not a neutral observer of these controversies over stylized group processes. I was once a group-process zealot, until my activist experiences brought me to a more skeptical, nuanced view.

What first attracted me to lifelong activism was participatory group process and prefigurative movement culture. In 1977, I was a Princeton student languishing without clear purpose when 1,414 Clamshell Alliance protestors were arrested at the Seabrook nuclear construction site and jailed in New Hampshire state armories for two weeks. The *New York Times* had reporters inside the armories, and they reported daily on the remarkable scene there. A group of us began reading those articles aloud in the dining hall every evening. The protestors were organized into affinity groups; they spent their time singing and leading workshops; and they managed to change jail policies such as gender segregation by mass noncooperation. Most amazing of all, they were making decisions by consensus—with hundreds of people. They used an elaborate system of small-to-large-group transmission of concerns and objections, which actually worked to make tricky decisions, such as refusing to be bailed out. Like the young activists galvanized by the beginning of the Occupy movement (Delvino 2011), I fervently wanted to be inside the armories with the antinuke occupiers.

I dropped out of college and joined Movement for a New Society (MNS), a national network of activists that had played a major role in organizing the Seabrook occupation and facilitating the group process in the armories. For the first year or two, I loved everything about MNS organizational culture: the playfulness of incorporating games into meetings; the freedom to challenge anything and process everything; the long deliberations over internal dynamics and political positions. For me, it was a tremendously empowering experience of participatory democracy.

Ten years later, MNS disbanded, fading away with a sad failure to flourish. My own evaluation, shared with some others (such as MNS cofounder George Lakey [Cornell 2011]), is that rigidity about consensus decision making was one of the reasons it languished. Consensus can be deeply conservative, as the status quo is the fallback position if consensus can't be reached on a change. I saw this first with gay rights: despite MNS's focus on "oppression/liberation" issues such as sexism and classism, the organization was about five years behind most of the Left in adding homophobia to its analysis of social problems. Why? Because one single person, in one local chapter, who as a boy had been molested by a man, blocked consensus on taking that stand. Wave after wave of younger people brought new political energy into MNS, only to have their ideas not achieve 100 percent consensus. There may not be many MNS veterans who would say this as strongly as I'm saying it, but I suspect that if we'd had a more flexible decision-making system, MNS might be alive today.

Many attempts have been made since then to modify the consensus process, preserving its channels for minority opinions but making it less time consuming and less conservative, for example in some feminist groups (Iannello 1992), in some self-managed collective workplaces (Buck and Villines 2007), and in some Occupy groups.

More broadly than just problems with consensus, I gradually realized that the movement culture that had charmed me did not charm others. And there was a pattern in who wasn't charmed: not only champions of the status quo, no loss to our movement, but also working-class people with plenty of critiques of social problems. My tastes for creative, ultraegalitarian process had grown out of my UMC background, and like all tastes, they separated people by class. The anti–nuclear power movement, for all its success, stayed smaller than it had to, given that a majority of Americans came to oppose nuclear energy. Those most threatened by radiation in their backyards and by rate hikes in their electric bills did not join in great numbers.

I remember my first glimpses outside my countercultural bubble. Building an antinuclear coalition with local working-class groups exposed me to coffee-and-donuts community organizing. Meetings were quick, teasing was rough, and leadership was seen as a good thing if it resulted in stronger action against unjust authorities. I was in culture shock. But the down-to-earth working-class organizational culture appealed to me, and I started to see MNS group process through these activists' eyes: stilted, overstylized, oversensitive to small imperfections and slights, and sometimes just bizarre.

Here's one memory that exemplifies the culture clash. My antinuclear group, a bunch of long-haired men and hairy-legged women, had gone to a senior citizen group to recruit them to help stop a local nuclear construction project. They were mostly white men retired from blue-collar jobs. The meeting was going well when someone proposed we take a coffee break. One of my esteemed counterculture colleagues said, "I know! For the break, let's all howl like wolves!" And even worse, several people did it! As a big "Owwwww-ooooooh" went up, I saw senior activists nudge each other and roll their eyes, as if they were thinking, "What's up with these wackos?" Their group did join the coalition, but no thanks to the howlers.

Something in my gut switched allegiance at that moment, from a previous enchantment with all things alternative to a skepticism about what is effective in movement building. I began pushing my sister and brother countercultural radicals to blend in more with the norms of less culturally distinct groups, in particular working-class groups; and to confine their howling (metaphorically speaking) to small groups just for howling devotees. We had thought of ourselves as prefiguring emancipatory participatory democracy, but in ways that were invisible to us, we were also performing class-exclusionary PMC counterculture.

I coined a term back then to describe alienating behavior such as howling: "inessential weirdness." By including the word "inessential," I was acknowledging that what alienated a movement's more mainstream potential supporters was sometimes essential to an activist's core identity, such as sexual orientation or a minority religion. But many other styles and actions that seemed bizarre to some constituencies outside the subculture were optional; in those posthippie days, the most common inessential weirdnesses were voluminous hair, crunchy granola food, and ultracasual behavior such as sitting on the floor. Within MNS and the antinuke movement, I advocated shedding inessential weirdnesses, and in particular not imposing them on others when building bridges to working-class communities and other non-counterculture coalition partners.

Now fast-forward to the 1990s and the rising anti-corporate-globalization movement and the growing anarchist subculture. Many of the same admirable qualities of MNS reappeared: the emphasis on creating positive alternatives, a comprehensive analysis in which all injustices are interconnected, and the courage to do nonviolent direct action with unpredictable tactics.

But sometimes it seemed that all MNS's mistakes were being made again, with a new set of inessential weirdnesses. I have seen process tastes intensifying the very problems they are meant to solve. Excessive rigidity in group process and strict equality have sunk many groups aiming to prefigure their ideal world. Polletta (2002) calls for a more sophisticated idea of participatory democracy, based on a more complex equality, to enable social movement groups to give all their members a voice, develop their deliberative skills, and do their work effectively and efficiently.

In MNS we had a checklist of skills that every activist should acquire. If I were amending that list for today's college-educated radicals, I would add the skill of participating in a brisk, leader-run, majority-rule, action-oriented labor or community-organizing meeting without whining about the process.

While I still advocate that facilitators think in advance about how to use a meeting to increase the group's creativity and cohesion, and while I still judge meetings by how many new or marginalized people's ideas are drawn out, I no longer think there's a formula for the right group process to accomplish those goals. In fact, I think that belief in a formula poses a problem for cross-class movement building.

So as I did the fieldwork for this book, I could not observe the most process-heavy meetings with a neutral eye. I had an agenda of discovering which participatory democracy methods work to activate disempowered potential activists—and an agenda of making PMC-background group-process proponents more aware of which of their class-culture-specific processes might be less effective with working-class and poor people. While my research uncovered some examples in which stylized group processes *did* work to activate new or marginal members, I also found many examples, summarized below, in which they seemed to make things worse.

How Stylized Group Processes Sometimes Backfire

The Action Against Empire (AAE) meeting described in the opening of this chapter exemplified how stylized group processes sometimes didn't simply fail but actually backfired. Several techniques Alton and Ira introduced had the unintended consequence of intimidating or marginalizing the less-active members.

First, rotating facilitation backfired. A different person facilitated each AAE meeting. The facilitator of this meeting, inexperienced activist Cass, was the only member from a clear-cut working-class background and the only transgender person in the group. Cass spoke so seldom that I didn't learn who was facilitating until interviewees told me later. With the facilitator almost silent, no one called on members to speak or asked them evocative questions. Only the three most active members presented information or suggested roles that needed filling.

Rotating facilitation is a popular way of sharing leadership and empowering marginalized members by giving them a turn to be in charge. Of twenty-six interviewees with an opinion on who should chair meetings, sixteen (including every VDM person) favored rotating facilitation; only ten interviewees favored a steady chair. But to rotate facilitation without any training, and without any explicit agreements about how facilitators encourage member participation, is to leave meetings too weakly chaired. Its effect on inexperienced one-shot facilitators like Cass is questionable; it may sometimes work to strengthen their facilitation skills and sense of enfranchisement, though sometimes it fails at this too. But its disempowering effect on other less-active members is undeniable. Many new and marginalized people didn't speak until someone asked them to, and rarely did anyone ask except a confident, skilled chair or facilitator.

Second, hand signals backfired. Hand signals communicate agreement, disagreement, and other messages during consensus decision making in many global/local cause groups with younger members. Four groups used hand signals; no two used identical versions. At AAE meetings, arms crossed over chest meant blocking consensus and wiggling fingers in the air meant consent.

One newer AAE member, Lowell, a Latino lower-middle-class (LMC) man, the only person at the meeting who was neither white nor Asian, and the only one besides Cass from a working-class-range background, was exactly the kind of quiet, marginalized member that the stylized group processes were meant to activate. In this explicitly antiracist group, whose leaders fretted about too little racial diversity, getting Lowell more actively involved might have been a top priority. But when a decision was made early in the meeting, everyone wiggled their fingers in the air except for Lowell, who stared at the wigglers, dumbfounded. Ira explained the signals only after this decision. Lowell was almost silent for the rest of the meeting, asking just one three-word question. Seeing eccentric hand motions, a classic inessential weirdness, used by everyone except himself may have marginalized him further. I asked Alton about hand signals, and he said, "If there are new people, we want them to get acclimated to the signals in the group. It's a responsibility that we should try and keep up-to-date, especially when there is a new person there. . . . We scan the room, go around and make sure that everyone is doing some kind of signal." But this attentiveness to shared understanding of hand signals had broken down at the meeting Lowell attended.

Third, it seems that strict consensus decision making didn't always have its intended empowering effect either. Unlike in more informal groups, in which the word "consensus" meant talking until a sense of the meeting emerged and those with minority opinions spontaneously quieted down, "consensus" was used at AAE in the stricter sense that any dissenting opinion could have the power of a veto. This veto power was key to how Alton described the enfranchising effects of consensus: "I really enjoy the consensus-based decision making. While it does make meetings longer, and maybe decisions don't get made as quickly, I think that it's important to make each individual feel that they have something to contribute to the group; and if you give an individual the power of veto . . . that really sort of gives people the responsibility, makes them feel like a participant."

But in practice, newer and less-active members had rarely if ever blocked consensus at AAE meetings, to Ira and Alton's despair. Alton described how nonleaders avoided expressing dissenting opinions: "I feel that the way to overcome people's concerns with the group, especially with this unspoken hierarchy, is to combat the habit of looking to [other] people for consensus. . . .

I feel that people sort of look around the room and then give their opinion, which means that if they see someone who they feel to be a larger part of the organization consenting, then they make their decision on that."

The phenomenon Alton described is not uncommon in strict-consensus groups, where only the most enfranchised were observed taking the dramatic step of blocking consensus. Blocking consensus is a much higher-risk action than casting a nay vote. The final authority granted to any individual's veto makes it harder for any new person except the very boldest to block. Given the very wide gap in participation levels in this group, it's not surprising that the less-enfranchised AAE members weren't exercising their veto power. The very process meant to level hierarchies was, in fact, reinforcing them.

These stylized group processes were the main tools that Ira and Alton had in their tool kit, and even after some techniques didn't work, they continued to suggest other similar processes to make the group more egalitarian and participatory. One process, separate race caucuses, reportedly did work to give a stronger voice to members of color: Alton said that everyone spoke during the first caucus of people of color. But it seemed that most of the other group-process solutions didn't have the intended positive effects.

I don't know what AAE's problem was, why so many members hung back from speaking or taking on tasks. Perhaps, as Ira and Alton suspected, the dynamics of a few dominating leaders, all white and/or male, had disempowered others; perhaps some personality clash or political disagreement was unspoken in the room. But in any case, most of the stylized group processes introduced by the informal leaders did not solve the problems, and some backfired and made things worse.

The antiauthoritarian wing of the globalization and antiwar movements developed some of the protocols used by AAE specifically for protest-planning meetings. Spokescouncils or general assemblies before direct action *do* require different processes than other meetings, because they are often one-shot ad hoc meetings; some have hundreds of participants; and sometimes the action under discussion is less than twenty-four hours away. Hand signals and speech restrictions (such as that only affinity group representatives can speak) are methods of coping with those special circumstances. Strict consensus, with an emphasis on individual veto rights, means that the majority cannot make a plan that puts the minority at risk of arrest or injury. But when processes developed for those unusual situations become the norm for regular meetings, as they have in some anarchist and Occupy groups, their downsides may have unintended negative consequences. Some VDM white anarchists saw these processes as a nonnegotiable characteristic of egalitarian activism without evaluating their effectiveness.

Breaking Up Natural Conversational Sequence

Another reason that some stylized processes backfire is because they interrupt the most common pattern of natural conversation, in which each utterance responds to the immediately prior utterance (Sacks 1992: 41–43; Furo 2001: 27–29).

For example, "keeping stack" kept conversations choppy. In this method, a separate stack-keeper or the meeting facilitator keeps a list of people waiting to speak and calls on them, ideally in the exact order that they raised their hands. The process is intended to equalize access to the floor, to prevent dominant personalities or informal leaders from talking more than their share. But with its lack of a mechanism for keeping the discussion on topic, the stack system made some discussions disjointed. I observed new people ask questions that were never answered because someone with a different point was next in the stack.

Some systems of hand signals have a signal for "direct response," pointing alternating forefingers at the prior speaker to indicate to the chair that there's a reason to break the stack to allow another comment on the same topic. But this signal was rarely observed in practice, and then only by the most process-savvy insiders. So the effect of keeping stack was to make the meeting less like a naturally occurring conversation. Group discussion became a series of individual solo statements, and joint productions (Sacks 1992) were prevented.

The same interruption of the conversational flow is often a feature of go-arounds. In the form common in PMC- and VDM-majority global/ local cause groups, the rest of the group listens silently until one person is done, then turns their gaze to the next person, which signals her or him to start speaking. The facilitator speaks only to restore the one-turn-each norm if a back-and-forth breaks out. Not only is the question usually asked just once, at the beginning of the go-around, and not only are most contributions greeted with silence, but the expectation is that each speaker will respond not to the prior speaker but to the original question, making the flow very different from natural conversation. While appreciative laughter or comments did sometimes happen during go-arounds in global/local cause meetings, such interruptions were less frequent than in working-class-majority community-organizing groups.

Overall, in PMC- or VDM-majority global/local cause groups, meeting participants tended to be left on their own to formulate their contributions, which stood alone, without a conversational preliminary or a follow-up response. Individuals were expected to perform a freestanding utterance during go-arounds, in small group report-backs, and when keeping stack was the means of calling on the next speaker. This requirement is reminiscent of the speech performances that Lareau (2003) found to be expected of middle-class children, who were continually quizzed by middle-class parents and teachers and asked to perform their knowledge. Lareau found working-class adults' interactions with children to be very different, without such demands for a solo performance. Thus, processes requiring solo speech performances may seem more comfortable to PMC activists and more foreign to some working-class activists.

There's a race and gender dimension to this cultural strain as well. Some working-class black communities have coached boys, though not usually girls, to compete in creative public solo performances from a very young age (Heath 1983); working-class African American men with this childhood experience might find solo-performance process demands more comfortable than would working-class whites and/or women, most of whom have been socialized into more interactive, collaborative speech norms (Tannen 1996; Belenky, Bond, and Weinstock 1997).

As the findings of this previous research would predict, those who ex-pressed discomfort with go-arounds were women from working-class back-grounds, in particular women of color. No one had problems with the ubiquitous, straightforward introduction go-arounds requiring only name and organization, just with substantive or icebreaker questions. At one meet-ing of Neighbors United, all those from PMC backgrounds, all men and all white women cooperated with a go-around about what the group should do next, but three Latinas from working-class backgrounds made these com-ments instead:

> STELLA: Uh—what was the question again? [*group laugh*]
> SHIRLEY: I can't think of anything right now. [*group laugh*]
> BLANCA: I kind of just walked in, so I'd like to hear what everybody else has to say, as far as that goes.

Though go-arounds are much more familiar than, say, hand signals, it seemed that these women felt self-conscious about being put on the spot by a go-around question. But all three offered opinions and volunteered to do tasks at other points of the meeting.

A review of empirical studies (Hackman and Morris 1978) on the effec-tiveness of group processes found that those that increased group creativity, such as brainstorming, did have positive effects, but that there were "process losses" when the methods "severely limit the amount of spontaneous interac-tion that can occur among group members and constrain interaction" (58).

Their conclusion is that it's worthwhile to put attention on how group processes can foster creativity and problem solving but that groups should use sparingly methods that stifle participants' responses to one another.

The two leadership strategies advocated by activists from more-privileged class backgrounds—holding back and facilitating stylized group processes— have in common attentiveness to how much each member is talking. The goal of sharing airspace equally was emphasized; sometimes it was equated with equal power. Equality in the number of utterances by each person, or as close to equality as possible, appeared to be a key measure of the group's effectiveness in involving the less-active members. But, as we shall see, this is not a goal central to everyone's concept of leadership.

Strategy 3. Trustworthy Championing of Member Interests with Protective Leadership: Accomplishment of Natural Involvement

The notion of leadership was much less problematic for another set of in-terviewees, mostly from working-class-range backgrounds. Some displayed a frank acceptance of power differences, though they frequently opined on whether particular leaders abused their power. Others opposed excessive power differences but nevertheless described effective leadership as cham-pioning member interests. Seven community-needs or labor groups appeared to rely primarily on this leadership strategy for activating the inactive. Twelve in-terviewees from those seven groups praised a strong, protective leadership style.

Early in this study I had hypothesized that there would be a correlation between class composition and the formality or informality of meetings, but that hypothesis proved to be wrong. The meeting styles of the seven groups with large working-class memberships and led by trusted protective cham-pions in fact varied widely, ranging from the casual family-style discussions common in small, low-income community groups to the simple majority-rule process taught in most community-organizing training to the more elaborate Robert's rules procedures common in industrial unions. In any case, their meeting processes tended to be less innovative and less time consuming than in the groups where the stylized-group-process strategy was observed.

When these interviewees advocated democratic input, they praised lead-ers for using their authority strongly to ensure all members had a chance to speak. Listening was closely linked to forcefulness, not opposed to it. For example, Slim said about an officer of the Tri-City Labor Alliance, "He's been around. He knows how to argue. He knows how to fight. He knows when to make his point, when to shut up . . . he's very effective as a political leader. . . . He makes his points and he listens."

Nicole from Neighbors United thought the question about leaders was a straightforward one:

INTERVIEWER: And who do you see as the leaders of the group?
NICOLE: Fred.
INTERVIEWER: Fred?
NICOLE: I see Fred as a leader.
INTERVIEWER: And how is he as a leader?
NICOLE: I think he does a great job. He's very organized. He knows
   how to recruit people to get them to where he needs them.

Note that Nicole's praise of Fred accepts that members *should* get to "where he needs them," but she sees him as a persuader, not a commander.

When Elaine, the much-admired founder of Women Safe from Violence, was asked, "Who are the leaders of your group?," she answered, "It's pretty clear I'm a leader of the group. I'm not going to act stupid about that [*in a funny little voice*]: 'Who, me?' I have power. I try extremely hard to get people to step up and do new things."

Working-class-background activists tended to evaluate leaders by the trustworthiness of their actions, not by how little or much they talked (except in cases of extreme overtalking). Phrases such as "walk the talk" and "the proof is in the pudding" expressed this watchfulness for actions of integrity with avowed values. Here's how working-class Latina Darla defended Carolyn, a Brontown Affordable Housing Consortium leader whom other members criticized:

Some people kind of take, like, "What the hell is she, a white woman from [a middle-class suburb], she doesn't even know what the hell she is talking about." "I'm sorry, honey, but once she's the one here at eight o'clock at night reading to kids, oh yeah, that cuts it for me.". . . . She works, she definitely puts her money where her mouth is, she absolutely does, she would be someone that would be here on a Saturday, she's here at night . . . talk is cheap . . . so for me it's like "You go, girl!"

A tiny number of labor and community group members criticized their current group's leaders for failing to make all members feel respected, for breaking the rules, or for abusing power. But more common was criticism of a leader of a group they had formerly been involved with. Voting with one's feet by quitting a voluntary group in which a leader had proved untrustworthy appears to be part of the strategy of entrusting strong, protective leaders. For most working-class activists, to stay in a group required trusting the leader(s).

"Exit, voice, and loyalty" (Hirschman 1970) are three possible responses to problems in an organization, and there's a class correlation in who tends to choose which option. Speaking up with complaints while remaining in the group was more common among college-educated activists. Working-class activists were more likely either to quit or to stay loyal, and less likely to voice criticisms while still in the group. The average number of negative comments made during full-length interviews about activists' own groups was more than six for lifelong PMC, three for lifelong working-class, and about halfway between for straddlers. (See online figure 6.1.) Because so many interview questions probed for problems in the group, it took some effort to avoid voicing complaints, which made this working-class verbal loyalty conspicuous.

Why were there so few criticisms by working-class interviewees? Most working-class interviewees seemed sincerely enthusiastic about their current group, more so than any other class group. But a few seemed to be exercising restraint in not expressing criticism. Closing ranks and loyalty to leaders were clearly working-class habits. There was probably reluctance to air dirty laundry to a stranger, a presumably middle-class interviewer, particularly on tape. One working-class interviewee snuck in a quick criticism of her group's leader after the recorder had been turned off.

Openly dissenting was sometimes interpreted as disloyalty. For example, Slim regarded it as a major betrayal when executive committee members failed to present a united front to the members of the Tri-City Labor Alliance. He was angry at executive committee members who revealed at membership meetings their individual dissenting opinions that had already been outvoted at the committee premeeting.

The old canard that working-class people are passive followers who prefer authoritarian or even fascist leadership (Lipset 1960), long disputed as empirically wrong (Miller and Riessman 1961), differs from the watchful conditional support given to trustworthy leaders only. Evidence against Lipset's stereotyped portrayal of sheeplike working-class people is found in interviewees' critiques of their *former* leaders. When the lifelong-working-class interviewees were asked about their current group or about their hypothetical ideal group, many of them answered by telling stories about how awful their former group had been before they quit. When their trust and positive bond with those leaders eroded, they quit, which reinforces the point that loyalty is a basis of working-class group affiliation.

Two lifelong-working-class members of Neighbors United, Nicole and Cecilia, had both quit the same group. Both avoided questions about Neighbors United by instead criticizing that former group.

INTERVIEWER: Do you have any pet peeves with people at the Neighbors United meetings?

NICOLE: I'm sure Cecilia told you about the other group we belonged in.

INTERVIEWER: She did. She did, yeah.

NICOLE: It was very one-sided. . . . [The leader] was very controlling. Nobody else's opinion mattered. [*story about beginnings of abuse of power*] I finally left. [*long story about the last straw*] So I'm very glad that [my current group] runs differently.

This pattern showed up over and over in working-class activists' interviews: someone joined a group, had a negative reaction to something the leaders did, walked out, and later used it as a cautionary tale.

Lifelong-working-class activists were also more likely to speak positively about their current group's leaders. Seven leaders of labor or community groups were especially praised by interviewees as strong leaders. Observing their leaders' behavior during meetings, as well as hearing them described by other group members, suggests that championing member interests and ensuring member input are components of a broader strategy of protectiveness.

All seven of the most-praised strong leaders lived in the same working-class or poor community as most members, but they had more privilege than the typical member. Five were white and one was mixed-race; four were homeowners; four had college degrees (although vocationally oriented and only acquired in middle age in two cases); five had decent-paying, steady jobs. Other members didn't tend to share all these class advantages, and leaders' protective acts could be interpreted as sharing them with members.

Their protective acts varied by gender. The four admired male leaders socialized with members, sometimes going to bars after meetings, sometimes buying refreshments or hosting social gatherings in their homes. These four men were also praised for skillfully standing up to authorities on behalf of members, as well as for forcefully intervening to prevent domination during a meeting. For example, in the Neighbors United incident described in the "Humor and Laughter" speech interlude, remember that Fred barked "Be quiet!" at the white PMC man who had repeatedly interrupted others. Working-class interviewees and interviewees of color expressed only positive reactions to Fred's authoritative handling of this incident. They appreciated his forcefulness in making space for the rest of them to speak.

The three women most praised as strong leaders (Elaine, Dorothea, and Brandy, profiled in chapter 1) played much more intimate roles in members' lives. They fit Collins's definition of "community othermothers" who use their power not to dominate but to uplift (1991: 131). Their protective acts included taking in a homeless member, lending a member money, attending at a member's childbirth, and providing food. Members also sometimes aided each other in these ways, as seen in chapter 5; leaders seemed to be the most active protectors within a network of mutual aid.

An anecdote from a meeting of Women Safe from Violence illustrates the link between leaders' protectiveness and members entrusting them with power. The founder, Elaine, was not at this meeting, as she was out trying to rescue a member from a dangerous situation. A timely issue on the agenda had to be decided at that meeting: accepting or rejecting someone's offer of sanctuary for group members, which could possibly endanger the person making the offer. The members vehemently disagreed with one another: roughly half opposed taking the offer and half supported it. Then the chair revealed that Elaine opposed taking the offer and suggested "just going on Elaine's judgment." Others spoke immediately:

NADINE: She's the one up close and personal.
RANDALL: We have a founder and leader, and she's the best. Elaine has to make decisions for the group all the time. We should trust her judgment.
LACI AND KATERI IN UNISON: We trust her.

The chair called for a vote: those who had supported the offer during the earlier discussion all abstained, so only votes opposing the offer were recorded. Loyalty and deference to Elaine were so strong that no one voted contrary to her opinion even when she wasn't there. The group discussion linked this loyalty to trust in Elaine's commitment to protecting members.

The downside of relying on trust in a leader, of course, is that sometimes trust isn't there. In particular, across race, it can be difficult to establish. Latina straddler Hannah described the dynamics in her mixed-class, mixed-race labor-community coalition: "People like Yvonne [*white staff member*] and Kevin [*white volunteer*], their legitimacy is always scrutinized, questioned by African Americans. . . .Are they serving their own power and getting ahead on the ladder? Or are they really trying to represent the people? . . . So there's always a lot of questioning, and there's not a lot of trust."

Note how Hannah emphasizes "questioning" and "scrutiniz[ing]" "legitimacy," an example of how trustworthiness is monitored in community and labor groups.

Sometimes leaders aren't trustworthy. Unscrupulous opportunists can gain excessive amounts of power or status if they manage to tap into a working-class community's propensity to follow a strong leader. Although no leaders were observed amassing or abusing power in these twenty-five groups, Lichterman

(1996: 122–26, 222) found a "centripetal cycle" in some grassroots toxic-waste groups, in which all energy and legitimacy were drawn into too few leaders.

Dissenters to the strategy of entrusting authority to trustworthy champions of member interests tended to be notably higher in class than the other members. For example, Sheila, a white LP woman, expressed a wish that her mostly working-class community group, City Power, wouldn't concentrate leadership functions in so few people.

What Processes Foster the Development of Empowerment?

Some working-class people described their own process of empowerment and praised their labor or community-needs groups or particular leaders for assisting them in that growth. For example, a working-class black woman, Pearl, said about Low-Income Women Rising:

> Everyone's a leader. We teach leaders. We promote leaders. So when I came into welfare rights, I wasn't a leader in anything but my house, of course. They make you—they don't "make" you—they empower you to stand up, speak out, and fight back. My first task was holding a sign. I never was holding a sign . . . so I held the sign, and then from there I listened to the protests, and I'm very much a speaker, I like to talk . . . so my first time was in reading a press statement from the people. I was so nervous, I was, my voice was chattering. . . . It's been a good experience for me, and I've been there for like seven years now.

The empowerment method that Pearl said worked so well for her—leaders asking new people to take on small, low-risk tasks, then gradually bigger roles and eventually leadership responsibilities—is the sequence recommended by the Midwest Academy and community-organizing manuals. Some leaders seemed inept at this facilitation of others' empowerment, while others were good at it; there was no class pattern in who did it well, only in who praised it.

In analyzing the participation of forty-eight lifelong-working-class or poor people attending their first, second, or third meetings, I found two techniques by chairs and facilitators that seemed to be especially effective in increasing participation.

Asking Tailored Questions and Suggesting Tasks

A middle-aged African immigrant woman in a low-paid job, Michelle, was reluctant to speak at her first meeting of the Local 21 organizing campaign, but by the end of the meeting she asked a question and agreed to attend a rally. What caused this change in her behavior? Owen, the PMC black union organizer, deliberately drew her out. He was chairing a meeting attended by seven new recruits, all inexperienced women of color with very low incomes, five of them immigrants whose first languages weren't English, and he was determined to get them as involved as possible. Owen went around the circle and asked each person directly, "What improvements are needed in [your workplace]?" Most workers could easily answer this question, even the first-time attendees. But Michelle answered by saying "I'm just a guest." Owen then asked her follow-up questions about her experience until he got a response from her:

> OWEN: You're a guest?
> MICHELLE: This is my first time.
> OWEN: Are you [employed in a workplace being organized]?
> MICHELLE: Yes.
> OWEN: For how long?
> MICHELLE: Eight years.
> OWEN: In that time, have you seen anything that changed?
> MICHELLE: This is my first time, I just listening.
> OWEN: OK. OK. What do you feel needs to be improved in the [workplace]?
> MICHELLE: More hours.
> OWEN: How many people do overtime? [*most hands go up*] How many get paid for overtime? [*one hand goes up*]

After each newcomer spoke, Owen responded with a general affirmation, such as "Great, great," with a restatement of what the person had said and/or with a probe for more, such as "More training, is that it? Anything else?"[3] Similarly, an elected worker-leader, Marion, asked a quiet working-class newcomer, "Let me ask you a question. Are you getting any benefits?"

Throughout the meeting Owen asked for commitments very specifically: "Put your name down and when you're available." His colorful wall-charts included the words "YOU need to get involved NOW!!!" Michelle was quiet through most of the rest of the meeting. But when a sign-up sheet went around for attending a rally, she signed it and asked, "Where do we get the bus?"—a small empowerment success story.

Effective organizers of inexperienced working-class people, such as Owen, make go-arounds more like natural conversation. In the form of go-arounds most prevalent in working-class-majority labor and community groups, marginalized people speak when someone asks them a direct question, and then they get an immediate positive response from one or many people, similar to what they would get in a friendly one-on-one conversation.

Fred and Dorothea also asked questions of less-active individuals during meetings, often customized to that person's knowledge and roles. Without patronizing them with gushing compliments, these leaders affirmed the value of new members' knowledge, gained from their life experience, by asking about things relevant to the group's goals that they would be likely to know. For example, Fred asked a Puerto Rican member whether passing out flyers was allowed at a Puerto Rican parade.

Asking direct questions seems like a promising empowerment practice, with two caveats. First, the most evocative questions are open-ended ones with no wrong answers. Once when Owen asked a question with a right answer, a feisty elected worker-leader answered it wrong and he corrected her; she then slumped in her chair, stared at the floor, and was uncharacteristically silent for a few minutes.

Second, putting people on the spot with direct questions can backfire if there's insufficient trust between the asker and the person asked, or if it seems that only certain marginalized people are being singled out. I once saw veteran activists Attieno Davis and Louise Dunlap do a skit to dramatize the excessive, patronizing attention sometimes given to newcomers of color by white activists. Louise, a white woman, used a fake-nice tone to say to Attieno, a black woman playing a new recruit, "Oh, we're so glad *you* came! I want to know what ideas *you* have!" The point was that putting an exaggerated or forced spotlight on a marginalized person can be alienating.

Hannah, the staff organizer of Labor and Community United, described an incident where that kind of patronizing attention backfired with working-class Latino union member Aaron: "When we went to that [high-level political] event, Aaron was there, he was invited, and he felt really uncomfortable. And they tried to bring him into conversation and they were like, 'Oh so, Aaron, where are you from?' and stuff like that. And it did sound a bit condescending. . . . And [he] was just like, 'Don't talk to me' [*laughter*]."

One lesson from these stories is that new people sometimes need some initial time to quietly hang back to get comfortable with a group; it can backfire to come on too strong too fast. The broader lesson is that no technique works without genuine, tuned-in respect behind it.

Spotlighting these methods of activation drawn from working-class activist culture puts Lowell's silence in the Action Against Empire meeting into a different light. Alton and Ira felt guilty and self-critical about their unwanted domination of the group, but they felt powerless to change the dynamic, given that their preferred solutions weren't working. But they never tried the common, everyday methods observed in labor and community-needs groups. No one spoke directly to Lowell during the meeting; no core member asked him to do any specific task; no one tapped into his expertise or any networks he might have, even though he was the only representative of the local Latino community present. Instead, suggestions for more involvement were spoken to the whole circle at once, often using the third person: "What time on Saturday would people want to meet?"

Why didn't the quiet new AAE members hear direct questions or get individual invitations to get more involved? I would guess that Ira and Alton, intent on making all members into peers in a horizontal group, would have thought they were being patronizing if they singled out a quiet new member, in particular if they as men tried to influence women's involvement, or if Ira as a white person tried to influence the involvement of a person of color. They would have rejected the idea that they were Lowell's leaders; who were *they* to empower *him?* They were in a double bind: trying to demonstrate equality within the group by their holding back behavior but prevented by that very ideal from playing active roles that would bring equality into reality. As with many LPs I observed, their discomfort with power ended up reinforcing their power.

Of course, it is easier to play a developmental role for new and disempowered members from a paid-organizer position. It was the job of Owen and Hannah to activate inactive workers; it wasn't Ira's or Alton's job to empower Lowell, and they were no doubt right that too strong a role might have been seen as domineering, given the group's antiauthoritarian ideology. But other most-praised leaders were leading from peer positions. Founding leaders Dorothea, Fred, Elaine, Toni, and Jasmine were all unpaid members of their groups, some of them elected to a board slot or officer position, but some leading entirely without formal position. Some of their empowering communication came across as friendly and curious, not directive, and thus could probably have been pulled off even in the most antiauthoritarian group.

MENTORING AND ENCOURAGEMENT

Empowerment also happened through intensive one-on-one relationships of friendship or mentoring. Contrast the weak, inexperienced rotating chairs described above, who were left on their own to flounder through the meeting, with the collaborative process recounted by Nicole: "I like the way we do it at the Interfaith [group]. Each leader has an opportunity to run the meeting. . . . We have a director. He's the only paid person. We're all volunteers. And he sits with us before that meeting and helps us to get our meeting together. And I like that."

Similarly, after Hannah noticed Aaron's disempowerment, she helped him prepare to chair meetings:

> I'm like "Aaron! Why didn't you say anything?" He's kind of taken a step back. . . . He's supposed to chair. I've seen him chair one time, you could feel it in him, he did not feel confident. . . . I always try to prep him beforehand. I'll meet with him, to let him know what's going to be on the agenda, what's the real politics behind stuff. Also like how to chair. . . . I've given him some information on like parliamentary procedure and stuff so he'll feel more confident.

One-on-one encouragement happened both inside and outside meetings. Owen credited his success in turning out workers for Local 21 organizing meetings to his one-on-one conversations outside of meetings: "[Workers] came as a result of my follow-up, because when I follow up with people I connect with them. I talk to them and I listen to them, and as a result of that that's what makes them return. . . . I ask them, 'What do you think about the meeting? Is there any way that meeting could have been better or more improved? Do you feel as though you got anything out of it?'" Local 21 achieved a huge victory soon after the meetings I observed, with a majority of workers voting to approve union representation— tangible proof of the effectiveness of organizers' and rank-and-file leaders' one-on-one outreach.

Why Would Approaches to Low Participation and Leadership Vary by Class?

Unlike the holding back strategy, which was advocated mostly by activists who fit a particular age/ideology/race/gender profile in addition to sharing the VDM class trajectory, the other two strategies were advocated across varied races, ages, and genders. There was a contrast specifically in *class* cultures between who favored facilitating stylized group processes and who favored trustworthy championing of member interests.

These two class-specific strategies for overcoming member inactivity parallel Lareau's (2003) two philosophies of childrearing, "concerted cultivation" and "accomplishment of natural growth." Activists' class trajectories predict whether their goal was cultivating equalization of speech or accomplishing natural involvement through a trusting relationship with a leader.

Monitoring how much each person speaks, attempting to equalize airspace by holding back or by equalization techniques, and requiring the creation of an original solo speech act are concerted-cultivation solutions to the problem of too little member participation.

Because professional and managerial occupations involve speech as a central work activity, activists from PMC backgrounds may tend to stress participants' amount of speech in meetings as the primary indicator of a central role in a group, as opposed to amount of work performed, amount of inside knowledge, or closeness of relationships.

While activists from class-privileged backgrounds were more likely to be monitoring who was taking up how much airspace, working-class activists were more likely to be monitoring trustworthiness and dedication to the cause, as expressed primarily in actions, not words.

Why would working-class labor and community activists be more likely to favor strong, protective leadership? Lamont found protectiveness to be one of the primary values of working-class white and black American men (2000). Providing and protecting were seen as ways to keep the world in moral order. This value did not appear in her earlier interviews of PMC men (1992).

Working-class activists tend to have a different relationship to power, with less of the ambivalence that many LPs feel about using the power conferred by their privilege in the service of social justice. In light of Croteau's (1995) finding that hopelessness about having an impact is why working-class people don't join social movements, evidence of power amassed on their side may give a jolt of energy to counteract such hopelessness.

Processes experienced as empowering by activists from PMC backgrounds are sometimes uncomfortable for working-class people, who may experience mandatory-speech requirements as facilitators' attempts to manage them (Ellsworth 1989: her article is titled "Why Doesn't This Feel Empowering?"). Well-meaning PMC people may try to resolve tensions by doing organized team-building activities that require stylized speech, explicit sharing of personal feelings, or tasks reminiscent of school assignments, not realizing that if the people they're trying to activate have felt alienated from school teachers or workplace managers, their efforts may make the environment *less* comfortable, more enmeshed in PMC culture. In addition, shy PMC organizers without a flair for informal social bonding may overstress formal community-building methods.

The class association with leadership concepts found in this study runs contrary to the traditional white/gender duality (Helgesen 1990; Belenky, Bond, and Weinstock 1997), which associates male style with directive, foreground leadership and female style with participative, background leadership. While the normative ideals of almost all activists in this study were on the participative end of the spectrum, for working-class activists, that didn't necessarily mean that leaders should stay quietly behind the scenes. The actual practices of the most-praised leaders in working-class-majority groups tended to be both forceful *and* nurturing of others' involvement (as Barbara Ransby described Ella Baker in her 2005 book on the civil rights leader).

Both individual class conditioning and movement traditions affected activists' concepts of leadership. Protectiveness and strong leadership were found in groups rooted in the historically working-class labor and community-organizing movement traditions, even when current members were class-diverse. Facilitator-managed equalizing processes and stylized speech requirements were most often found in global/local cause groups; in addition, they were advocated by PMC and VDM individuals within all kinds of groups.

The class incongruity in who dissented from each strategy provides evidence that class was often a stronger influence than movement tradition. Most dissenters were quite different in class from the majority of their groups' membership. When these class-incongruous dissenters came from a higher-class background than the group mode, as with Sheila in City Power, or when they were currently in a higher class, as with Gail in the Action Center, they were more likely to prevail in getting the group to modify its leadership style. When the dissenters came from a lower-class background, as with Olivia in the Parecon Collective or Mack and Laverne in Easthaver Demands Justice, their different approaches didn't have much effect on how meetings were run.

What can an activist do about passive, inactive members? Occasionally it works simply to hold back from dominating. Sometimes it works to facilitate group processes that require everyone to speak. Sometimes it works to provide strong, trustworthy leadership and offer one-on-one mentoring. But overemphasis by class-privileged activists on equalizing airspace may obscure the importance of building empowering relationships of trust.

Class Speech Differences II
Abstract and Concrete Vocabulary

One of the most clear-cut class-cultural differences among the activists in the study was in their type of vocabulary. Remember that the professional-middle-class (PMC) facilitator profiled in the introduction used general organizational words to guide a labor coalition's goal-setting process, while working-class-background members responded with concrete political issues and operational details. This pattern was found throughout all the meetings and interviews.

Lifelong-working-class activists referred to more specific people, places, and events, even when answering general questions, as Bernstein (1971) also found in his studies of British teenage boys, one component of his so-called "restricted code" of working-class speech. In contrast, lifelong-PMC and VDM activists used more abstract words and phrases in their speech, even when asked concrete questions, as in Bernstein's "elaborated code" (77–109).

For example, when a Neighbors United meeting chair asked people to go around the circle and "say some of the major ways you think that [the group's goal] can be done," here's how two members began their answers (with notably concrete or abstract terms in italics):

LOWER-MIDDLE-CLASS WHITE WOMAN: [*Governor's name*]'s campaign had a *calendar* of where he was going to be, what he was going to do. I think if we do some standard routine things like be at the *supermarket* on a *Saturday morning* or *afternoon*— everybody goes *shopping*! [Emphasis added]

PROFESSIONAL-MIDDLE-CLASS WHITE MAN: I think it's important for *media time, being visible,* I just think being a *catalyst* for getting other people real excited so ... they can start *spreading the word. [Emphasis added]*

A listener to the first answer could picture first the governor and then the group recruiting support outside the supermarket at a particular time. The second answer doesn't lend itself to such visualization.

Of sixty-one interviewees, thirteen included notably concrete answers to questions where more abstract answers might be expected, and sixteen included notably abstract answers to questions where more concrete answers might be expected. Such especially abstract or concrete speech correlated very strongly with the nonmobile class trajectories, with lifelong-PMC activists much more likely to speak abstractly and lifelong-working-class activists much more likely to speak concretely.[1] Class background also had a strong correlation.[2] Current class had a weaker correlation but was still statistically significant.[3] Abstract versus concrete speech was not associated with any gender,[4] race,[5] or movement tradition,[6] only with class.

Tastes, not just habits, accounted for this class speech difference, as this quote shows:

INTERVIEWER: Does anyone in the group drive you crazy?
LOWER-MIDDLE-CLASS WHITE WOMAN: There's someone who used to come. She's going to be a lawyer. She drives me mad.... I couldn't make head or tails of what she said. . . . Maybe it was her language . . . like "stakeholders have to buy in." She'd be linking concepts up in the air, and we'd be like, "What does that mean we do?" No action steps! She would talk to [community members] and they would look at her—they respect how erudite she is, but they couldn't understand her. She can't put things into the common man's language.... Dern's a lawyer, but he talks in steps, like 1, 2, 3.

To pin down these abstract and concrete speech styles to particular classed vocabulary, I created word-frequency lists to measure how many times certain terms were used per 10,000 spoken words by interviewees within each broad class trajectory. Lifelong-PMC interviewees used these words far more often than lifelong-working-class people:

- "Network" (6.3 times as often by PMC as working-class interviewees)
- "Outreach" (5.4 times as often)
- "Activist"/"Activism" (5.1 times as often)
- "Context"/"Contextualize" (4.7 times as often)

In some cases, it was not only lifelong-PMC but all more class-privileged activists (those with four-year college and professional/managerial occupations in the prior generation and/or in the current generation, that is, all VDM and straddler as well as PMC interviewees, shorthanded below as "college-educated") who used the following abstract generalizations more often than working-class people did:

- "Strategy"/"strategize" (8.1 times as often by college-educated interviewees as lifelong-working-class interviewees)
- "Principle" (7.4 times as often)
- "Connection" (5.7 times as often)
- "Perspective" (5.5 times as often)

Stout (1996), who grew up in poverty, refers to one of these very words when she discusses "the different languages of class," which she noticed when she first worked with middle-class activists:

I remember getting frustrated with words like "strategies and tactics." . . .
I came to terms with the language problem by translating what I was
taught into my own language. For "strategy," I thought, oh, this is what I
call a "plan." I realized that I had different words for the same concepts
and that, in fact, some of the things I was doing as a community organizer,
and which felt to me like just common sense, were being taught as complicated concepts. (119–20)

Some PMC activists used jargon, in particular from the nonprofit organizational development field (e.g., "operational decisions" and "management and evaluation"). They answered questions about their group's goals with abstract phrases such as "capacity building" and "symbolic impact."

Fortunately for cross-class communication, some general words were used with similar frequency by all classes:

- "Coalition"
- "Goal"
- "Issue"
- "Community"
- "Situation"
- "Conflict"
- "Decision"
- "Power"
- "Story"
- "Task"
- "Recruit"

Besides organizational development jargon, the other source of abstract vocabulary was leftist theories. Those with college-educated trajectories were much more likely to use the words "nonviolence"/"nonviolent" (35.5 times as often) and "oppress(-ion/-ive)" (6.5 times as often). "Socialist"/"socialism" was used 20 times more often by PMC than by working-class activists, and 7.1 times more by straddlers. VDM activists used certain anarchism-associated ideological words far more often than working-class interviewees did:

- "Anarchist"/"Anarchism" (49.6 times more often than working-class)
- "Hierarchy"/"Hierarchical" (19.1 times more)
- "Autonomy"/"Autonomous" (11.5 times more)
- "Consensus" (8.7 times more)
- "Vision" (5.1 times more)

It's a very sad commentary on the state of the labor movement that the word "solidarity"—the rallying cry of unions around the world—was used more than 14 times more often by college-educated activists than by working-class activists.

It was not just the presence of certain abstract words that made the speech of those from more-privileged backgrounds distinct but the relative scarcity of concrete referents. Sometimes an entire sentence would have no people, times, places, or actions in it, such as this sentence by Zoe, the PMC facilitator of the Tri-city Labor Alliance annual meeting: "That's a whole big category of developing a plan in order to achieve a number of these goals." Working-class activist speech is less likely to include such entire sentences or paragraphs without any concrete referents.

Thus there is no equivalent list of words that working-class interviewees said at least four times more often than other classes. Instead, there is a steep drop-off in their frequency list, as thousands of specific proper nouns are used a small number of times each, with each interviewee supplying different concrete specifics. Contrary to a controversial study of poor children's vocabulary (Hart and Risley 1995), the number of distinct vocabulary words used by working-class interviewees was not smaller than the more formally educated PMC people's vocabularies, due to the many proper names of neighborhoods, people, organizations, nationalities, and other specifics that each working-class interviewee mentioned.[7]

Of all the words spoken in interviews, the lifelong-working-class activists as a group used only 11 percent of their total vocabulary words twice or more per 10,000 words spoken. Straddlers, despite their college educations, had a very similar rate of using non-repetitive words, using only 12 percent of their vocabulary words twice or more per 10,000 words spoken. By contrast, lifelong-PMC activists as a group used 16 percent of their vocabulary words twice or more per

10,000 words spoken, relying more on repeated words, such as the abstract terms listed above.[8] This is evidence against Bernstein's early theory of a "public language" (1971: 42–43), deficient by comparison with middle-class speech (Macaulay 2005), in which working-class British boys repeated stock phrases instead of inventing original utterances.

One particular interview question, "What are the goals of your group?," turned out to be especially revealing of abstract versus concrete class speech differences. Some young white or Asian American men from PMC backgrounds in globalization and direct action groups described their groups' goals in very abstract terms. For example:

> INTERVIEWER: What are the goals of your group?
> WHITE LOWER-PROFESSIONAL MAN: Just social consciousness . . . to organize around social justice issues like broadly and to do actions, take action in solidarity with different struggles that are taking place internationally and locally, educate about radical political issues and struggles, and be a space where that kind of conversation can happen.

Especially striking was the contrast in goal statements between people of different classes *in the same group*. In the next examples, notice how two African Americans start with their group's focus on stopping the war in Iraq; but the woman from a working-class background (who earned a vocational degree only in middle age) then shifts to more concrete, local aspects of the issue, while the lifelong-PMC man then moves to a more general level:

> INTERVIEWER: What are the goals of your group?
> LAVERNE (STRADDLER): We don't want to see the war in Iraq; we want to see that come to an end. We don't want to see the recruiters harassing the kids in the high school, which they do.

> INTERVIEWER: What are the goals of your group?
> RODNEY (PMC): One, we want to end the war; two is to become a multiracial, multiclass, multiethnic peace movement for social and economic justice.

In place of abstract generalizations, working-class people tended to make points with examples, metaphors, and especially analogies, typically starting with a phrase such as "Say you and I were . . ." These extended hypothetical scenarios were never once heard from a lifelong-PMC informant but were heard over and over from lifelong-working-class activists, and occasionally from straddlers.

For example, working-class African American Rhonda explains why she advocates reparations for slavery:

RHONDA: Until there is true reparation for slavery, it's not going to happen. If you stole my TV, you and I going to have a conflict. Now if you
were sorry for stealing my TV, you came and told me you were sorry
for stealing my TV, what's the first thing you think you need to do to
make it right?

INTERVIEWER: Buy you a new TV.

RHONDA: Right, until you replace what you took from me, would I think
it's sincere? No.

When a labor coalition debated two pieces of health legislation, hypothetical scenarios (such as "If you were in the hospital...") were used by five people
during the debate. The point of these ministories usually did not have to be
spelled out; it was obvious what the speaker was arguing for.

Colorful metaphors eloquently expressed working-class interviewees' political choices. Lifelong-working-class Brandy used a metaphor to explain why she
felt compelled to organize against extreme poverty: "[It] is like seeing kids on
a railroad track, and when you push those kids off that railroad track, is that a
choice or did you have to do that? I have to do that." Some of these metaphors
were familiar clichés, as Bernstein (1971) would have predicted: "other fish to
fry," "heavy foot on the gas," "hit the roof," and "stepping stone." Others were
culturally specific traditional sayings, especially common among African Caribbean immigrants and older African Americans. Martina said, "Back home they
say, 'You want good, your nose has to run'; you have to put that effort in it." But
other working-class metaphors seemed freshly coined, such as "I'm a pebble in
their shoe." Such creative, vivid speech contradicts Bernstein's assertion that
working-class speech is largely restricted to repetitive, learned stock phrases.
His early idea that working-class sentences use "low-order symbolism," while
the middle-class elaborated code has a "complex hierarchy for organizing experience" (Macaulay 2005: 41–42) also turned out not to apply to US activists.
The political ideas expressed by working-class activists were just as likely to
be complex and nuanced as PMC activists' ideas, just expressed differently. In
fact, a repetitive abstract word, such as "imperialism," occasionally flattened
out a PMC activist's speech into simplistic generalizations, unelaborated with
examples.

Class Speech Differences III
Racial Terms

One example of abstract versus concrete speech plays a key role in the next chapter on class differences in approaches to antiracism. Activists of different classes tended to use different terms for ethnic groups. Why? One explanation is that certain broad racial terms, such as "people of color" and "Latino," are in fact abstract generalizations, more common in the vocabulary of college-educated activists.

The only racial term for which activists of all classes shared nearly universal usage was "white." More than 90 percent of references to those of European ancestry by all class groups used "white." To refer to people of color, lifelong-working-class activists used markedly different terminology than college-educated activists.

Racial terminology for the ethnic groups targeted by discrimination has been controversial throughout US history (Smith 1992), with gradual changes in what is considered a respectful term and what is considered a slur. The terms favored as respectful by most professional-middle-class (PMC), voluntarily downwardly mobile (VDM), and straddler activists in 2007 and 2008—"people of color," "African American" and "Latino"—were all less common among working-class activists. Working-class terminology was more mixed, and in some cases much more nationally specific.

Many progressives have worked to promote the terms "Latino" and "Latina," which are inclusive of Latin American indigenous peoples and Brazilians in a way that the term "Hispanic" (literally meaning "Spanish") is not. This effort has been very successful among the college-educated activists: 69 percent of PMC, VDM, and straddler interviewees' references to people of Latin heritage used "Latina/o," compared with only 4 percent using "Hispanic." Lifelong working-class people of all races, however, used "Latina/o" only 17 percent of the time, overwhelmingly favoring specific national terms, such as "Cuban" and "Mexican." Even when working-class people said "Latino" or "Latina," often they also said a specific nationality in the same sentence.

Two Latinas from the same group in a Puerto Rican neighborhood exemplified this contrast in race terms—and in reasons for mentioning race, whether to refer to particular people or to discuss a political generalization:

> WORKING-CLASS LATINA: You don't find many Puerto Ricans up there.... We lived in the Italian section of the town; we were one of two Latino families, Puerto Rican families in the entire town.
> PROFESSIONAL-MIDDLE-CLASS LATINA: I just went to a meeting with [the governor] and a group of Latino leaders in education. . . . I think there's an openness there for Latino voters.

There was a similar class breakdown in how African Americans were referred to. While "black" was the most common term among all races and classes, college-educated activists said "African American" 42 percent of the time, compared to only 14 percent of the time by lifelong-working-class activists, a statistically significant difference.[1]

College-educated people referred to people of color as a general category far more often than working-class people did. Overwhelmingly, when working-class people of all races mentioned race, they were referring to one specific ethnic group or nationality,[2] and often to a specific person or people. Variations of the term "people of color" were used three-quarters of the time by college-educated activists, but only 58 percent of the time by lifelong-working-class activists of all races.

Within each racial category, there were also class differences in racial terminology. When referring to their own ethnic group, working-class African Americans were more likely to say "black," and college-educated African Americans were more likely to say "African American." But no matter their class, they didn't use "Latino/a" to refer to people of Latin American heritage; in all the interviews and meeting transcripts, there's not a single example of a black activist saying "Latino/a." Latino activists of all classes only rarely said "Hispanic"; they either used nationalities or "Latino/a." Among white activists, college-educated people were more likely to say "Latino" and "African American" than were working-class whites.

These differences in racial terminology are striking in comparison with the absence of gender-term variation. Regardless of race or class, activists all used the word "woman," never "lady" and rarely "girl"; they said "man" or "guy," not "boy."[3] Within the trinity of race, class, and gender, in 2007 and 2008, race terms were contested, gender terms had been settled, and (as discussed in Class Speech Differences VI) class terms were not even on the map.

CHAPTER 7

Diversity Ironies

Clashing Antiracism Frames and Practices

City Power members were frustrated. They depended on progressive foundations to pay their staff, but one of their regular funders had returned their grant proposal with an additional set of questions about race and racism that they had to answer before the proposal would be considered.

Their meeting about this funder demand was a rare instance of open class-based resentment discussed at length by lifelong-working-class activists. It revealed class differences in approaches to identity politics, in particular to race and antiracism, which turned out to apply to many groups in the study.

In this racially diverse group, it was interesting how few racial differences there were in talking about race. Both black and white members seemed to think the funders' questions reflected misunderstandings of City Power's work. One question in particular was met with gales of whole-group laughter and cries of "Oh, my God!" City Power had recently won a major victory that gave low-income people of color more influence over local policies. The foundation asked them to explain how that campaign was "link[ed] to institutionalized racism." The incredulous response implied that if the foundation had to ask, they just didn't get it.

In the following exchange, note that members presumed that counting members of color and going to a workshop would be the kinds of antiracist activity that a funder would like:

RANELLE (working-class black): They're just going after racism this
  year.

DOROTHEA (working-class white): We went to that workshop.

SHEILA (lower-professional white): Yeah, we went to that workshop,
  and it fucking sucked. [*group laughter*]

MAN'S VOICE: It was boring.

DOROTHEA: They will ask some questions about racism to every single
  group, but the questions will be a little different depending on how
  the Emma Fund perceives the group. [*group groan*]

ADRIANA (working-class black): These questions seems like they know
  everything that happened within City Power.

DOROTHEA: They think they do.

SHEILA: I feel like walking in there and calling them on their shit and
  not falling into this trap and saying, "Oh look, look, look, look, let
  me show you, we have Courtney, we have Quincy, we have Adriana,
  we have Ed, we have Ranelle, and in the past we had Carmen."

THELMA (working-class white): "Yeah, fuck you, give me the money!"
  [*group laughter*]

SHEILA: Right, I feel like walking in there and saying we are doing the
  best that we can.

RANELLE: We're a grassroots organization that's really stepping up.

ADRIANA: And we're still around.

Another funder question was why City Power didn't have any Latinos
on its board despite organizing in a city with a big Latino population. Only
the lone professional member Sheila expressed the excuses in broad societal
terms and in the third person: "We can't be expecting those of the most
oppressed classes, of the most oppressed groups, to be able to find all of this
free time." Working-class members, on the other hand, brought up specific
information to exonerate the group, for example mentioning particular col-
laborations with Latino groups. Bastian mentioned that City Power's food
giveaways had attracted Latinos. Darius, a working-class African American,
asked defensively, "What's the makeup of *their* organization?"

Sheila's college education and other cultural capital were needed to put
the group's work into terms that would satisfy the funder. She was one of
only two members who used the funder's term "institutional racism," a frame
predominant among college-educated activists. Atypically, this frame was
brought up first by Dorothea, the working-class white leader with abundant
self-taught cultural capital and radical politics. In the following exchange,
these two white women of different classes stressed institutionalized racism

to a similar degree, but only Dorothea included a class analysis and a critique of class-privileged single-issue antiracists:

> DOROTHEA: I will say this in favor of the Emma Fund. They made a commitment to tackle institutional racism in their organiza- tion. . . . I think that they are missing the class analysis because of this absolutely nonstop focus just on race. Do you remember, Ranelle, when we were at [a national gathering of poor people's groups], remember there was, in one of the workshops there was this guy. . . he was African American, [and his organization had] strong leadership of color?
>
> RANELLE: I was shocked when I seen all those colored people in the front. I mean in the *front*. Some of the main organizers are either Hispanic or African American.
>
> DOROTHEA: They just said, "You're on the wrong track, we have to focus on what unites us, not what divides us."
>
> SEVERAL PEOPLE: Yeah, right.
>
> DOROTHEA: I think [the Emma Fund is] really sincere, but at this point in time I also think . . . the pendulum has swung too far.
>
> SHEILA: They are very focused on like a multicultural model, which I feel is getting outdated. We are operating under a system of white supremacy now. . . . We're not just talking about racism; we're talk- ing about white people's dominating all over the place.
>
> RANELLE: Right.
>
> DOROTHEA [*bringing class back in*]: *Rich* white people!

This City Power discussion of the Emma Fund's antiracism questions was only one of several examples of a low-income community-needs group criticizing funders' approaches to diversity and stressing unity instead. White working-class leader Brandy's rant about funders gives the impression that identity politics as a whole is an elite preoccupation:

> We live in a silo nation where people are very much organized around identity issues and are awarded by funders for organizing around those identity issues, never working together; and people will fight with their life to never cross urban and rural issues, race issues, women and men, unity doesn't pay, unity doesn't get you a foundation grant in this country. . . . There's definitely no money in having actual poor people involved in our own fight for our own lives.

Is there in fact a class difference in activists' approach to diversity as Brandy and City Power members believed? This chapter explores how the

activists in the study—all too progressive to openly espouse racial prejudice or even the common color-blind denial of its existence (Bonilla-Silva
2010)—differed in how they defined racism and how they thought it should
be opposed.

Classed Approaches to Social Identities

Every organization has choices to make about how to relate to the social
identities within it. For example, a social change group can try to keep racism and racial identities in the forefront, on the back burner, or out of sight
entirely. Debates over identity politics have raged over the last half-century,
including on the left. Retrospective analyses of the movements of the 1960s
and 1970s are sharply divided on the question of how much they should have
focused on marginalized subgroups. At one extreme, some former activists,
such as Todd Gitlin (1996), blame the failure to win more lasting structural
change on the splintering of diverse movements into separatist black power,
women's liberation, gay rights, and other identity-based groups. Countering
him are many observers of the sexism and racism within sixties movements,
who saw a much-needed emergence of suppressed voices (Evans 1980; Epstein 1991).

The feminists of color who pioneered intersectionality analysis (Moraga
and Anzaldúa 1981; Collins 1991; Crenshaw, Gotanda, and Peller 1995)
documented how spotlighting only one marginalized identity at a time (for
example, convening a women's caucus to create a program on sexism, then
convening a caucus of color to create a program on racism) denied the realities and suppressed the power of multiply marginalized people, such as black
women.

Around the turn of the new millennium, one progressive ideal was mixed
coalitions (Anner 1999; Warren 2001) that advocate vigorously for oppressed
subgroups of members. Even when an organization's members share only
one identity, as with a women's group, systematic attention can be paid to
raising the voices and the leadership of the members with other oppressed
identities, such as women of color. But more often, the multiply marginalized remain on the sidelines (Vaid 1996; Strolovitch 2007).

What do lifelong-working-class activists tend to think about these controversies over dealing with diversity? Empirical studies by Kurtz (2002) and
Ward (2008) offer insights into how a working-class-influenced approach
might look different than today's typical practices.

In the labor movement, "do it but don't talk about it" seems to be the
usual mode of dealing with diversity. In the Columbia University unions

that Kurtz observed, workers and union leaders stressed worker unity across race and gender, rarely talking explicitly about identities other than "worker." These unions did bargain for the concrete needs of the multiply marginalized members, such as child-care benefits needed by single mothers and race-based affirmative action. But they framed these simply as workers' issues, as if no other identity needed to be verbalized to tackle them.

I saw a similar "we're all workers" frame in the Tri-City Labor Alliance, where a recurring meeting topic was how to get more conservative rank-and-file members to support TLA's advocacy for oppressed subgroups of workers. On the controversial public issues of immigrant rights, same-sex marriage, and transgender discrimination, progressive TLA members discussed framing each issue as a workers' rights problem, calling on the members to show solidarity with workers who were getting a different kind of flack from employers but who had the same needs for job security and benefits as every worker. *Action* on behalf of subgroups was not always controversial, though too much identity talk often was.

This working-class culture of diversity action without diversity talk is not found only in unions. Ward (2008) studied three Los Angeles lesbian, gay, bisexual, and transgender (LGBT) nonprofit organizations and found that diversity attitudes and practices tended to break down by class. She found that working-class people were further marginalized by the diversity practices in each organization. Ironically, sometimes people of color were marginalized by antiracist ideas and activities. Two of her cases illuminate my findings so well that I summarize them at some length.

One of her cases is especially analogous to the groups in my study because it concerns an all-volunteer group: Christopher Street West, which planned the annual gay pride parade. The board of this group was taken over by a new and very different group after the old board was charged with incompetence and insensitivity to diversity. The longtime board had been made up of white and black working-class gay men (none with a university degree). The accusations were a mix of understandable concerns (such as drunkenness at board meetings and money unaccounted for) and classist over-reactions to the "lack of professionalism" in working-class gay subculture. Politicians, journalists, and other prominent people criticized the working-class board members for their awkward public presentations and poor fund-raising and publicity skills.

Ward (2008) defends the old board as more truly "queer" than the professionals who replaced them (2). She describes the situation as an example of the "politics of vulgarity" (60), class nonconformity as a basic element of US queer culture in its earlier decades. One of the old board's copresidents said that LA Pride wasn't "political like San Francisco"; instead, he described LA Pride as "You pay, you drink, you fall down" (57). The board had five- or six-hour meetings with dramatic, emotional exits in the middle; once the board secretary walked out after another member called him "Mary" (59). Ward mourns what was lost in the transition to the new respectable, family-friendly LA Pride board.

When community disapproval rained down on the old Christopher Street West board, some criticisms were couched in classist terms. Ward quotes articles and letters in local gay newspapers: "Everyone knows that they are better suited to work at 7–11 [convenience store] than to be on that board"; "There's this lack of skill on the board, they are afraid of people who have good minds and ideas"; "Maybe you're all as dumb as dirt" (62).

The contrast between the old and new boards was not just in degree of slickness but specifically in attitudes to race and gender. The old board, while ignoring race in a mainstream color-blind way, was in fact quite racially diverse, black and white, and won praise from a Latino community newspaper for including a Latin dance party in the LA Pride celebrations. But they were lacking in some diversity competencies that the new white members brought to the board: connections to ethnic and female community leaders and to politicians of color; lingo about diversity in public descriptions of gay pride festivities, and in particular in communications with funders and corporate sponsors; and emphasis on visually obvious demonstrations of diversity, such as the Native Americans and Latinos in "ethnic costumery" (74) proposed by the new board. When many in the LGBT community insisted that people with professional skills join the board, they didn't mean only financial and public relations expertise but also diversity expertise.

Enough college-educated professionals joined the board to outnumber the old board members, most of whom stayed on for a while before quitting. Ironically, the long-standing working-class African American board copresident was pressured to step down for a new white president known for his "diversity skills" (70) and his connections with diverse community leaders and politicians. The new board won more funding from corporate sponsors, more city council approval, and national recognition for producing a "polished" Pride festival (72). The kind of diversity success that counted most was making connections with the most class-privileged people of color and the most class-privileged women. Class diversity not only counted for little but in fact often proved an embarrassing liability.

Some aspects of this story rang true to what I observed in activist groups. Diversity work was often professional-middle-class (PMC) turf; think of white lower-professional (LP) Sheila writing up City Power's antiracist credentials in the grant proposal. Approved forms of diversity expertise earned what Ward calls "liberal capital" (6) and I call "movement capital." Class identities were rarely talked about, and almost never as a positive form of diversity. The diversity competencies of working-class people were invisible, in part because they tended to be rooted in a tolerant antibigotry frame that avoided explicit race talk. But, in fact, working-class white people often had more multicultural social networks than PMC white people did.

Ward's (2008) second case, though it concerned a workplace instead of a voluntary group, also resonated with my findings. The LA Lesbian and Gay Center, the largest LGBT social services agency in the world, held an annual Diversity Day. One of its purposes was to overcome the agency's reputation as a "white organization" (78), which persisted even though most staff members, including many top leaders, were people of color. Mention of Diversity Day, which was mandatory for all employees, brought groans at a staff meeting. Staff of color in particular expressed resentment at the idea that they had to be forced to think about racial diversity. In interviews with Ward, some staff mentioned bizarre racial stereotypes peddled by the supposed diversity experts brought in to facilitate (e.g., that African Americans listen with their eyes closed).

As in corporate diversity programs, the emphasis was on how multicultural differences improved service to clients; inequality of power and money as an injustice in itself was downplayed. White progressives, as well as some managers of color, tended to believe that Diversity Day should be run by trained experts, not by well-meaning amateurs; a white manager said, "It would be as if we attempted to call together a group of Center employees who didn't have management expertise and turned them loose with developing a strategic plan for fundraising" (91). Just as in the first story I selected from Ward, diversity skills were regarded as another form of professional expertise. The professional approach involved gathering data, facilitating dialogue, and using human resources expertise to recruit and hire the right staff of color. The knowledge gained by actually living with racism or sexism didn't count for much.

Lower-level employees of color favored more action and less talk. It didn't make sense to them that the organization had to psych itself up via a prolonged multiyear process just to hire diverse staff and serve diverse clients. Instead, they suggested "just do[ing] the right thing" and "doing it now" (79). When Diversity Day speakers called on the Center to form more relationships with organizations of color, some staff members of color were offended by the implication that the Center was a white organization, asking, "Isn't *this* an organization of color?" (101).

All these negative reactions sounded familiar to me; some working-class activists in my study also expressed suspicion of talk-heavy diversity sessions and favored a more pragmatic approach.

Ward worked as a grant writer at the Center, and she learned that the organization had to satisfy funders' diversity demands in order to survive. Affirmative action policies and Diversity Day were selling points to diversity-conscious funders.

Just as Ward did, I found a hot frame contest on race and racism in progress in the groups in my study. Activists' ways of framing racism in particular tended to differ by class.

Class Differences in Framing Racism

The word "racism" can be understood in several different ways. Is it primarily bigotry and discrimination? Is it an absence of multicultural diversity? Or is it also the economic and social disadvantages built into US society by centuries of biased policies, leading to white supremacy in every institution, including activist groups?

Most references to race or racism in the meetings and interviews fell into one of those three broad frames, each tapping into deep cultural resonances (Gamson 1992: 94–103, 149–50): an institutional-racism frame, a multicultural diversity frame, or an antibigotry tolerance frame. At the time of the study, this distinction was one of the most important of all concepts to leftists, especially leftists from PMC backgrounds.

In the first frame, the problem is all-pervasive institutionalized white advantages and systemic subordination of entire communities of color, even where intentions are good. The solutions are both macroeconomic and political policy changes *and* micro changes to organizational culture to give more clout to members of color. In the second, the problem is racial segregation, in particular excessively white organizations and neighborhoods, and the solution is encouraging more diversity and celebrating minority cultures. In the third, the problem is prejudice and discrimination, with hate as its worst form, and the solution is tolerance of all races and cross-racial unity against injustice.

A growing movement of antiracists has been vigorously promoting the institutional white supremacy frame since the 1990s. I've been part of this public education effort through United for a Fair Economy's Racial Wealth Divide project,[1] including coauthoring *The Color of Wealth: The Story behind the US Racial Wealth Divide* (Lui et al. 2006).

Some of my interviewees were among the 130,000 people who have attended workshops put on by the People's Institute for Survival and Beyond, one of the main groups that favor the institutional-racism frame in the United States since they were founded by two African American community organizers in 1980. Their statement of their approach clearly distinguishes the institutional-racism frame from the other more mainstream frames:

> The People's Institute is one of the few existing programs in the U.S. that focuses on institutional and structural forms of racism. The model makes important distinctions between individual expressions of prejudice, bias and discrimination, and institutional or systemic forms of racism. It critiques the dominance of individual-level approaches that fail to address the more prevalent, less visible, systemic dimensions of racism.[2]

The People's Institute is also explicit about racism being the *primary* oppression in US society: "Racism is the single most critical barrier to building effective coalitions for social change" (2002). I have encountered a few People's Institute graduates who downplayed class and gender oppression compared with the primacy and severity of racism. This race-first focus has spread along with the institutional-racist frame; the two often go together.

While for many years activists of color (such as those affiliated with the Center for Third World Organizing) took the lead in antiracist organizing with an institutional-racism frame,[3] over the last decade white antiracists have become more vocal and visible within the US Left (Thompson 2001; Kivel 2002; Wise 2005; Warren 2010). While activists of color shifted away from race-specific organizing in the 1990s and the first decade of the 2000s and toward more multicultural coalitions (Anner 1999), simultaneously more white radicals began to do specifically white antiracist work. The annual White Privilege Conference has steadily grown in size from 1999 to 2013.[4] Gradually, the institutional white supremacy frame seems to have become more common among white leftists.

Class and Racism Frames

I heard each of the three racism frames from activists of every class, but not at the same rate. For example, in a Women Safe from Violence meeting, when a side conversation about racism broke out among white and black people from working-class backgrounds, less-experienced white liberals brought up slurs and social discrimination, reflecting the antibigotry frame, while the longtime radicals raised systemic problems and used abstract terms reflecting the institutional white supremacy frame:

ELAINE [*white straddler radical leader*]: An all-white out-of-state jury ruled against [a falsely accused person of color]. The judge was so horrified, . . . "2007 and this much racism!"

BETTE [*working-class African American radical*]: The judge said, "Mr. Welton, you were treated wrong. Prosecutors should right wrongs, not win cases."

LOUELLEN [*LMC white woman; nonactivist—reframing an institutional court story into a bigotry frame*]: I lived in backwoods Tennessee—we're supposed to be the backward ones!

ELAINE [*shifting back to institutional frame*]: You're talking to the right place. We get white privilege and white supremacy here. Ignoring problems doesn't make them go away.

LY-ANNE [*LMC white woman, more politically mainstream—shifting the topic to interpersonal discrimination*]: I worked in a large office, black and white working together, all nice. I joined this white group for lunch—I removed myself from that group. Ed, this African American dispatcher, they called him "n———", but to his face they were nice, "Oh, how are you doing?" [I felt toward the lunch group,] "I don't want to talk with you people!"

LOUELLEN: In 1993 in *Tennessee* people said "n———"

RONDELL [*working-class African American experienced activist—returning discussion to the institutional frame*]: We've gone from individual racism to corporate racism.

ELAINE: There was always corporate racism.

LOUELLEN: What is "corporate racism"?

If this example were typical of racism conversations in the groups I studied, the liberal-to-left political spectrum would predict racism frames and class would not. However, in the meetings and interviews as a whole, people like Rondell and like Dorothea in the City Power story at the beginning of the chapter—lifelong-working-class people who clearly use the institutional white supremacy frame—turned out to be quite rare. Less than one-quarter of the mentions of race or racism by lifelong-working-class activists invoked that frame, compared with two-thirds or three-quarters of the other class categories. (See table 7.1.) Most of those working-class mentions were by the same three radicals with an outlaw identity, and very few involved an abstract generalization such as "corporate racism." Instead, lifelong-working-class people of all races disproportionately used the most mainstream bigotry frame, injecting the ideal of tolerance and opposition to racial discrimination and hate speech.

Table 7.1 Mentions of race or racism in meetings and interviews, percentages for frames by class trajectory

Frame	Lifelong working class	Straddler	Lifelong PMC	VDM
Institutionalized racism and white supremacy	24	**74**	63	67
Multicultural diversity	33	22	25	33
Antibigotry and tolerance	**42**	4	12	0
Total number	44	20	64	6

Note: Because of rounding, percentages down each column may not add up to 100%.

There is a strong correlation between the three college-educated trajectories and the institutional-racism frame, as well as between the lifelong-working-class trajectory and the antibigotry frame.[5]

All twenty-five groups studied for this book were open to people of all races, so all the working-class members of color expected to encounter white people in their groups. Their nonracial rhetoric signaled that they had no problem working with whites. For example, working-class Latina Cecilia took offense in a Neighbors United meeting when she misheard white working-class Devin and thought he said she had advocated the colors of the Puerto Rican flag for the group's t-shirts:

> CECILIA: I said, "Well, how 'bout red and white and somethin'," right? . . . And I thought he said, "Oh, she want, she's always tryna get the Puerto Rican colors in." And I was like "What? I ain't tryna get no Puerto Rican colors!" He's like, "I didn't say that. I said Republican color." . . . But you know, when he said that at first, I was like, "What is his problem about Puerto Rican colors? Why is it have to be, you know, about nationality?"
>
> INTERVIEWER: That's how you took it.
>
> CECILIA: That's how I took it, like, "Why you tryna make it into something that it's not?" You know? I mean, I'm proud of my heritage. I like being proud of it. But I'm not going to force it upon you.

To Cecilia, an ethnically diverse group was a stronger group, and avoiding partisan race talk helped protect that multicultural strength. Valuing multicultural diversity for its own sake was a minority view among my interviewees of all classes (table 7.1), without the class pattern found by Lamont (2000). None of the working-class white and African American men she interviewed referred to multiculturalism as a positive thing, but her professional and academic interviewees did (58–59). The members of these twenty-five groups, as progressive activists, tended to have broader definitions of racism and to take a more political antiracist stance than Lamont's nonactivist informants.

Additional evidence that these racism frames correlate with class trajectory comes from rates of usage during interviews of the most common words associated with the frames. Lifelong-working-class interviewees were more likely to say two words associated with the antibigotry frame: (1) "prejudice" (said by working-class interviewees 3.2 times as often as by all college-educated interviewees and 4.2 times as often as by lifelong-PMC interviewees); and (2) "discrimination" (said by working-class interviewees 1.7 times as often as by all college-educated interviewees and 4.8 times as often as by lifelong-PMC interviewees).

These higher working-class rates of saying the general words "prejudice" and "discrimination" are especially remarkable given the relative scarcity of abstract words in working-class interviewees' speech overall, documented in the "Abstract and Concrete Vocabulary" class speech interlude. Since working-class interviewees used more specific unique words, working-class multiples as high as 3.2 times the college-educated rate are extremely rare in the entire word list, which makes the higher rate of saying "prejudice" stand out.

Interviewees in the three college-educated trajectories were more likely to say these words associated with the institutional white supremacy frame: (1) "privilege" (said 4.7 times as often by college-educated interviewees as by working-class interviewees); and (2) "oppressed" (said 1.6 as often by college-educated interviewees as by working-class interviewees and 2.3 times as often by VDM interviewees).

Key terms associated with the multicultural frame did not have dramatically different rates of use by interviewees of different classes, except that "diversity" was said 1.6 times as often by lifelong-working-class interviewees as by lifelong-PMC interviewees. The multicultural frame wasn't strongly associated with any class trajectory; but the institutional white supremacy and antibigotry frames were.

Working-Class Activist Worldviews Manifested in Attitudes toward Antiracism

Why would lifelong-working-class activists be more likely to use the antibigotry frame? There are several possibilities. In some cases, such as the Women

Safe from Violence meeting, use of the dominant mainstream antibigotry frame by inexperienced working-class people stemmed from their performance of respectability through demonstrating their rejection of hatefulness. Some of the respectable lifelong-working-class meeting participants weren't multi-issue radicals but people recently mobilized on one issue. To some extent these various race frames fell along the familiar blue-red, left-right spectrum; and some of the working-class activists weren't very far to the left.

White working-class activists in particular seemed more comfortable sticking with tolerant actions and avoiding explicit race talk. Like the community volunteers observed by Eliasoph (1998), some of them felt it was best "not to make an issue of including minorities but just treat them like everyone else" (35) while working together on concrete community projects. In addition, some white resistance to the institutional frame may have stemmed from unspoken racist attitudes (Van Dijk 1987; Bonilla-Silva 2010).

However, some experienced lifelong-working-class progressives promoted the antibigotry or multicultural frames on racism for what seemed like well-thought-out reasons related to their overall social change strategies. In most cases, it wasn't that they disagreed with the structural analysis behind the institutional white supremacy frame but that they saw that frame being pushed in counterproductive ways, such as jargon or alienating group processes. In particular, worry about divide-and-conquer tactics by power holders led them to stress racial unity. Brandon, the young Caribbean American loan administrator in the Interfaith Workforce Improvement Task Force, newly lower-middle-class (LMC) after a working-class childhood, stressed pragmatism in explaining his disagreement with high-professional straddler Jeremiah over how much to stress racial differences: "He comes from the civil rights era mentality, which is great . . . but the spin has to be for 2008 as opposed to '88 or '68. . . . Differences can get in the way, but you can't get hung up on it. You have to look past it sometimes."

When working-class activists (usually activists of color, but occasionally whites) raised charges of racism, it was virtually always at the macro level, externally against people in authority in the wider world, not the micro level, internally within the group. Police, politicians, courts, mainstream media, employers, and teachers were accused of abusing power, using hate speech, and fomenting divisions. Congruent with their prevailing antibigotry frame, the forms of racism most worthy of their notice seemed to be the most dangerous and extreme ones, often as experienced by their own family and friends. For example, low-income Native American Kateri said she knew her son wouldn't get justice when beaten up by thugs after a prosecutor called him "nothing but a damn Indian." A LMC white woman was shocked when her daughter's black friends reported that guidance counselors told them they couldn't go to college. At times working-class activists seemed to regard college-educated people's sensitivities to subtle internal racial dynamics as the sheltered naïveté of hothouse flowers who didn't know how hateful the world outside the group could be.

Working-class interviewees of color who mentioned cultural differences were referring to ethnic food, music, and social occasions, not different inter-action styles. These references were usually quite specific and descriptive. For example, Darla said her working-class Puerto Rican relatives "look Italian but [the neighbors] know you're not Italian . . . your Christmas dish is not lasagna! . . . We had certain cultural things that other people didn't. They had theirs and we had ours." When working-class activists of color brought up cultural differences in the context of their activist group, the point was usu-ally to figure out how people of different ethnicities could socialize together as part of building up group cohesion.

By contrast, college-educated activists, especially unassimilated straddlers and those in more radical groups, tended to bring up racism as an interper-sonal power dynamic within their own groups. Whatever their race, they were less likely to bring up racist violence and discrimination in the wider society and more likely to talk about low turnout by people of color and the whiteness of the group's internal culture. Their presumption, in keep-ing with their predominant institutional white supremacy frame, could be summarized in the phrase "as above, so below": the pervasive racism of the wider society was just as present inside their groups as outside. Often these references to internal culture had a guilty tone. White lifelong-PMC activ-ists in particular seemed to be performing racial humility. Ira said he regret-ted the "white ethos" within Action Against Empire. With a similar guilty tone, Sharon spoke defensively about her disagreements with her group's Antiracism Subcommittee, "I can't deal with it, not because I haven't dealt with my racism, though I'm sure that's part of it." Melissa told a story about five Jewish women in a radical collective who realized that their cultural style of simultaneous talk was silencing members of color from cultures with one-at-a-time speaking norms, such as a Haitian American member. She and the other four Jewish women made a pact to hold back and leave room for others to speak. These examples show how PMC whites often saw racism as a cultural dynamic inside activist groups.

Only one lifelong-working-class person, frequent outlier Dorothea, brought up white cultural norms within the group, and she put it in much more concrete terms than lifelong-PMC people did: she said she got "a mes-sage from one of the women of color . . . 'Well, you don't understand. This is just what black people do; we yell at each other.' So that was where I'd say, 'Alright. Maybe that's true. Maybe I really don't get that.'"

Contrast the specificity of Dorothea's quote with the abstract references to racism that Sheila used to describe City Power's mission: "using the classism or the racism that they're feeling in their everyday experience and give them an opportunity to understand that as part of a larger social structure that is oppression." As with concrete and abstract speech generally, PMC activists more often framed racism as a general property of organizations, less often as particular incidents with times, places, and people.

Arguing over Racism in a Mixed-Class Group: How Is an Antiracist Commitment Expressed?

These class differences in approaches to racism were clearly visible in a conflict at one meeting, a special session to talk about racism. The mixed-race, mixed-class group Easthaver Demands Justice had a commitment to be antiracist, but members disagreed about the implications of that commitment.

The least controversial form of antiracism was getting involved with low-income grassroots groups of color in their urban neighborhood, such as joining a picket by an environmental justice group against placing a toxic incinerator in a mostly black area. Such involvements as hands-on allies to grassroots campaigns (advocated as a best practice by Piatelli 2008) were one of the few things that everyone in this fractious group could enthusiastically agree on.

But all other ways of expressing antiracism were the subject of vociferous conflict during the study period and the two prior years. Workshops and special sessions to talk about internal diversity had proponents and opponents, as did hanging diversity-related behavior guidelines on the wall. Affirmative action to deliberately recruit new members of color was controversial. Publicly describing their wider movement as "white and middle class" was controversial. And what happened at this specially called session was particularly controversial. Analyzing who took which position, by class and by race, reveals the different approaches to race found in other activist groups as well.

When I arrived at this special antiracism session, the first thing that jumped out at me was how much whiter it was than the prior meeting, with just three people of color instead of six. Almost all the community activists of color who had been drawn in by EDJ's concrete work on local problems skipped this meeting, as well as a later public event on institutionalized racism.

The special session had been convened by the Antiracism Subcommittee, which had mostly white college-educated members. The facilitator, Judith, was a friendly, humble white straddler who had often served as a bridge person between the working-class community of her youth and her chosen community of mostly PMC radicals. The subcommittee had chosen Judith and LP Deborah to lead the session instead of a sharp-tongued white member, perpetually angry at EDJ for insufficient antiracism, described by two interviewees as "blasting" other white members.

The subcommittee had circulated ahead of time a statement that began, "The power elites of this country . . . have successfully used white supremacy to keep white people from uniting with people of color" and ended with a call to white activists to "support and follow the leadership of activists of color." The subcommittee's intention was to increase the acceptance of the institutional white supremacy frame within the group. Judith introduced the proposal with words that exemplify the macro/micro linkage in that frame:

> In a white-dominated society, it's easy for white people to dominate discussions and groups. We have privilege that comes with our white skin that sometimes we don't even notice. This [proposal] is a conscious effort to follow activists of color, to listen more than lead in our collaboration, in an effort to move towards something where we can truly be equal partners, recognizing the inequality in the society that exists right now.

But at the meeting, the proposal got overwhelmingly negative reactions, in particular to the last part about "follow[ing] the leadership of activists of color." All three members of color present opposed it, along with most white people not on the Antiracism Subcommittee. Dissecting the varied objections provides a cautionary tale for how *not* to promote the institutional-racism theme in a mixed-class group.

Two politically inexperienced white members from working-class backgrounds, impoverished Stuart and late-straddler Doris, both speaking with heavy working-class accents, quickly interjected the antibigotry frame into the discussion. Stuart responded to the written statement by saying, "Dr. Martin Luther King was one of the greatest heroes in America. . . . If we can't build unity between the races, that's going to further divide America, and that's one thing America doesn't need"—a mainstream liberal view with no political kinship to the leftist written statement.

Stuart and Doris's liberal antibigotry frame on race is the predominant one in mainstream media. The subsequent ideological debate in the meeting involved cultural capital that Stuart and Doris didn't have and references that were foreign to them. More radical antiracist ideas were brought into the conversation by people with college degrees and international travel experience.

A politically sophisticated member from a working-class background, the white contrarian Mack, injected the labor movement's variant of the multicultural frame, the strength-in-numbers emphasis on unity, exemplified by the old union rally chant "Black and white, unite and fight." Promoting an anti-ideological, pragmatic-action orientation, he said, "I agree racism is a very powerful force of disunity . . . [but] we need . . . a tactics that isn't very strictly bound by some long-term vision."

When the disagreement heated up, the one and only working-class person of color in the room, a black experienced activist, Wendy, who had remained silent for most of the meeting, said, "Maybe we should forget about it because it's divisive." Given that the purpose of the meeting was to strengthen cross-race ties, neither her silence nor her suggestion to drop the proposal seemed like a healthy sign.

Putting together Wendy's concern about divisiveness with Mack's "powerful force of disunity" comment and Stuart's call to unity for the good of America, it is clear that the working-class members (diverse in race, movement tradition, and political experience) shared a strong value on unity. In their varied ways they were cautious about overemphasizing racial differences.

To the dismay of the more radical meeting conveners, both Stuart and late-straddler Doris also returned the discussion to its most superficial level, the presence or absence of African Americans at EDJ's meetings. (In the following dialogue, when Judith is startled by Doris's response to her initial statement, note how Doris assumes that the problem was her terminology.)

DORIS: I'll bring my black friends next time.
JUDITH: I'm sorry? [*laughs*]
DORIS [*correcting her terminology to match Judith's*]: I'll bring my friends of color.
JUDITH: Your friends of color. For an illustration of this?
DORIS: No, so they can begin to work with us.
JUDITH: Oh, okay. [*laughs uncomfortably*]

While the working-class members were introducing the antibigotry and multicultural frames, while they were raising concerns about the impact of approving the statement on solidarity and pragmatic action, the PMC members were arguing about the wording of the statement, its ideology, its negativity, and especially the passive-follower role it proposed. One PMC white man initiated an abstract discussion of whether imperialism or structural racism caused more problems in the world.

Two PMC people of color, as well as several PMC whites, objected to the way that the statement lumped all activists of color together and romanticized them. PMC African American Rodney also objected to the implication that EDJ was a white group. He said in a later interview that he had taken offense at this erasure of members of color:

> There are people of color in the group, and often we hear this voice that "we're this sort of white, middle-class, middle-aged group," and it drives me up the wall. . . . This "where are the black people?"—there are black people there, okay, so what are you saying? . . . That's a pretty disturbing speech. One, because you're not leveraging the existing assets that are within the group. Two, because you're almost . . . through your own speaking, marginalizing the very people [*laughing*] that you're trying to bring in.

The other controversial part of the proposal was a vow to shun coalitions with groups that didn't agree with a particular political platform, including a strongly worded version of the institutional white supremacy frame. This too was rejected, not because of disagreement with its political values, but because of the constraints it would have put on EDJ's local work, which involved collaborating with groups of varied ideology. Radical analysis on paper seemed fine with all members, but not when it limited their program options. The abstract, ideological way the pledge was framed didn't make sense to the most culturally working-class members of EDJ, nor to people of color of all classes.

Three white PMC women with more elite professions than Deborah's or Judith's, including two older Quakers—the polite faction—all spoke in favor of softening the tone of the pledges and rejecting the commitment to shun some groups. Irene said, "Working *with* people is better than refusing to work with them." Thus, in a different way, the most race- and class-privileged people in the group also rejected the antiracist pledges.

For their part, Judith and Deborah had a frustrated tone at times, as if they couldn't believe how hard it was to sell EDJ members on the self-evident sense of an antiracist organization making an antiracist commitment. Their first loyalty was to organized groups of color not in the room, not connected to EDJ, with whom most members were unacquainted. To them, being white allies against racism meant acting in solidarity with radicals of color, being accountable to them, even at the expense of the goodwill of their fellow group members. But it proved impossible to get others to sign on to such a commitment when presented in the abstract.

The special session about the proposed pledge was not the first time EDJ members had argued about antiracism. In recent years the Antiracism

Subcommittee had organized workshops led by outside diversity trainers. Their most vocal critic was Mack:

> We've had more programs than I feel comfortable with on dealing with racism . . . people of color are pretty cynical about it. . . . There *are* cultural issues, I just don't feel that it's very easy to address them by . . . codes of behavior or inward assessing. . . .We've had a number of programs which were considered like training . . . which I personally find really, really off-putting. . . . That approach is . . . well-meaning but sometimes odd, patronizing, paternalistic. . . .A lot of black people don't appreciate it either. . . . It's something just odd about these white people wringing our hands all the time. [*laughs*]

Arguments over antiracist practices came to a head between Mack and Deborah; they were two poles of a polarized group. Deborah felt that Mack and many other EDJ members (mostly but not only whites) didn't see the cultural racism within their group or the multifaceted meaning of solidarity with people of color. Convincing other members of the institutional white supremacy frame and the meaning of being a white ally (Myers 2008) was an ongoing mission for her.

Deborah fit the profile of a long-term white antiracist described in Thompson's *A Promise and a Way of Life* (2001) and Warren's *Fire in the Heart* (2010). She described a conversion experience of being convinced by another white radical that most white activism ignores racism and betrays the interests of people of color. Deborah's life exemplified the low-key, plain-dressing, moderately VDM, LP white women profiled in chapter 2; her speaking style and self-presentation came across as sincere but lacking in pizzazz; and she had made occupational choices that lowered her income somewhat in order to keep her time flexible for activism. Most recently she had poured hundreds of volunteer hours into EDJ's urban grassroots partnerships in the Easthaver neighborhood. While Thompson, Warren, and others praise white antiracists almost without reservation, emphasizing their importance in ridding the United States of racism, Deborah's difficulties in persuading EDJ members suggest caveats about how the most committed white antiracists are sometimes perceived by other activists, and why their persuasive efforts sometimes fail.

Deborah, Judith, and the rest of the Antiracism Subcommittee convened the special meeting and proposed the antiracist pledge because milder forms of persuasion weren't working. Yet the very form and language of their proposal—ideological, abstract, and speaking in a humble voice more fitting for class-privileged whites—backfired, increasing the resistance of the rest of the group.

The common ground for this impressively varied group was combining work on global justice with local community-organizing projects. In theory, all members saw connections between international and local injustice; and in practice, they were all happy that EDJ worked at both levels. But their reasons for connecting those usually distinct political realms were so different and sometimes conflicting that they were unable to put out a joint statement explaining their dual focus. The strength of EDJ was its political, class, and race diversity, but that variety turned this discussion into a Tower of Babel, with different political languages being spoken.

Up Close and Personal, and with No Excuses

The class contrast between approaches to racism can be seen very clearly by shifting attention from the EDJ disagreement back to the working-class-majority City Power meeting described at the beginning of this chapter. After the discussion of the funder's questions, white working-class leader Dorothea opened up a broader question of race dynamics within the group, setting off a rare metaconversation about race talk by working-class people.

To make the class contrast more vivid, first picture Deborah asking EDJ to sign on to a general vow to follow the leadership of unnamed activists of color and calling EDJ a "white middle-class group" despite the presence of people of color in the room. Then picture white LP Ira giving general definitions of the words "oppression" and "privilege" at the Action Against Empire meeting spotlighted in chapter 5 and never speaking directly to Latino newcomer Lowell. Now notice how very *personally* Dorothea spoke to the black members at the City Power meeting, with how much less social distance:

> DOROTHEA: This is not to put you guys on the spot at all, but you know, if you got something to say about, "Well, hey, I do think City Power is sort of like not letting me develop as a leader the way I want to, or not having given me the opportunities I deserve," nobody is going to take that bad, you know, we got to think about this stuff.

Most members of color had positive reactions to what Dorothea said. However, low-income African American Adriana very clearly rejected the cultural domination theory and replaced it with an economic "invisible walls" (Stout 1996) explanation, speaking in the first and second person: "I don't believe you're not allowing. . . . For me things just keep being thrown in the way, and I know everybody else has things thrown in the way, but for me it just seems hard sometimes. . . . Speaking honestly, I can't come here comfortably when I'm not going to have any lights tomorrow. . . . I have to go and take care of my business first, and then still try to come to City Power second."

Working-class African American Quincy agreed with them that economic hardship was an obstacle to activism but pointed out that poverty also drew people to City Power: "When they're having the hardships and don't have nowhere else to go, and they need information, we're going to be probably the main networking for people." Thus, after working-class outlier Dorothea made the typically PMC move of putting a spotlight on the cross-race dynamics within the group, working-class members of color shifted the spotlight back to wider-society hardships by tying involvement by people of color to their concrete life circumstances.

Then the City Power conversation took another revealing turn. Court-ney, a lifelong-low-income black woman, was sitting quietly, not intending to participate in this discussion, until Dorothea asked her what she was think-ing. She hesitantly made a controversial comment that then became a hot topic in all five subsequent interviews with City Power members:

> Stop listening to me. I don't think you want to hear what I want to say. I don't want to say *all*, but some black people are lazy, and they just don't want to give it as much as it should be given to get where they need to be. . . . [They] make excuses. Everything is hard, yes, but if you want to do it, you make the time to do it.

Ranelle chimed in, speaking as one black woman to another: "We know the way to struggle, to make our way out of no way." Dorothea said, "*You're* at the table right now." But most of the members didn't respond to Courtney's comment at all. White women Sheila and Thelma both made long statements that weren't directly related, that carried the conversation in other directions; and in their interviews both expressed discomfort about not knowing what to say in that awkward moment. They assumed Courtney was speaking from internalized racism, a negative stereotype of African Americans as lazy, which may have been true. But her rejection of cultural and economic explanations for low participation also gave more agency to black nonactivists.

Courtney was at the far end of the disempowerment spectrum. (She's the one who said, "I never want to be in charge. . . . I'm just a helper in the background.") But she was not the only working-class person of color to repudiate the argument, heard almost entirely from college-graduate activists, that it is white cultural domination keeping people out of, or from taking leadership in, activist groups. A similarly tough, "no excuses" argument was also heard in another group, Labor and Community United, by a more empowered working-class African American activist, Rhonda: "When I'm in primarily black or solely black groups and they'll say, 'I'm having this clash, blah blah blah, the white person blah blah'. . . . I'll say, 'That supervisor don't [dis]like you because you're black, that supervisor don't like you because you're a butt.' [*laughs*] Sometimes you just have to be frank with people and just tell them, 'It don't have anything to do with your color, it has a lot to do with your attitude' [*laughs*]."

Instead of cultural domination (the micro dimension of the institutional white supremacy frame), all the working-class City Power members, both black and white, along with many working-class activists from other groups, had a distinctive way of talking about race and racism: factually descriptive of particular people's ethnicity, loyal to their organization, blaming the powers that be for injustice, and pragmatically emphasizing unity. Working-class activists of all races tended to favor concrete help to protect specific individuals from external racial injustice.

PMC and VDM diversity practices, while occasionally appreciated for their good intentions, were criticized by working-class activists sometimes as too rigid and formalistic; sometimes as too filled with weird or boring group processes or too jargon laden; sometimes as too guilty or condescending; and sometimes as impractical, taking the group's energy away from action and into endless talk and ideological conflict.

But talk-centered PMC diversity practices, not working-class approaches, were the ones that funders and large employers seemed to prefer. In a postindustrial society, where knowledge and management skills are the basis of class power (Wright 1985: 107–8), the abstract diversity lingo and stylized workshop processes known and practiced almost entirely by progressive college graduates are an example of Bourdieu's point that cultural practices sometimes classify, rank, and exclude people (1984: 223; Lamont and Lareau 1988). Just as we have seen that some activist groups studied here treated group process and organizational development as the turf of the PMC members or staff, so similarly a focus on internal diversity and "isms" was also frequently PMC turf—which is ironic, given that the ostensible purpose of organizational diversity work is to boost up marginalized people within the group.

In my opinion, the institutional white supremacy frame favored by many PMC and VDM activists includes some important aspects of the reality of racism that are missing from the antibigotry and multicultural frames, such as structural explanations and historical context. Since it is often learned at universities and is most prevalent among more class-privileged activists, spreading it means sharing cultural capital across class lines. The question is how this can be done more effectively, in ways less distorted by PMC cultural dispositions, especially to persuade politically inexperienced working-class whites—the huge demographic group that would have to be convinced before that frame could gain mainstream prominence (Teixeira and Rogers 2000; Metzgar 2010). An antiracist practice that wasn't class exclusive would look very different from the accepted practices in social movement groups today.

Class Speech Differences IV
Talking Long, Talking Often

Most groups had norms about how much people talked in meetings, which varied by the group's predominant class. Members of mostly professional-middle-class (PMC) groups used more words but talked less often; members of mostly working-class and lower-middle-class (LMC) groups talked more briefly but more often.

In conversation analysis, one principle is that "turn size is not fixed, but varies" (Sacks 1992); in other words, there's no typical number of words people speak at a stretch. But even though all groups had some almost silent and some talkative people, participants' typical wordiness corresponded with the group's predominant class. When three mostly working-class meetings are compared with three mostly PMC meetings,[1] the median lengths of members' longest speaking turn are strikingly different: 36 to 65 words in the working-class groups, and 151 to 364 words in the PMC groups. Race differences don't seem to account for this difference, as the median lengths for each class are about the same regardless of racial composition.

In terms of how many speech turns there were in the meetings as a whole, there was also a class pattern: in the same three working-class groups, the total number of speaking turns was very high, averaging 298 per hour, much higher than in two of the same three PMC groups, which averaged 151 speaking turns per hour.[2] Whiter groups also seem to have a lower number of speaking turns per hour. In working-class-majority community-needs groups in particular, production of joint utterances by several simultaneous and overlapping speakers (Sacks 1992: 57–59) was common, resulting in a great number of brief speaking turns.

This pattern in group norms was mirrored in individual speaking behavior: regardless of the group's class composition, PMC and other more-privileged people spoke longer but less frequently at meetings, while working-class, poor, and LMC people spoke more briefly but more often.

Individuals' median number of speaking turns per hour was almost twice as high for lifelong-working-class meeting participants (median 13) as for lifelong-PMC participants (median 7).[3] Given that quite a number of working-class or poor meeting participants, in particular people newer to activism, were almost or entirely silent, and that those quiet people pull the median down, the median of 13 turns is surprisingly high. Those working-class people who did participate verbally tended to speak more frequently than more-privileged people.[4]

There was little difference in frequency of meeting speech between LMC meeting participants (median 12 speaking turns per hour) and those who are working-class or poor, even though these categories encompassed a very wide range of class life experiences, from those stuck in deep poverty to homeowners in skilled trades. This suggests that the key factor in less-frequent speech may be the experience of academic higher education, which may train people to restrain themselves and wait their turn.

The class pattern for brevity or length of speech is that professionals tended to speak longer at a stretch, taking "multi-unit turns," meaning speech that continues past the first possible moment of completion (Liddicoat 2007: 286). For lifelong-PMC or UMC meeting participants, the median length of their longest speaking turn was 139 words, compared with 51 for lifelong poor, working-class, or LMC participants, who tended to stop or be interrupted sooner.

Thirty-five percent of lifelong-PMC people, but only 17 percent of lifelong-working-class people, used more than 174 words (triple the overall median of 58 words) in their longest speaking turn.[5] There wasn't a strong race pattern in who talked especially long at a stretch, but men were more likely to use a lot of words than women, and older people talked longer than younger people.[6]

Was talking long a function of enfranchisement in the group? This is borne out by looking at the four most extreme long-talkers, those using 540 or more words in their longest speaking turn: all were founders or longtime core members of their groups. However, 15 of the 24 longest talkers were not founders, officers, or otherwise identifiably leaders, but rank-and-file members.

Confirmation of the class difference in length of speech, independent of role in group, can be seen by looking at how many words the chairs of meetings used. Two lifelong-working-class chairs used 72 and 155 words in their longest speaking turn, while the two chairs from the highest UMC backgrounds used

342 and 352 words. Class background is associated with wordiness at all levels of involvement in the group.

In interviews as well, PMC people gave longer answers. An archetypal example is how African American labor organizer Owen, raised by college-educated homeowner parents, answered the question, "What did you like about that meeting, and what did you dislike?" (a question that, needless to say, most interviewees answered by mentioning things that happened at the meeting). When I first heard him make the long statement excerpted below, I felt I had witnessed a spontaneous work of art:

> The true value lies from the bottom up, not the top down, you know, and an agenda should be worker-centric as opposed to organizer-centric. Everything has to come out of the context of the struggle that you, that people find themselves in, like Paolo Freire says, *Pedagogy of the Oppressed* . . . Jesus sayeth in order to follow him we have to deny ourselves and take up our cross daily. Now I'm one who has had to bear the cross; I grew up in certain neighborhoods, so I understand what that's about. . . . It's important to me that if I organize that I be in the community that I organize; and this goes back to the tradition of Dietrich Bonhoeffer, who talked about the cost of the discipleship; he lived in Harlem, you know; it goes back to Langston Hughes, even though he grew up middle class, he still lived in Harlem; goes back to Miles Davis, even though he was from Juilliard music school and his father was a dentist, he went down into Harlem to work with Charlie Parker and to learn from him. . . . If you're going to be true to your art, if you want to be true to your social justice, then it's important that you are engaged with those people that you say that you represent. That's the fallacy and the travesty of communism and socialism is that, for the most part, as it was advocated in Eastern Europe, most of the people who spoke on behalf of the proletariat were not proletariat themselves. Most of them were a part of the bourgeoisie . . . you have to be organically related to the people that you represent.

While Owen's answer is exceptional in its number of intellectual references and its elaborate cogency, and while he drew on the eloquent African American rhetorical tradition in particular, it exemplified not only the PMC tendency to wordiness but also the verbal facility, use of abstract ideas, and inner-directed distance from other group members common among PMC interviewees.

When was talking a lot a problem, and when did it pass without complaint? Chapter 8 shifts the spotlight from simply describing varied class speech norms to an analysis of the behavior most annoying to activists, overtalking.

CHAPTER 8

Overtalkers

Coping with the Universal Pet Peeve

Activism brings many pleasures, but the downside is rubbing elbows with fellow activists whose behavior is annoying or offensive. In this chapter I explore class differences in how activists responded to problematic behavior, first analyzing the most common of all annoyances, overtalking. In chapter 9 I look at more extreme violations of group norms.

When fifty-five interviewees from twenty groups answered the questions "Do you have any pet peeves about how people act in meetings?" and/or "Does anyone in this group drive you crazy?," the great majority, forty-one of them, mentioned people talking too much. In addition, eight group members were heard during a meeting objecting to someone's overtalking. Overtalking dwarfed all other complaints put together.

Analyzing overtalking—who overtalked in meetings and in what ways; how other members reacted; how chairs and other members intervened or didn't—revealed some subtle class-culture patterns. Few contrasts between the two broad class categories, the working-class and the professional range, appear in this chapter. Instead, the class-culture traits of smaller subgroups, such as outlaw working-class women leaders, self-confident upper-middle-class (UMC) men, and soft-spoken lower professionals (LPs), pop out. It turned out to matter whether activists were class congruous or class incongruous in their groups. Some of these class-culture patterns persisted in the face of extreme behavior violations, but others didn't, giving us a window into how class predispositions sometimes break down under stress.

Who Was Seen as an Overtalker and Who Wasn't

Not all talkativeness violated group norms. Eleven active members, diverse in race, class, and gender, may have been overtalkers by objective measures,[1] speaking an average of four times their share of the meeting's total speech turns, but they got no negative reactions from other members either during the meeting or in interviews. In fact, interviewees praised some of them. They stand out for their long tenure with their groups; eight of eleven were founders.

These eleven frequent-talking leaders provided information on most agenda items, usually staying on topic. Other members often addressed questions to them. Many less-active people seemed motivated to come to meetings in order to hear updates from those closer to the heart of the action, so these leaders' frequent speech was welcome. It appears that in many groups, talking frequently was expected from those with long-term core involvement, and frequent tuned-in, on-topic speech was appreciated as contributing to the mission.

Criticism of overtalkers was targeted at a very different profile of meeting participants, mostly not group leaders. Thirteen overtalkers were criticized by name; for eleven of them, their speech behavior is also documented in meeting transcripts.

Acquaintances who heard I was writing about overtalkers presumed the offenders would fit a certain profile: an older, white, highly educated man. But only one fit that profile, Rufus from Labor and Community United. It is true that the eleven resented overtalkers were disproportionately white and male, but virtually every race, gender, class, and age bracket was represented among the eleven.[2]

The eleven resented overtalkers spoke a mean of 2.66 times their equal share, making them less talkative than the frequent-speaking leaders. Clearly, something besides sheer volume of speech causes group members to see someone as a problematic overtalker. They were far more likely to be off topic or in other ways out of sync with the majority of the group. They seem to have been resented for their unawareness of what kind of talk others in the group valued.

Is overtalking a class dynamic or just a matter of personalities clashing with group styles? Strikingly, nine of the eleven resented overtalkers were class incongruous, distinctly different than the class mode of their group, whether higher, lower, or with a mobility trajectory moving in the opposite direction.[3]

Another class pattern was that the median class-background score of the eleven resented overtalkers was far lower than the median class composition of the 362 meeting participants as a whole. Sometimes an overtalker fit in with the group demographic in every way except for a class difference. For example, Hilda, a working-class Latina, was named by several interviewees in her majority-professional, majority-Latina group as a person who drove them crazy. She shared a town, a type of occupation, and a national heritage with most of the group, but she had less class privilege and talked twice her share.

Similarly, Doris, a white woman from a working-class background, was in the class minority in the PMC-majority group Easthaver Demands Justice, though she matched the group in its majority gender, race, and generation. While some working-class women, African Americans, and others tend to say supportive back-channel minimal responses such as "*uh*-huh" and "yeah" while others speak (Mesthrie et al. 2000: 198), these unobtrusive responses were never criticized as overtalking. But Doris had an exaggerated version of this speech practice in which she frequently exclaimed or asked clarifying questions while others spoke, in a full-voiced way too intrusive to be called back channel. Doris's speech style might have fit in at a community-needs meeting of working-class women, where multiple members frequently created joint productions by overlapping speech (Sacks 1992), but in this group she was seen as disruptive. Not just the chair but also two other members intervened repeatedly to try to curb her overtalking.

It is notable that in three of the five conflict stories viewed through a class lens in chapter 1, the lighting rod person was a class-incongruous overtalker. First, in the Action Center, the ad hoc convention protest group, in which several members didn't realize that Dirk was virtually their only lifelong-working-class active member, the recent efforts to curb Dirk's dominating behavior had been focused in part on his aggressive overtalking. Dirk's number of speaking turns was more than four times his equal share of airspace.

Second, during the conflict at the Workforce Development Task Force meeting, Jeremiah was resented not only for scolding the group and trying to thwart their plans but also for overtalking. A straddler from a low-income black family in a mostly lifelong-professional group, Jeremiah was class incongruous in the meeting where he spoke both very frequently and very long.

Third, the white man who raised the upsetting criticism in the Women Safe from Violence meeting, Randall, was a habitual overtalker. The context of the quarrel was that Randall had already gotten on everyone's last nerves by overtalking earlier in the meeting. His verbal patterns were reminiscent of someone with Asperger's syndrome:[4] he had exhaustive knowledge of one topic that he interjected over and over, despite its limited relevance to the discussion. Before the meeting, he saw my recorder and literally backed me into a corner as he rapidly told me many facts from his life story, seemingly oblivious to my attempts to escape. Despite having highly educated professional parents, Randall worked as a driver, an occupation with no regular coworkers to resent his aggressive overtalking. His critique of the public presentation might have been received better if it had come from a better listener, someone more tuned in to the group's conversation.

Randall was not the only involuntarily downwardly mobile person from a professional family to be heard overtalking in a mostly working-class community group. In Safety Net for All, there seemed to be a collective effort by the class-diverse members to cut off frequent overtalker Angelica, a white woman from a very high UMC background, who kept a stream-of-consciousness monologue going throughout the meeting. Both Randall and Angelica were involuntarily downwardly mobile activists in groups dedicated to empowering low-income people. Perhaps the same personality problems that led these two to their extreme off-topic overtalking also contributed to their alienation from the PMC social and professional networks into which their privileged background might otherwise have led them.

A picture emerges of uprooted individuals joining a voluntary group unconnected with their own neighborhood, workplace, or social-identity group. Some class-incongruous resented overtalkers may also fit Jasper's (1997) definition of a crank: a stubborn personality who persists in activism even when lacking a supportive activist community or a promising political climate.

But unlike the activists who offended others by more extreme breaches of basic norms, profiled in chapter 9, virtually all of whom were unrooted, some class-incongruous resented overtalkers, such as Doris and Hilda, were actually deeply rooted in their communities and matched the predominant race and class of the neighborhood, if not of the group. Frequent interrupter Doug, a young white professional resented overtalker, was also very enfranchised in his community group. Overtalking is a lesser offense that neither requires nor causes exit from root communities. Thus it is not being an uprooted transplant generally, but specifically being *class* incongruous within a group that is associated with being resented as an overtalker.

Class Patterns in Reactions to Overtalkers

When someone violated group norms against overtalking in a meeting, reactions varied strongly by class. Most working-class interviewees unambivalently wanted stronger chairing to keep people on topic. Their praise for chairs tended to stress firmness in cutting off overtalkers. For example, Alonzo from the Local 21 Organizing Committee—using the word "teacher" to mean facilitator, as some other working-class interviewees, mostly older African Americans, also did—said: "There's nothing more aggravating to me than a meeting that's supposed to go one or two hours that runs for three hours. . . . Teachers have the skill to move the conversation on, saying something like 'I want to make sure we get to everything.'"

Similarly, Olivia complained: "There's someone in the Parecon Collective who likes to facilitate but is really, really bad at it . . . they just forget there's a facilitator or they don't listen to the conversation, and they're the ones who are [side-chatting by] making [social] plans with their friends."

But some working-class nonleaders, especially women of color, sounded disempowered and hopeless about this topic, as if disruptive overtalkers were an unfixable problem. Much as they wished for less overtalking, they didn't sound confident that anything would work to curb it. Even when asked directly "If you were in charge of leading the next meeting, what would you change to make it go better?" some of these working-class nonleaders had a hopeless tone about effectively implementing their own process ideas. Myra, a middle-aged working-class Latina immigrant in the Brontown Affordable Housing Consortium, answered that question by saying, "One person would speak a lot more than others, and they would take a lot of the time. I don't know how [*pause*]. . . sometimes it could be a little bit rude, if you're trying to interrupt somebody when they're trying to express themselves. . . . It's hard sometimes to do; people get offended, 'Geez, let me finish.'"

Many PMC people, by contrast, put themselves into the chair role in their answers even without being asked to, suggesting things they had done or would do to limit overtalkers. But their relatively higher sense of empowerment didn't mean they acted decisively. In fact, many of them squelched their own annoyance and let overtalkers keep talking. A strikingly high number of LP, medium- and lower-PMC, and VDM interviewees, mostly white, expressed ambivalence in their attitudes toward overtalkers, revealing inner tension between wanting everyone to be able to express themselves but also wanting to keep the meeting on track. No poor, working-class, or LMC interviewees expressed any such self-criticism nor described straining to be even-handed.

Some PMC interviewees felt irritation and frustration at overtalking, but they also said that they shouldn't feel those negative emotions; they seemed to be holding back their reactions, sometimes tying themselves in knots. Two said their ideal selves wouldn't be annoyed by anyone. When asked "Does anybody in the group drive you crazy?" a white professional in the Brontown

Affordable Housing Consortium, Charlotte, said, "I'm a therapist, nobody drives me crazy."

A seesaw pattern characterized these professional-background interviewees' comments on dealing with overtalkers: on the one side this, on the other side that. The word "but" and silent pauses interrupted many of their statements, revealing a midstream shift in opinion. Listen to how Rupert, a young white man from a UMC background, switched course midstream as he described his pet peeve in the Parecon Collective this way: "Chronically getting off topic and chronically focusing on minutia . . . and that's why I think it's important to have a good facilitator. . . . But [*pause*]—I think it's more important that [everyone] get practice facilitating than to make sure everything runs smoothly as I'd like it to. *But* I certainly do appreciate a good facilitator. You know, 'This has nothing to do with what we're supposedly talking about.'" Note that something about pulling members back on topic went unsaid during the pause after the first "but." Bernstein (1971) quantitatively analyzed hesitations and pauses in the speech of working-class and middle-class British teen boys; he concluded that middle-class speech is more hesitant because it involves planning what to say while speaking. First LP- and PMC-background interviewees would express their desire for meeting participants to talk less, then they would pull themselves back and state their support for all members expressing themselves. Some interviewees openly described their inner resistance to their wish that meetings could be tighter and how they reoriented themselves to the belief that it's more democratic to hold back from intervening. Complaints about particular overtalkers by LPs often also contained praise for the same individuals, sometimes seesawing back and forth. For example, a white LP said of a working-class white man in City Power, "Sometimes Bastian would start saying things, and it would seem to me like it was totally off topic, which is . . . a pet peeve of mine when people start filibustering . . . but I learned pretty quickly that he's a pretty insightful guy. . . . And so now it's kind of more like if I find myself getting annoyed, like 'Oh, here we go', I think, 'Wait, I have no idea where this is going to end up.'"

Self-conscious ambivalence and self-questioning appears to characterize PMC activists, in particular white LPs. This LP class disposition also plays a central role in responses to extreme behavior violations, discussed in the next chapter.

Class Patterns in How Chairs Dealt with Overtalkers

When someone was overtalking, the most common intervention by chairs of all classes, races, and genders was simply to restate the agenda item the group was supposed to be talking about. But when the chair or another leader intervened in some additional way, class and race patterns showed up.

The most direct confrontations of overtalkers were by white working-class founders. These formidable women sometimes snapped at talkative members, at times using the imperative verb form to issue commands. They were not observed shushing or scolding people who were less privileged than themselves, such as people of color or currently poor people. At a WomenSafe meeting, when LMC white newcomer Ricki persisted in repeating her own awful story of violence, Elaine interrupted her, saying, "Hold on, hold on, hold on." Another white working-class leader of that group barked "Focus!" at overtalker Randall; by contrast, Adaline, a college-educated white woman from a PMC background, made a more indirect comment to steer Randall back to the meeting topic, "That's a whole other deal."

Other blunt interventions by working-class white women leaders used the second person "you" to stop overtalkers, as well as the imperative. Toni from Safety Net for All interrupted overtalker Angelica's wordy reveries on her lunch choices by snapping, "You don't need to tell us what you're ordering . . . just pass the menu around." City Power founder Dorothea said to an overtalker, "You just interrupted the last three people."

At the other end of the class spectrum, blunt interventions to stop overtalkers were also heard. For example, Blake, the Ivy League–educated white facilitator of an Easthaver Demands Justice meeting, snapped, "Hey! Shhh! Folks!" Thus the most forceful, directive intervention to stop overtalking came from white people at the two ends of the class spectrum.

People of color tended to intervene with politer language than whites,[5] though still assertively in the case of those at a higher class level. This race contrast can be seen in two reactions to Doris, the white very frequent talker from a working-class background in Easthaver Demands Justice. When Blake was facilitating, he became increasingly annoyed at Doris as the meeting wore on. When she started another digression, he twice barked, "Doris! Doris! Doris!" But another of the most class-privileged group members, Mia, a South Asian high professional, handled Doris's overtalking differently. She moved to sit next to her and whispered answers to her many informational questions, keeping up a steady but quiet side conversation with her. Once when Blake cut Doris off, Mia suggested gently, "You could raise your hand and you will be called on." Doris immediately raised her hand for the first time during the meeting.

Working-class African Americans usually used courtesy words or laughter to soften their interventions. During the heated conflict between Jeremiah and members of the Workforce Improvement Task Force, the black LMC chair, Brandon, called two combatants' names and then said, "Please hold for one second." At a Safety Net for All meeting, when overtalker Angelica began to read a long letter aloud, a LMC black woman, Lidia, used a lighter tone, different from Toni's sharp lunch menu intervention, laughing as she said, "You don't have to read every word!"

All this direct communication stands in stark contrast with the indirectness of *all* LP chairs, as well as some other white and/or female PMC-background chairs. Listening to some of them, it would be impossible to tell whose speech they were attempting to curb, as they rarely used names. For example, when one Easthaver Demands Justice meeting went off topic, an older white PMC woman, Nancy, made tentative statements into the air: "Probably we do need to get going"; and later, with an upward inflection, "I don't know if we want to stick to our schedule?"

Professional-range chairs tended to use third-person speech to refer to people in the room. The UMC leader of Neighbors United, Fred, said, "Let's go around and people can put the ideas out." Also note Blake's third person, "Folks!" When a Parecon Collective meeting went into an extended side conversation, Rupert murmured ineffectively, "Shift coverage! Who wants to talk about shift coverage?" Using third-person words such as "folks," "people," or "everybody" for people in the room seems to reveal a greater social distance than the working-class second person (Mesthrie et al. 2000: 503). It may also be that PMC activists use indirect speech to avoid domination and to communicate respect.

For LPs and some white PMC-background activists, there appeared to be a long, convoluted pathway from thought to speech. They took more words to say their thoughts, contradicted themselves more, and spoke more distantly to and about others in the room.

Speech practices and norms can rarely be correlated with huge demographic categories because the contexts of speech vary so widely (van Dijk 2008: chap. 4). Intersecting race and gender differences could reasonably be expected to wipe out any class correlations. The class patterns in overtalking and reactions to it were found to cut across other identities, a finding that strengthens my overall conclusion that distinct, crosscutting class-culture differences do exist.

Chapter 9 asks whether the classed ways of approaching life and activism revealed by analyzing overtalking also show up when activists react to more dramatically problematic acts.

Class Speech Differences V
Anger, Swearing, and Insults

Within every class category, a subset of activists got angry, swore, and used hostile language. But class differences showed up in different ways of expressing anger and antagonism.

Professional-middle-class (PMC) activists were more likely to talk about being angry, using emotion words such as "pissed off" and "angry."[1] Lifelong working-class people usually expressed anger in other ways besides describing their emotions in words, such as with tone of voice, body language, and loud volume. There was a race pattern in volume: everyone who yelled was white or African American; no Latinos, Asian Americans, or Native Americans yelled.

One word in particular shows up frequently in college-educated activists' quotes about conflictual situations: "frustrated" and its variations (said 1.6 times per 10,000 words in interviews, compared with .5 times by working-class activists). This may be an acceptably polite euphemism for being angry among people taught to value emotional restraint.

Swear Words

A subset of interviewees in every class swore, but which swear words they used varied by class.[2] Working-class activists were more likely to say "shit," "bullshit," and "hell," usually in the phrase "what the hell." Lifelong-PMC activists were more likely to say "fuck(ing)"; working-class people rarely said the f-word and never said "screwed." I can't explain why scatological terms would be more common among working-class activists and sexual terms more common among PMC activists. Among some respectable working-class people, "fuck" may be the most proscribed word, never to be said in a public setting.

Class-mobile activists swore more than those lifelong in any one class.[3] Straddlers—mostly the uprooted, unassimilated subset of straddlers—combined the high rate of saying "fuck" of their current PMC class status with an even higher rate of saying "shit" and "bullshit" than those with whom they shared their working-class background. Adding in less common words such as "ass(hole)" and "goddamn," straddlers have a very high total rate of swearing, 3.23 per 10,000 words. As chapter 9 shows, this speech pattern is consistent with more combative behavior overall by uprooted, unassimilated straddlers.

Swear words were the most obvious difference between the speech styles of the respectable and outlaw working-class activists. The working-class outlaws tended to pepper their routine speech with swear words that the respectable working-class activists tended to avoid. For example, a one-hour interview with Brandy included these seven sentences: "It was like a greater force that made this damn thing come here. You can't have poor people who have been taught that they are a piece of shit thinking that they can lead unless you first deal with that shame. Hell no! That's all a bunch of crap. They don't give a shit. The hell with this. A lot of people don't give a shit that you're poor."

These working-class outlaws' blunt speech reconfirms Lamont's finding that working-class American men prize directness and the courage to risk giving offense (Lamont 2000: 36–37). But despite their casual use of swear words, even the toughest outlaw working-class activists showed some restraint in their language. They tended to avoid expressing hostility toward individuals, instead just sounding rough and tough, refusing to tame their speech to polite manners.

Halfway between the working-class outlaw frequent swearers and the respectable nonswearers fell the most common degree of moderate respectability among working-class interviewees. For example, middle-aged, working-class Latina Cecilia explained this moderately respectable viewpoint in a story about a hip-hop recording by a local youth organization. (Note that she says "shit" herself, evidently a less offensive word, as she describes her negative reaction to youth profanity.) "There was a CD . . . and I told my boyfriend, 'Get that shit out [of the CD player].' Because I didn't feel that for youth to send out a message you need to use profanity. . . . You can express yourself positively, without using negative words. . . . You don't use the foul language. . . . These kids . . . can express themselves, without using profanity of course . . . letting out all that anger." The most common working-class standard seemed to allow for an occasional restrained swear word, within reason.

Classist Intelligence Slurs

College-educated people were more likely to use insult words maligning someone's intelligence. Lifelong-PMC people in particular used these slurs more than twice as often per 10,000 words as lifelong-working-class people.[4] The rate of saying the word "stupid" per 10,000 words was 6.8 times as high for the combined college-educated trajectories as for lifelong-working-class interviewees. The word "idiot" was used by PMC activists but never by working-class activists. Only "dumb" showed no class difference.

Intelligence-based insults evoke resonances of institutionalized classism and racism, in particular of tracking within public schools. Thus a classism alarm should ring at this finding that insult words implying stupidity had a strong class association.

Privilege as Putdown

One common conversational gambit by activists was to invoke someone's privileged identity immediately before or after criticizing them or disagreeing with them. For example, during Easthaver Demands Justice's conflict over antiracism, profiled in chapter 7, when Deborah found herself in the awkward situation of being a white person pushing an antiracism frame that some people of color disagreed with, she sometimes used the higher class backgrounds of members of color to undermine their case (a dubious move, in my opinion, as racism is experienced by people of color of every class):

> DEBORAH: There's a few people in the group that haven't gotten past feeling guilty every time these [race and class] words are uttered and don't want to hear about it.
> INTERVIEWER: Do you mind saying who had a negative reaction to [a public antiracist statement]?
> DEBORAH: [Member's name], he's not white but he's upper class.

Typically it was a disliked person who was presumed to have higher-class status, as when working-class black woman Rhonda criticized union staffer Suzy and described her as a "rich white woman" "on the higher economic status than the rest of us." In fact Suzy had only a high school diploma and listed her race as "American Indian"; she was a homeowner, but her parents had done working-class hourly wage jobs. In a similar presumption, Cecilia characterized resented straddler Shirley as a high-level professional, exaggerating the difference between their direct-care and program-manager human services occupations. Often these were honest mistakes. But in an environment without much coherent talk about class, it's easier for unscrupulous activists to use references to privileged social identities to attack and score points.

The rancorous conflict among groups protesting the 2008 Democratic National Convention,[5] explored in the next chapter, was rife with privilege putdowns. For example, McKayla of The People's Convention (TPC) mischaracterized a Stand Up Fight Back (SUFB) member who in fact came from a working-class background: "This may just be gossip, it may be true, I don't know, that she's more of a trust fund kid. . . . She's a giant pain in the ass."

The most talked about incident among DNC protestors was an exchange of hostile words in a local newspaper's forum. SUFB founder Tye was quoted in an article characterizing TPC as a "white, middle-class group"—a fairly accurate description but one that TPC members took great offense at. In response, a hothead TPC member, Nanette, researched the assessed value of Tye's suburban home and posted this comment online: "Be careful who you categorize as white and middle class, considering you are white and you live in a home in [wealthy suburb] that you paid $331,000 for. . . . Does that not make you white middle class?" Tye then posted an online response in which he defended himself against the charge of being middle class and called Nanette an "ignorant fool."

In contexts other than left-leaning movements "white" and "middle class" might not seem like insult words. Why would mention of suburban homeownership be offensive enough to warrant a rude response like "ignorant fool"? Privilege as putdown only makes sense in a context in which an oppressed status confers movement capital. If social standing within a group could be gained by claiming an identity such as being a person of color, queer, or poor, sometimes the converse is also true: to say activists were privileged could tarnish their reputation.

CHAPTER 9

Activists Behaving Badly
Responses to Extreme Behavior Violations

The most eccentric person I met while re-
searching the 2008 convention protests was Anthony, the full-time bicycle
billboard. For several weeks before the Democratic National Convention, he
spent all his daylight hours riding around Denver wearing sandwich boards
that read "Tye Lies," referring to a founder of the militant convention protest
group Stand Up Fight Back (SUFB).

Anthony was a surprisingly normal looking middle-aged white man, very
buff from all that bicycling; his way of talking sounded sane. But his explanation for his total dedication to harassing a protest leader made no sense.
During two SUFB meetings, Anthony told me, he stood outside the building
holding a sign that said "Beware, sheeple: SUFB spreads fear" and blowing an
extremely loud air horn. If esteemed scholar Jasper (1997) can use "crank" as
an academic term for a stubborn lone-wolf activist, I can add my own term
to the social movement lexicon: Anthony was not just a common crank but
a full-fledged whack-job.

Such obnoxious harassment would grate on the nerves of the most easy-
going activist, and SUFB members Tye and Brenda, both uprooted, unassimilated straddlers, were not easy-going. According to Anthony, Tye and
Brenda came out of their meeting and shoved him across the street, threw
flyers at him, threatened to "kick his ass," and then called the cops to get
him removed. This last accusation surprised me: Stand Up Fight Back was

so militantly antipolice, with such certain expectations that they would be brutalized just for peacefully protesting (justified expectations, as it turned out), that I would have sworn they would never turn to the police to resolve a dispute. Their organizational t-shirt urged people not to snitch. But eyewitnesses corroborated that they called the police on Anthony. What people do under extreme provocation is sometimes different from their everyday behavior, and these unexpected reactions may give a unique glimpse into how flexible or rigid their class predispositions are.

As the date of the 2008 Democratic National Convention grew closer, protest planners were under more and more stress. It was Barack Obama's moment, not the antiwar movement's moment. When I first met protest planners six months before the convention, their weak support from funders, media, city officials, and potential recruits was already upsetting them. By the final weeks before the convention, organizers were tearing their hair out. As it turned out, the protests were spirited, but the biggest only drew a few thousand people, and some events had tiny turnouts, which is always hard on organizers' morale.

But most activists I interviewed from the Denver protests were far more upset about the behavior of other activists than about the wider political environment or low turnout. They had expected activists to treat one another honorably. In their interviews, many tried to convince me of how outrageous the breaches by other groups and individuals had been, patrolling moral boundaries and articulating the limits of what was acceptable and what was intolerable.

This DNC-protest situation was a perfect opportunity to see how activists, many thrown together as strangers at an unsettled time, reacted under pressure—and to test ideas about how and when group expectations are formed. Because ad hoc coalitions begin without a group style, the interplay of movement traditions and members' class and other cultural predispositions could be more plainly seen as strangers worked out ways to operate together. Activists faced with extreme behavior violations sometimes tapped their preexisting conflict-resolution repertoires, drawn from their class predispositions and/or their movement traditions; but at other times they reacted to emotionally upsetting situations in out-of-character ways, improvising new responses to offensive breaches within or among their groups.

Intolerable Violations of Norms

As the rivalry between DNC protest coalitions degenerated into open enmity, activists made many accusations of intolerable behavior. Recall the example of privilege-as-putdown in which Tye called The People's Convention (TPC) a "white, middle-class group," and in retaliation Nanette of TPC posted the price of Tye's house online; then Tye called Nanette an "ignorant fool." Members of both groups had a strong negative reaction to the personal attack in Nanette's post. Lissa, a professional-middle-class (PMC), white TPC member, said, "I was appalled, I was absolutely appalled." Some but not all thought that Tye had also misbehaved by publicly calling TPC a "white, middle-class" group. As noted, most Denver interviewees seemed to take it for granted that to point out someone's dominant identity in public was a form of unfair attack. Bo, a PMC, white member of the TPC, said, "That kind of race and class baiting should never be in any kind of organizing. . . . We have members from all classes in our group."

In addition, DNC activists made dozens of other accusations of intolerable acts, including threats of violence, threats to sue, hate language and insult words in public and in private, "spying," and "stealing bands" from other groups.[1]

While these DNC protest groups had the greatest number of alleged violations of activist norms per group, several other groups that I studied also had some incidents regarded as intolerable, including drunkenness, stealing, hitting, and yelling.[2] In total, I heard approximately thirty individuals be accused of intolerably bad behavior, twelve of them DNC protestors.

In what follows I look at who did and didn't perpetrate these low blows; at how activists of different classes explained such intolerable behavior; at differences in group conflict norms; and at how activists responded when someone breached a basic behavior norm, using the worst conflict I encountered, the SUFB/TPC clash, as a case study.

Who Crossed the Line and Who Didn't?

There was no class pattern as to which activists perpetrated which kind of problematic behavior. I had hypothesized that perhaps threatening to sue would be a PMC act, but I found two examples where working-class activists threatened to sue an activist. I wondered (perhaps falling into a classist stereotype) whether alcohol or drug violations would happen more commonly in low-income groups, but I found at least one story of public intoxication in each class trajectory. Extreme offenders were atypical of every class. Nor were there any race, gender, or age patterns in who was accused of behaving badly.

Each class-trajectory category contained at least one offender. However, five of the twelve DNC protestors accused of intolerable acts, a disproportionate plurality, were unassimilated straddlers, the first in their family to graduate from a four-year college but not then going on to a professional job—a slight class pattern.

Looking at who *didn't* behave outrageously helps explain the precondition for extreme breaches. There were entire categories of DNC protest activists who had zero incidents of hostile behavior toward other activists, despite some intense provocation: members of religious congregations, salaried employees of nonprofits, union members, parents with kids in the local schools, people who grew up in Denver and whose parents and/or extended families still lived there. In short, *rooted* people of all classes didn't take public hostile action during the DNC conflicts.

By contrast, the twelve DNC offenders' greatest commonality was that they were exceptionally unrooted. All lived on the fringes of society in some way. Most had no employer; they were either unemployed or self-employed. For example, one was a nonunion carpenter. Some were students many miles away from both their college towns and their hometowns. Two were voluntarily downwardly mobile (VDM) and nomadic. None of these dozen offenders had dependents. Most rented; a few were just crashing in Denver to organize the protests; only two were homeowners. None practiced their parents' religion. Most belonged only to an ad hoc protest group that would disband after the convention.

Who were such unrooted activists accountable to? If they behaved abominably under stress, whose displeasure did they have to face? They answered to no employer or co-workers or neighbors or religious congregants or family members—none of the ties that bind more rooted activists. The preconditions for intolerable breaches of activist behavior expectations lie in this lack of community interdependence. Lone cranks can join groups, act out, and disappear; hot-tempered activists can crack under stress, do things that appall others, and face no consequences except for some criticism from acquaintances or, at worst, from friends.

Even though intolerable misbehavior happened in every class category, this lack of community accountability is a class issue, because unrootedness is a feature of PMC and VDM lives. Among my 362 survey respondents, the relationships between rootedness or unrootedness and all college-graduate trajectories were statistically significant.[3]

It is typical for PMC and straddler young adults to move far away from their families to go to college, often never returning to their hometowns. By contrast, working-class people are more likely to live near where they grew up. Immigrants, of course, are the exception, but like other working-class people, they are more likely to move with multiple family members, less often as lone individuals. As described in chapter 3, in the last two generations, college-educated people have left their ancestral religions in droves, while the working-class population has shifted to being secular at a slower rate; thus working-class people disproportionately belong to religious congregations.

PMC and VDM *activists* are even more uprooted than PMC nonactivists. Becoming a college-educated activist often means breaking family ties. And the way that global/local cause groups form, with each individual motivated by a personal commitment to the cause, means weaker ties among members than in working-class groups. The setting most likely to breed hostile misbehavior toward other activists is a short-term group whose members joined one by one, as strangers.

When activist groups grow out of the shared life experience of a workplace, a neighborhood, or a particular hardship, they tend to have some members who are tied to one another over the long term, including clusters of relatives; those ties make openly hostile behavior riskier. In working-class-majority groups, when offensive behavior crossed the line into criminality (such as violence or theft), some perpetrators had to leave town afterward; they had broken the trust of their neighbors or co-workers or family members too severely to remain part of the community.

Rootedness and unrootedness also varied by the four broad movement traditions, with labor-outreach groups including the highest rate of very rooted people. Not surprisingly, unrootedness strongly correlated with age.[4] The most typical unrooted activist was a VDM member of an anarchist group in his or her twenties. The most typical rooted activist was a lifelong-working-class union member in his or her sixties.

Unrootedness is a double-edged sword. Having been uprooted is also what allows many activists to think and act boldly and independently. People from PMC backgrounds turned to progressive activism in greater numbers precisely because they were relatively free from dependence on conservative extended families and because they were less embedded in hometown community and religious traditions. Some unions, community-needs groups, and staff advocacy coalitions were relatively cautious in their demands and tactics because of their embeddedness in community ties. Radical analysis and action more commonly came from unassimilated straddlers, working-class outlaws, and PMC and VDM activists who had moved far from home. But weak community ties also created the environments where hotheads, cranks, and whack-jobs could act out.

Of course, most activists, no matter how unrooted, would never dream of threatening or harassing another activist. The offenders were unusual people. A disproportionately high number of the individuals accused of extreme misbehavior, more than one-third, were class incongruous within their groups, either higher or lower in background or current class than most other members.[5] A picture emerges of problematic personalities wandering the movement in search of trouble, or escaping from past troubles encountered in groups demographically more like themselves.

Emotional Reactions to Activists Behaving Badly

Activists reacted with anger, fear, and other negative feelings to extreme misbehavior, which is not surprising. We know from Garfinkel's famous breaching experiments that people tend to get upset when someone violates their expectations for ordinary behavior. When his experimenters repeatedly asked clarifying questions about whatever subjects said (e.g., "What do you mean, you had a 'flat tire'?"), subjects became more and more heated, red in the face, angry and yelling; one said, "You know what I mean! Drop dead!" (Heritage 1984: 80). Subjects expected experimenters to draw on shared background knowledge of what "everyone knows" to supply recognizable, common sense understandings of what the subject said.

Such emotional reactions have been documented across a wide variety of social settings (McKinnon 1994: 127–38; Garfinkel 1967). But there is a reason why moral breaches are upsetting to activists in particular. Whether or not the group is intentionally prefigurative (reflecting qualities of the sought-for better society in its operations), there is a widespread expectation that social change groups will live by the values they espouse and create an island of positive social relations within an oppressive society. Union members expect worker solidarity; peace activists expect peaceable relations among members; anarchists expect an absence of coercion; and so on. Breaches of these expectations may be experienced as betrayals of the cause.

As other activists responded to intolerable behavior, face-to-face confrontation was less common than talking about breaches behind the offenders' backs. But occasionally trouble led to more trouble, as yelling and insults about earlier breaches erupted. The context of yelling was usually a conflict so rancorous and intractable that it threatened to break up the group. The two cases in which groups actually split (the SUFB/TPC separation and the end of the Workforce Development Task Force) were the only groups in which more than two people yelled. There were yellers in every class, gender, age, movement tradition, and in the black and white racial categories.

In these most rancorous conflicts, activists surprised themselves by acting in ways outside their own class predispositions *and* outside the norms of their movement traditions. For example, young white UMC McKayla, a leader of the mostly civil TPC, surprised herself by yelling for the first time in her life during a long, conflictual DNC coalition meeting.

Class Differences in Explanations for Outrageously Bad Behavior

While no class had a monopoly on offensive behavior, there was a revealing class difference in what activists believed caused extreme misbehavior. When they thought another activist had behaved intolerably, many interviewees from working-class backgrounds turned to individualism as the explanation, while some activists from PMC backgrounds turned to a failure of self-restraint.

Fourteen working-class and straddler interviewees used terms like "selfish," "individualistic," "ego," "competitive," and "self-promotion" in explaining a whole range of bad behavior, from power grabs to public denouncements, from lawsuits to embezzlement. For example, in both Cecilia's and Nicole's explanations of why they had left their former antiviolence group, the leader's self-centered attitude was seen as leading to her malfeasance. When Nicole told a story about the leader yelling at her in a church during a funeral service for someone killed in street violence, she said, "Everything was always about her grandson and nobody else's murder victim." Cecilia was offended that the leader renamed the group after her murdered relative, saying, "No one ever voted that in, and it just came to be a personal thing." Brenda was eloquent about what she believed was wrong with The People's Convention: "This group has the dysfunction of America. . . . 'We're individuals, we're bad-asses, we're number one,' instead of being community oriented. When something happens, people don't think community, they think 'How can we be individuals? How can we stand on our own?'"

The word "ego" was especially common in these working-class explanations of activists behaving badly. Eight working-class people, including Slim, Dorothea, Tye, and Reginald from TPC, all used the term "ego." So did three straddlers or semistraddlers: Brenda, working-class-identified Elaine, and Emilio who was half a generation away from his family's working-class roots. By contrast, only two people from PMC backgrounds ever used the word "ego." Working-class communitarian values were clearly at play in these explanations. Despite the lack of explicit working-class identity among working-class and poor activists, this anti-individualistic stance hints at an embryonic culture of solidarity (Fantasia 1988). A working-class communitarian ethic has also been noted by other class-culture analysts (Lamont 2000; Rose 2000; Jensen 2012).

In some cases working-class-background activists explicitly linked individualism to a more privileged status. For example, when Tye accused the Immigrants United group of "only thinking about themselves" after they changed an event date to conflict with a SUFB event, he made a classic privilege-as-putdown statement that many members were not actually immigrants but US-born Chicanos.

By contrast, PMC and VDM activists virtually never used egoistic individualism explanations for behavior breaches. Instead, they tended to see hothead personalities as exercising insufficient restraint on their emotions or their behavior. An anarchist leader from an upper-middle-class (UMC) background, Brian, described the nasty disputes among DNC protest groups as "the politics of bad manners." Eight activists from PMC backgrounds referred to uncontrolled personality problems or lack of emotional restraint to explain problematic behavior, using terms such as "poor form," outbursts "without thinking," "negative personality," and "argumentative."

When lifelong-PMC activists advocated emotional restraint, they were usually talking about a working-class person's or a straddler's outbursts. Corazon called Irene "abrasive"; Gail said Dirk could be "brutal"; Deborah said Mack "can't control his anger." Whether or not there actually was a class difference in expressing or restraining anger, clearly some PMC activists believed there was. They were right that some working-class activists vented emotionally during meetings, but they may have been overlooking that sometimes college-educated activists did too—another red flag for possible classism.

Groups' Conflict Cultures as Resources and Impediments to Repairing Breaches

To last beyond one event or campaign, groups must have ways to cope with ordinary conflicts: the personality clashes; the cultural differences; and the disagreements over tactics, messages, and group process that so often arise in voluntary groups. But groups' usual methods of coping with conflict often didn't work as well with extreme breaches. Groups were seen scrambling to invent new rules covering the new situations and taking previously unacceptable actions. Individually improvised reactions to unanticipated situations seemed to be less class specific than groups' habitual anger norms and conflict cultures. For example, City Power had a written protocol that called for a mediation committee to sit down with both parties to a conflict, which was used for some very intense conflict situations; but when some misbehavior crossed the line into criminal acts, the group kicked some members out and socially shunned them without first going through the mediation process.

I began the research for this book with some hypotheses about conflict resolution, such as that straddlers and women would tend to be mediators and that working-class people and African Americans would tend to be the most bluntly confrontational. Almost all turned out to be wrong, at least in situations of violations of basic norms. For example, although many African Americans of all classes were forthright and emotionally expressive in ordinary conversation, most tended to become cautiously polite and diplomatic during hot conflicts. One by one my prior hypotheses bit the dust. But both class and movement tradition *were* associated with approaches to conflict, just in different ways than I had anticipated.

One typology of conflict cultures, created by Rothschild and Leach (2007), includes two useful categories of conflict cultures within voluntary social change groups: cultures of avoidance and cultures of candor.[6] In cultures of avoidance, conflict is seen as a negative thing. Touchy topics go unspoken, and problematic individuals are not confronted. A premium is put on harmony and unanimity, even when that means problems fester indefinitely. This conflict-avoidance profile matches the conflict culture defined as "white" by Kochman (1981) in his research on middle-class whites.

Cultures of candor favor talking openly about disagreements, but in a respectful way. Domination and hierarchy can be curbed, but without trashing individuals. In a culture of candor, it is important to prevent the false appearance of agreement that is characteristic of the culture of avoidance. Everyone is expected to speak up honestly and not to take disagreements personally. Communication has to happen openly with no clandestine talk. The culture of candor ideal resembles the best practices advocated in the iconic negotiation book *Getting to Yes* (Fisher and Ury 1981) and by other conflict-resolution experts (Breslin and Rubin 1995): forthrightly getting all interests and concerns on the table, listening across differences, and cocreating compromises that hadn't originally been considered.

These conflict cultures are not fixed features of groups but can evolve over time. Rothschild and Leach tell a story of a Quaker Friends meeting that started with a polite culture of avoidance until an intractable fight over same-sex marriage erupted; they finally reached a culture of candor that members saw as true to the Quaker ideal of egalitarian group process. Such evolution is evidence that new group styles can be created through interaction, as Eliasoph and Lichterman (2003) claim: these mostly white PMC people moved away from their traditional Quaker culture of avoidance into two modes not learned in their childhood conditioning.

For fifteen of the twenty-five groups, enough conflict was observed and discussed by interviewees to allow categorization as a culture of avoidance or a culture of candor. A very strong pattern was found associating groups' class composition with the conflict culture.

I diagnosed a culture of avoidance when members referred to conflict as a negative thing; when interviews revealed surprisingly different opinions about the very issues that had ostensibly been discussed at the meeting; and when there was talk behind someone's back about criticisms not brought directly to the person. Five groups clearly had a culture of avoidance by this definition. In four of these, the majority class was lower-professional (LP). (See top shaded area of table 9.1.) No predominantly LP group had a culture of candor. For example, in the anarchist Parecon Collective, lifelong-poverty-class Olivia thought that the mostly LP white

Table 9.1   Conflict cultures, class composition, and movement traditions

Group pseudonym	Conflict culture	Modal class trajectory	Movement tradition
Action Against Empire	Avoidance	Lower professional (LP)	Global/local social change (G/L SC)
Convention Protest Coalition	Avoidance	LP	G/L SC
Parecon Collective	Avoidance	LP	G/L SC
Brontown Affordable Housing Consortium	Avoidance	LP	Professional advocacy
Safety Net for All	Avoidance	Straddlers	Community organizing
Easthaver Demands Justice	Candor	Professional middle class (PMC)	G/L SC
Green Homes Green World	Candor	PMC	G/L SC
The People's Convention	Candor	PMC	G/L SC
Workforce Development Task Force of Citywide Interfaith Coalition	Candor	PMC	Hybrid: professional advocacy within community organizing
Local 21 Organizing Committee	Candor but avoidance of power issues	Working class	Labor
Tri-City Labor Alliance	Candor but avoidance of power issues	Lower middle class (LMC)	Labor
Neighbors United	Candor but avoidance of power issues	Working-class background risen to LMC	Community organizing (CO)
Women Safe from Violence	Candor but avoidance of power issues	LMC*	CO
City Power	Candor	Working class	CO
Immigrants United	Candor	Straddlers	G/L SC

Note: Table includes only the fifteen groups with both a clear-cut conflict culture and a majority class composition. Notable patterns are shaded.

* Excluding several student interns, who mostly acted as observers at meetings. Modal class trajectory of this group including interns would be lower professional.

men in the group were terrible conflict avoiders. When a potential member was visibly drunk while representing the group to the public, members found another pretext to stall his official membership so they didn't have to bring up the drunkenness to his face. Both Parecon and another majority-LP group allowed situations in which someone was misspending the organization's money drag on for years without confronting the offenders. While sometimes avoiding conflicts may help preserve group cohesion, clearly these stories show a degree of conflict avoidance harmful to the organization.

I characterized a group as having a culture of candor if many areas of disagreement were discussed openly and respectfully at meetings and if interviewees said or showed that they felt free to express dissenting views. By these measures, four predominantly lifelong-PMC groups had cultures of candor with no topics forbidden. (See second shaded area of table 9.1.) These groups' typical members, both in their class backgrounds and current class, were well above the average class of the most conflict-avoiding groups, including many from UMC backgrounds. For example, during Easthaver Demands Justice's disagreement over how to practice antiracism, discussed in chapter 7, one of the members who used a sharp, critical tone had gone to an Ivy League university; another was a doctor.

Once again I see a cultural divide between the high and low portion of the professional range—sharply contrasting class cultures near each other on the class spectrum. The self-confident upper-PMC and UMC people were much more comfortable with giving and receiving criticism than the more tentative, soft-spoken self-censoring LPs.

Five working-class-majority groups also displayed a lot of candor, openly discussing many areas of disagreement, sometimes with the bluntness and rough teasing characteristic of some working-class communities. But in four of the five groups, there was a distinct limit to the candor: questions of decision-making power and leadership within the group were never mentioned during meetings, and usually not during interviews either. (See third shaded section of table 9.1.) For example, rank-and-file members of the Local 21 Organizing Committee openly hashed out disputes, sometimes raising their voices, but none questioned the right of the international union's management to control the strategy of their unionization campaign. Another example is Women Safe from Violence, whose members argued with Randall and each other so openly but never questioned that Elaine would chair most meetings and informally set the group's priorities.

The one exception to this working-class avoidance of power and leadership issues within otherwise candid groups was City Power, where everything, including internal power dynamics, seemed to be on the table—apparently a full-fledged culture of candor.

The twelve groups included in table 9.1 that were clearly thriving—growing in membership and/or winning their goals—varied in their conflict norms: some had a culture of avoidance; several had cultures of candor. The other three groups, those shrinking or failing,[7] were also varied in conflict culture. Although a culture of candor seems to be roughly associated with growth and success at self-defined social change goals, it does not appear to be a requirement.

Stand Up Fight Back, which shrank during the observation period, was an outlier in its conflict culture, as in so many other ways. The group some-times went beyond the boundaries of candor to a tumultuous and conflict-affirming internal culture. "They *wanted* to yell and point fingers," said Jason after he tried to serve as an outside facilitator for a SUFB meeting. While SUFB's internal culture repelled many potential and former members, its most loyal members seemed to regard its conflict norms as a positive feature of the organization. It seems unlikely to be a coincidence that the only group with an ideal of uncontrolled open conflict was also the only one whose core members' predominant class was unassimilated, unrooted straddlers, such as Brenda, who expressed the SUFB ideal this way: "People should and do call each other on stuff. I've called people out on stuff. I've been called out; it's not that serious. You bring it to the table ASAP, and don't hold grudges . . . sometimes the hard things are going to be said. Sometimes we have stuff to iron out, but everyone's fine afterwards. . . . We're there for each other . . . for the next round too."

Class patterns of *individuals'* conflict behavior corresponded with the group conflict cultures described here. (See table 9.2.) During some con-flictual mixed-class meetings, the class dynamic looked like a tennis match: verbally aggressive unassimilated straddlers and judgmental critics from high-PMC/UMC backgrounds traded shots, while diffident LPs and politically less-experienced respectable working-class people looked from one combat-ant to another with frozen faces, as silent, uncomfortable spectators. Clearly, class cultures are neither a duality nor a spectrum but reflect specific life experiences.

With this helpful framework in mind, we now return to the Denver con-flict, the best setting for seeing both typical and atypical responses to conflict. Like the other irreconcilable rift at the final meeting of the Workforce De-velopment Task Force, this schism was between groups predominantly com-posed of the two class subcategories with the most distinct and problematic modes of approaching conflict: lower professionals and uprooted unassimi-lated straddlers—the class category most associated with a culture of avoid-ance and the one most associated with uncontrolled open conflict.

Table 9.2   Conflict behavior and attitudes typical of four class-trajectory subcategories

	Working-class followers	Unassimilated, unrooted straddlers	Lower professionals	Higher professionals and upper middle class
Most typical behavior during conflicts and breaches	Quiet on sidelines; felt disempowered; voted with feet by quitting group	Waged conflict for moral certainties linked to working-class backgrounds	Tentative, conflict avoidant, and self-doubting; talked behind backs	Waged conflict confidently; felt entitled to express opinions strongly
Likelihood and vehemence of waging verbal conflict	Low	High	Low	High

Note: Except for upwardly mobile straddlers, the other three class subcategories include only those lifelong in one class. Because informants who moved between lower and higher professional or were downwardly mobile are excluded from this table, because some columns are just subcategories of classes, and because the sample is only those activists observed during a conflict, the numbers are smaller than the number of informants in each class category in the study overall (see table 4.1, right column, for totals). This pattern is based only on the meetings at which open conflict was observed.

The DNC conflict is also an example of a clash between the militant anti-imperialist and progressive movement traditions, a conflict of worldviews that played out in the national movement between United for Peace and Justice and the ANSWER Coalition in the first decade of the twenty-first century, and which no doubt will erupt again.

A Perfect Storm of Conflict-Escalating Factors: Stand Up Fight Back

Stand Up Fight Back was the first DNC protest coalition to form, and for a while it was the largest. But over the months that I followed the coalition, the list of endorsers on its website got shorter and shorter as groups withdrew. One much-admired national group threatened to sue to get their name taken off the SUFB website. The People's Coalition started late as a split-off from SUFB and grew steadily until the convention.

To summarize a complicated conflict, there were three contested issues: (1) the terms of nonviolence pledges (SUFB's pledge allowed for self-defense against police attack, while TPC's was unconditional); (2) the name of the coalition (as with the pseudonym Stand Up Fight Back, the actual name could be interpreted literally to suggest violence by activists, or metaphorically interpreted, as the founders intended, to suggest militant resistance to injustice); (3) internal democracy and roles for women. The last issue grew out of arguments over the first two: when the most vocal and visible SUFB leaders, white males Tye and Arthur, refused to budge on the nonviolence pledge or the name, they were accused of sexism and autocracy. In their interviews, Tye, Brenda, and Emilio vehemently denied these charges.

After two disastrous multigroup meetings at which voices were raised and no resolutions were reached, some activists walked out and then met privately to form The People's Convention coalition. Some other SUFB members were able to talk calmly about and with TPC members after this rift, but Tye, Brenda, and Emilio remained in a state of rage for months until the convention, especially toward one TPC member who had been very active in SUFB in its early months, Elijah.

Approximately equal numbers of accusations of outrageous misbehavior were made *against* SUFB members and *by* SUFB against members of other groups. But the reactions to such accusations were very different, reflecting different anger norms and conflict-resolution resources in different movement traditions and class trajectories.

SUFB was the only group to have all the conflict-exacerbating factors I've identified so far: several leaders who were very unrooted, unassimilated straddlers; under extreme stress and provocation; in an ad hoc group with militant ideology. Tye and Brenda were archetypal unassimilated straddlers, people from working-class backgrounds with virtually nothing PMC-like about their life stories except bachelor's degrees (and Tye's famous home-ownership, which was a recent development). As profiled in chapter 3, Emilio was the child of straddlers, a young student whose parents had become professionals and homeowners by the time he was twelve; but the peer influence of low-income youth of color in his urban neighborhood created a culture clash with older white PMC progressive activists similar to what many unassimilated straddlers reported. None of the three had employers, dependents, religious affiliations, or permanent group memberships. All expressed symbolic class loyalties to their working-class roots in their anticapitalist politics, but none were currently tied to their childhood working-class communities.

SUFB's explanation for the rifts was that other groups were "liberals," meaning sell-outs to the powers that be. Talking about the disagreement over nonviolence ground rules, Emilio linked more idealistic politics with class privilege: "A lot of people who are in these groups, like [TPC], have never really been oppressed, and when you come from an oppressed community and you have experienced oppression in your life, then you tend to believe more in self-defense. So you lived a sort of sheltered life, and you're doing this activist thing . . . to make yourself feel good about yourself . . . yeah, they kind of have these ideals that are a little unrealistic."

I was struck by the similarity between the behavior that offended these three SUFB unassimilated straddlers and their own verbal behavior. Brenda was hurt by TPC members talking behind her back, yet she didn't object to how SUFB members often talked scornfully about TPC at their meetings, and sometimes she herself joined in; the only difference I could see was that milder language was used at TPC meetings. Emilio was furious when TPC member Dina rejected one of his solidarity overtures by saying, "I don't appreciate you coming to our meeting and doing this"; he said he was "almost appalled" by what she said. Yet "don't appreciate" is much milder language than how he talked about TPC, for example calling their reasons for separating from SUFB "bullshit" and saying about Elijah that he wanted to "kick that kid's ass."

Brenda, Emilio, and Tye were simultaneously touchy and aggressive—a recipe for trouble. "High offense–low defense" is Kochman's (1981: 162–64) phrase for people who aggressively criticize others but are touchy when criticized. When he surveyed white and black men and women, he found that white males were the most likely to be high offense–low defense. White women tended to be "low offense–low defense," careful not to offend and sensitive to criticism. Black men tended to be "high offense–high defense." "Don't say no more with your mouth than your back can stand," one black male informant told Kochman (164). I found a less clear race and gender pattern than Kochman did. The most high offense–low defense people I observed, Brenda, Emilio, and Tye, were varied in race and gender, similar only in militant politics and unassimilated straddler class trajectory.

These three SUFB unassimilated, unrooted straddler interviewees had no criticisms of each other or of any SUFB member's behavior—not for calling the police on the whack-job Anthony or shoving him or threatening him; nor for wrongly accusing Elijah and McKayla of being government infiltrators; nor for threatening to kick Elijah's ass; nor for Tye's trashing TPC in the media. Brenda and Emilio were uncritical followers of leaders Tye and Arthur. Under attack, they closed ranks and remained uncritically loyal to one another. While some TPC members, especially Porter, acted swiftly to confront the offenders in their own group, requesting better behavior and expelling repeat violators of the group's written civility code, no SUFB members did anything equivalent, as far as I know.

These three militant uprooted straddlers in SUFB were unaware of how partisan and clannish they appeared. They couldn't see their double standard on rude language and hostile behavior practiced by their own group versus when it was directed at them. Their working-class roots showed in their intensely personal loyalties, activism tied to particular relationships, trustingly following particular leaders and quick to mistrust outsiders, but without the tempering effects of ties to a working-class community and the pragmatic approach that usually accompanied such ties. Their ideologically partisan militancy reflected their uprooted lives and their college educations, without the tempering effects of having to fit into a professional workplace. They combined the self-confident righteousness gained from PMC cultural capital with working-class rage, directed not only at unjust power holders but also at rival progressive activists.

This combination of faults showed up in class-incongruous less-assimilated straddlers in other groups as well, such as Jeremiah in the Interfaith group, Mack in Easthaver Demands Justice, and Carrie, the peace activist who threatened Action Center member Lea. While many other straddlers were the steadiest and most easy-going of activists, these straddlers seemed to combine the worst of both their class cultures. These cases are too few to conclusively prove a class-culture correlation. But I suspect that if hundreds of conflicts within and between social movement groups were examined, other very unrooted, unassimilated straddlers would be discovered at the heart of many of them, combining the righteousness and ideological invest-ment gained from upward mobility with gut-level impulses to loyalty and mistrust learned in their working-class childhoods. Especially in situations of extreme movement stress, such as government repression and rancorous splits, I would guess that people fitting this profile would be found unleashing this troublesome combination.

Maintaining Civility in a White Lower-Professional Convention Protest Group

In contrast to SUFB, the predominant emotional tone in The People's Con-vention was the low-key, restrained politeness often seen at the lower end of the professional spectrum. And indeed, the most common class trajectories in the virtually all-white TPC were LP (a plurality), modestly downwardly mobile PMC, and students from PMC backgrounds. Their conflict resolu-tion repertoire lined up with the class cultures of those typical members.

First, TPC relied on *private* communication with the hotheads in their own group. As a multi-issue coalition with low ideological barriers, TPC attracted cranks, who were welcome as long as they remained civil. But extreme misbe-havior, no matter whom it targeted, got swift negative reactions by e-mail or one-on-one conversation. When Nanette posted the price of Tye's house online, several TPC members spoke privately to her about how unacceptable they thought that was. When a loose cannon threatened to secretly cancel the plane ticket of a SUFB rally speaker, straddler Porter said privately that he would personally buy a replacement ticket, which prevented the threat from being carried out.

The next line of defense for TPC was severing ties. People who had quit SUFB then founded TPC, so the founders were by definition people willing to initiate a rift. When serial haranguer Stanley circulated e-mails accusing various activists of being infiltrators, "Stalinists," or other negative things, at first several TPC members e-mailed him privately to ask him to stop. But eventually white assimilated straddler Porter—a gifted mediator who only resorted to severing ties in extreme cases, after lots of one-on-one conversation—invoked TPC coalition's civility code and banned Stanley from the listserv, an example of someone going outside their habitual conflict responses in the face of unacceptable breaches.

Outright counterattacking was rare in TPC (except by the few hotheads seen as problem people by other members). Public confrontation in the whole group was also rare. When a white member spoke against a potential rally speaker by calling him "an angry black man," the group responded only with stunned silence at that meeting, then did lots of hand-wringing and behind-the-scenes conversation about racism, and finally resolved the incident via private conversations with the offender and only a brief discussion at a meeting. Talking behind people's backs was very common and seemed to occupy a lot of some TPC members' time.

TPC hammered out more written policies governing members' behavior than any other convention protest group. But they continued to need new policies as the convention approached. Even after the convention had started, TPC was still scrambling for new policies to handle last-minute conflicts. Under intense stress and time pressure, they added threats, abrupt expulsions, and public confrontations to their more comfortable conflict-resolution repertoire of private one-on-one communication and written civility guidelines.

Ambivalent Conflict-Avoidant Class Culture: Why Lower Professionals and Not Others?

As we have seen, LP groups were those most likely to have a culture of conflict avoidance. Individual LPs, in particular whites, were also conflict averse, even in situations where conflict seemed hard to avoid: they were more likely to speak privately than publicly with offenders and conflicting parties, and it was very rare to see one of them confront someone in a whole group or to facilitate a conflict-resolution process. Lifelong-working-class people, straddlers, VDM, and higher-PMC/UMC people were all more likely to advocate direct feedback or talking out disagreements than LPs were.

To combine the prior chapter's findings on responses to overtalking with this tendency toward conflict avoidance in the face of extreme violations creates a vivid LP class-cultural profile. Remember that in the overtalking analysis, LPs sometimes self-censored and self-critiqued their own responses to overtalkers and other violators, telling themselves not to have the emotional reactions they had, and as a result they spoke in an ambivalent see-saw way. In situations of extreme behavior violations as well, some LPs and low-end PMCs reported biting their tongues to avoid expressing critical thoughts.

Why would LP and lower-PMC life experience lead to such inner tension over one's own and others' speech and behavior? Many analysts of middle-class culture emphasize self-restraint, suppressing emotion, and avoiding conflict. Middle-class children are taught to internalize self-control (Rose 2000: 16; Lareau 2003). Managers are expected to avoid conflict while also being competitive, a contradictory set of expectations (Lamont 1992: 35–36): "The goal is to maximize integration in the workplace by playing down power differentials. . . . Only when associated with humility and at least a formal egalitarianism does professional success become equated with moral purity" (38).

Professional education includes training in self-restraint, deference, and conflict avoidance (Schmidt 2000: chaps. 9 and 13). Professionals are rewarded for not rocking the boat (Derber, Schwartz, and Magrass 1990). Professional positions rely on an internal locus of control instead of the external supervision more typical of working-class jobs (Zweig 2011; Aronowitz 2003). UMC people conditioned to have a sense of entitlement and self-confidence may be able to override these contradictions; but LPs end up with an inner monitor that self-silences any impulses to intervene.

Such double binds may tie up professional-range *activists*, particularly whites, even more than LP people as a whole. To come from a class-privileged background and be a social change activist, particularly in a mixed-class group, is a social location filled with conundrums not faced by working-class activists. PMC activists assert their political goals in the face of power holders' opposition while simultaneously avoiding dominating the very social change groups in which they want to express their alternative ideas. This contradiction between downplaying dominance and fighting injustice may explain LPs' more convoluted and conflicted thought processes and their more indirect, infrequent, lengthy, and ambivalent speech.

Working-class activists, particularly women and people of color, on the other hand, usually face no such conundrum. They may or may not be stuck in the disempowered position where society has placed them, depending on their degree of empowerment; but in any case there is no contradiction between self-empowerment as an activist and self-empowerment as someone in a subordinate social role. They need to draw fewer distinctions between their activist subcultures and the mainstream society that marginalizes them; thus prefigurative goals for their groups' internal functioning are less central to them. Since working-class activists have less need to avoid reproducing social hierarchies by dominating their own groups, they can carry the style of their root cultures into their social change groups, even if it means being confrontational, blunt, or a strong leader. For them, activism can be a direct shove against their own oppression, pushing outward with all their might; while for PMC-background people, especially white male LPs, activism is a sideways move, simultaneously pushing against unjust authorities and stepping away from their advantaged social position.

When Do Class Predispositions Prevail? Degree and Rarity of Offense

These patterns of class-culture differences explain more of the variation in responses to *everyday* offenses than to the more unusual and shocking situation of *extreme* behavior violations.

With the very common pet peeve of overtalking, remember that I found several very clear-cut class patterns: working-class people unambivalently wanted overtalkers quelled, while lower-PMC and especially LP activists had mixed, ambivalent reactions; strong working-class chairs used direct second-person and imperative language to shush overtalkers, while PMC chairs used the third person and LP chairs objected only indirectly. Everyone runs into overtalkers at meetings, and thus people turn to the habits of their class predispositions when responding to something so familiar.

But when faced with a shocking breach of accepted norms, some people were swayed by the overheated situation to act outside their class character. It seems that the relative rarity of extreme violations led to a less-developed repertoire of responses. In addition, hot emotions, such as anger toward and fear of the violator, may also have brought out class-atypical behavior. As Bourdieu put it, class predispositions ("habitus") "may be superseded under certain circumstances—certainly in situations of crisis which disrupt the immediate adjustment of habitus to field" (1990: 108).

When City Power abandoned its mediation process and expelled a member whose breach was too extreme; when SUFB leaders called the police; when McKayla found herself yelling in a meeting for the first time in her life; in those cases, out-of-character behavior emerged under stress. Most of the ad hoc convention protest groups evolved new ways of responding to conflicts and breaches that were not identical to what any member had done before, typical of neither their movement tradition nor their class disposition. Faced with a challenging new situation, they developed new standards and responses.

On the other hand, some activists actually intensified their class predispositions even in the face of extreme behavior violations, as when white lower-professional TPC members created more and more written policies and spent more and more time bemoaning people's misbehavior behind their backs. Many class-incongruous people brought sturdy, even stubborn, class predispositions to their groups, going against the group grain with long-internalized attitudes and habits characteristic of their class backgrounds. When lifelong-poor Olivia talked more bluntly about Parecon's problems than her LP fellow anarchists; when PMC Adaline pushed the mostly working-class Women Safe from Violence to do explicit organizational self-evaluation instead of closing ranks against criticism; when uprooted, unassimilated straddlers insisted on a blunt high-conflict group style in convention protest coalitions, even when they were outnumbered by LP peace activists who favored written civility codes; in these and other cases, we saw class cultural habits persist even when removed from the contexts that formed them. Remember that nine working-class-background activists explained breaches as individualism and ego, while eight of their PMC counterparts explained breaches as inadequate emotional restraint—clearly class-cultural lenses applied to activist troubles.

But the varied responses to the more unusual and upsetting violations, and especially the out-of-character innovations in ad hoc groups where strangers were thrown together, show that the habits that individual activists brought to groups from their class backgrounds and movement traditions were only jumping-off points for attempts to develop a shared group culture that could resolve problematic behavior.

Class Speech Differences VI

Missing Class Talk

Discussion of class dynamics was almost nonexistent in these groups. If class-culture differences played such a central role in the intragroup problems most troubling to activists, as seen in the last five chapters, why weren't they discussed more often? One reason was a lack of shared vocabulary for class identities.

Ironically, the word "class" was especially uncommon among lifelong-working-class activists' speech. Working-class interviewees said "class" only .34 times per 10,000 words,[1] compared with 9.55 times for college-educated interviewees, a large ratio of 28:1.[2] Straddler interviewees used the c-word more than any other class trajectory, 35 times as often as working-class interviewees.[3]

The phrase "social class" in particular was completely unfamiliar to some respectable lifelong-working-class activists who answered the question "How would you describe yourself in terms of your social class?" with nonclass answers about their social life. For example, working-poor African Caribbean immigrant Martina answered, "Well, for me it's good, I get along with everybody; I try to socialize myself, let people know me." LMC white activist Martha answered, "I was a social outcast," and then proceeded to describe her social life in each grade school classroom, starting with her first-grade class. If one goal of this study was to learn what does and doesn't communicate across class lines, the interviewers learned one thing very quickly: don't say "social class" without explaining yourself.

Nonclass Answers to Class Questions

But even clearer questions with prompts such as "poorest and richest" some-times got garbled answers, especially by lifelong-working-class activists. The members of the group Martina is describing in the following exchange in fact had education levels ranging from fourth grade to master's degrees, and a fairly wide range of income and assets as well:

> INTERVIEWER: What about educational background, class?
> MARTINA: That would be about our race, our culture, our skin color; they say we're African American or whites.
> INTERVIEWER: How about owners versus renters, people that have more opportunities than others.
> MARTINA: You're absolutely right.
> INTERVIEWER: Is there anybody that you notice that has more or less?
> MARTINA: I don't think so; I guess everybody is on the same level.

Some interviewees resisted the class questions for principled reasons, not wanting to buy into unfair inequalities by naming them.

> INTERVIEWER: How would you describe yourself in terms of social class?
> COURTNEY (impoverished African American): I don't have a social class. I'm just me. I don't compare myself with anyone, and I don't put myself above anyone.

Overall, lifelong-working-class people were more likely than college-educated people to answer an interviewer's questions about class with a nonclass answer, resisting the question, misunderstanding it, or answering about race instead of class.[4] Race, gender, age, and movement tradition made no difference; only the interviewee's class was associated with nonclass answers.[5]

Other researchers have found similar nonanswers to class questions. "Open-ended queries about class identification tend to yield confused responses, re-fusals to answer, and even explicit denials that classes exist" (Grusky 2005: 68).

But most PMCs, VDMs, and straddlers, once prompted, did use conventional class terms. Asked how they describe themselves in terms of class, most gave without hesitation responses such as "I consider myself working class" and "I probably grew up more middle class.... I have a lot of class privilege."

Unknown Class Identities in the Rest of the Group

When interviewees were asked about the class diversity in their group—which seemed to be the hardest interview question to answer—many of all classes avoided the question; there wasn't a statistically significant class difference in who hazarded a guess.[6] Several interviewees of varied classes expressed uncertainty about the class backgrounds of others in their groups, saying things like "I don't know their backgrounds" and "I'm not good at noticing class." But such uncertainty was more commonly heard from people from working-class backgrounds.

The college-educated interviewees who did answer the question used more conventional class terms in their answers, such as "It tends to be middle class; I mean people come from middle-class backgrounds" and "Edie is pretty solidly working class, but Beatrice is probably more middle class."

Contrast those answers with working-class white Reginald's two nonanswers when he was asked twice about class diversity in The People's Convention: "Just average white people" and, when pressed about class, "There's never any discussion about class as far as within the group itself."

White activists were more likely than others to specify other group members' class, and African Americans were less likely to,[7] but there was no correlation with gender, movement tradition, or age in how interviewees answered questions about class diversity in the group. Only class and race predicted answers to questions about others' class identities.

Class as the Facts of Everyday Life

It's not that most working-class nonclass talkers didn't talk about class issues at all, of course. Working-class activists were somewhat more likely to bring up concrete, proximate class-related facts, such as particular occupations, hardships, amounts of money, and neighborhoods.[8] A usually talkative white working-class man, Slim of Tri-City Labor Alliance, was uncharacteristically silent on the general question of class identities in TLA before answering a follow-up question with a dollar figure:

> INTERVIEWER: How would you describe people in terms of social class?
> SLIM: [*long silence*]
> INTERVIEWER: Like, are there differences in homeowners, renters, education levels, etcetera?
> SLIM: Well, I make twenty-six dollars an hour. Okay? I would assume that some of the service-sector people don't make nearly that much.

Many working-class and especially impoverished people openly told the stories of their own hardships. Adriana, an impoverished African American, said, "It's hard for me when I have my lights getting ready to get shut off. And my car, Lord knows I've been trying to get it running for the last two years."

Even when making general points about society, not just about themselves, working-class people were more likely to use concrete language and human details and to omit general class categories. For example, Aaron, a working-class Latino member of a labor coalition, said: "Look at the crisis in medical care . . . some people are actually going bankrupt. People in their sixties who want to live their golden years in peace cannot even enjoy their golden years because they have to mortgage their homes, sell everything to pay their medical bills."

Martha, the LMC white woman who answered the social class question by talking about her childhood social life, made this insightful comment about class diversity in activist groups without ever saying the c-word: "Usually the people that a group is *about* aren't there. Like the farmworkers group didn't have any farmworkers. The criminal justice reform group—people with drug histories, the homeless, ex-offenders—they bring them in to speak, not that they stay engaged. They have to get on with their lives, I think."

Occasionally working-class people used colloquial terms for class identities, as when Brandon said, "I wasn't born with a silver spoon in my mouth, and to be honest with you, I don't have a silver spoon to sell right now if I wanted to."

But there's a striking shortage in many working-class activists' speech even of such informal class talk that might indicate a class identity. Older working-class long-term leaders like Dorothea and Brandy claimed poverty as their identity. ("We're poor people, nobody wants to identify with poor people," Dorothea said.) But very few rank-and-file members of their group spoke similarly.

A few African Americans old enough to have lived through the civil rights movement made inspirational statements about the larger class group on whose behalf their group worked. For example, an elderly impoverished African American in Grassroots Resistance, Terrell, said, "We speak for the common people as a whole." It was uplifting to hear such general class statements from people currently affected by class oppression; but such references were rare, and almost nonexistent among people under age sixty. Most vocal champions of working people or poor people were straddlers staying true to their roots or PMC radicals, in particular those in labor and community groups, *not* anyone lifelong in the working-class range.

With one exception, each class-identity term heard from a working-class activist was seldom or never heard from anyone else in the same class category. College-educated people, by contrast, often used the same terms as other college-educated people. Once again, shared general vocabulary seemed to come along with college education, not through living through the experience of class subordination.

The one exception was the word "poor,"[9] which lifelong-working-class interviewees were more likely to use than any other class category. They used that word more than three times as often as "working-class," usually unprompted, suggesting that it's in working-class activists' everyday vernacular—the only general class term they used regularly. "Low-income" was used at a lower rate by both lifelong-working-class and college-educated interviewees; VDM activists used it most often.[10] Of the three words or phrases for the lower-class range, lifelong-working-class and PMC activists favored "poor," straddlers and VDM activists favored "low income," and no one used "working class" very often.

There didn't seem to be *any* common vernacular terms for the vast range of the class spectrum above poverty and below PMC, except perhaps the vague, all-inclusive term "middle class," used by only a few interviewees. For some black interviewees, ranging from working-class Rhonda to third-generation-PMC Rodney, their comparison group was chronically poor African Americans. Having more financial security than those trapped outside the primary labor force was a very significant class boundary, often marked by that term "middle class."

The frequently heard idea that almost all Americans call themselves middle class is an exaggeration; by my calculations, approximately 30 percent of American households are in fact PMC, and only half again as many (about 45%) pick out "middle class" to describe themselves on multiple choice surveys if "working class" is also an option (Metzgar 2003). "Middle class" is a term commonly used by politicians and the media for anyone not rich or poor, a slippery public euphemism. It sprang comfortably to working-class Latina Cecilia's lips, but she then took it back:

CECILIA: I think that this group is a little mixed, a little bit middle class and a little bit more upper class. Like just a step, not two step, just one step higher. . . . I know Pamela and Fred are above us; I think Shirley is one too. . . . And Clayton is right with me. [*laughs*] He's at my level, he ain't goin' nowhere.

INTERVIEWER: And so you call yourself middle class?

CECILIA: Um-hum.

INTERVIEWER: What do you think about that definition? People use that word . . .

CECILIA: And I hate, and I hate to use it too because I really don't. I call myself actually the working poor. That's where I'm at. . . . You got your little working poor like myself that's making only twenty-five to thirty a year, that would be the working poor. Then you have the poor, and they're on the welfare system or whatever, tryna survive. I'm one of the working poor.

INTERVIEWER: Do you think that most people are in that same working poor boat?

CECILIA: I would say at least four, five of us out of that group. . . . Living check by check.

INTERVIEWER: So there's maybe three people that you think aren't living check by check?

CECILIA: Well. Um, yeah. Yeah. Three or four . . . that are living, that they don't need that check that bad. It can wait. If they didn't get paid they'd be alright: "I'm good, I'm settled." Yeah, I'm like, "No, I want my money and I want it now. Gotta pay my rent."

Like most working-class interviewees, Cecilia reverts to describing class realities in concrete terms such as "gotta pay my rent." She switched from the public catch-all term "middle class" to "the working poor" after only a tiny bit of encouragement. Other researchers have found similarly fluid and changeable class self-identities (DiMaggio 2012: 16–17).

The scarce class talk and inconsistent class identities found in these activist groups don't seem like a healthy sign among activists of any class, but such a situation is especially disturbing among working-class and poor activists. Historically, the discourse within US working-class mass movements often included an explicit working-class or poor people's collective identity (Piven and Cloward 1979; Lichtenstein 2002). If the bottom half of the 99 percent could name and claim their class identity, it would open more possibilities for building and strengthening working-class-led movements.

Conclusion

Building a Movement with the Strengths of All Class Cultures

The years of this study, 2007 and 2008, fell during a time of relative movement drought when more progressive energy went into electoral politics than into social change groups. But after the drought came the inspiring movement resurgence of 2011. Against the backdrop of the Arab Spring uprisings across North Africa and the Middle East, union members, students, and local supporters took over the Wisconsin State Capitol to try to stop a union-busting initiative. Then in the fall, Occupy Wall Street began in Zuccotti Park in New York City; "Occupy" went viral, and hundreds of local encampments sprang up and held their ground. Longtime homeless people, longtime radicals, students, and some recently foreclosed and laid-off people, living together in crowded tent cities, experienced cross-class contact of the most 24/7 immersive kind. *Time* named the protestor the "Person of the Year."

As a casual observer, I saw many movement traditions coming together in the early Occupy movement. The labor movement was there: it seemed that every time Jobs with Justice or a union local visited an encampment or endorsed a local Occupy, the leftist blogosphere lit up with excitement (e.g., González 2011). Activists from progressive groups and nonprofits were there, offering workshops and bringing food, sometimes occupying, sometimes recruiting. The pagan anarchists were there: Starhawk (2008) and others who had brought rituals of deliberate community building to the globalization movement and the 2008 convention protests began coordinating a nation-wide effort to train hundreds of thousands of Occupiers in nonviolent direct action and participatory decision making. And in many cities, community-organizing groups teamed up with Occupy groups, at least briefly.

My favorite Occupy Boston action was when the Occupiers came out in support of City Life/Vida Urbana, a kick-ass community-organizing group, whose Eviction Free Zone campaign against foreclosures had been organized long before the recent housing-market bubble burst, so the group was poised to intervene to protect vulnerable homeowners in its urban neighborhood. With mixed-class leadership, City Life has mobilized directly affected neigh-borhood residents and their allies to block evictions and foreclosures through protests at banks and auctions. Their October 2011 march to the Bank of America had hundreds of extra protestors because Occupy Boston joined in. Once City Life added the crucial ingredients of opponent targeting and action planning—strengths of the community-organizing tradition that had been in dire short supply at Occupy Boston up to that point—the Occupi-ers' exuberant rebellious spirit made a real difference to particular people in trouble, which made them into local heroes.

But I was discouraged by some of what I saw as well. Some Occupy groups had gotten bogged down in group process quarrels and ideologi-cal quicksand by late 2011, reminiscent of the discouraging death throes of SDS, SNCC, and the Clamshell Alliance (Epstein 1991). Some of my ini-tially enthusiastic friends dropped out of Occupy Boston because they were burned out by endless internal debates. Looking through a class lens at the complaints—long meetings, jargon, eccentric hand signals, and a shortage of specific winnable demands—reveals the familiar downsides I have described in groups dominated by PMC and VDM activists.

One cold, windy November night at Occupy Boston, I watched a three-hour general assembly move at a painfully slow pace to decide whether to change the beginning times of general assemblies. To their credit, the facili-tators explained the sequence of consensus steps and the hand signals at the beginning. However, of the two hundred or more people participating, it appeared that only a couple dozen were fluent in the process. I could have predicted who did and didn't gain the floor by using the appropriate hand signals (for example, fingers curled into a "C" to signal a clarifying question). Like the facilitators, the successful hand signalers were all white people with newscaster-standard accents and all their teeth. Also present in the crowd were people with missing teeth, people of color, and people with working-class accents; I didn't see any of them use any hand signals or hear them say any consensus jargon terms. Most were silent or had side conversations with people near them; a few simply called out, speaking in violation of the process. Someone who snuck in a negative opinion as a "point of process" was chastised by many downward-twinkling hands for not sticking to the order of steps. The clarifying questions, points of information, and points of process took so long that only in the second hour were any pro or con opinions permitted on the minor internal proposal on the floor.

One gaggle of weathered older black and white men wearing worn clothing were clustered at the edge of the lighted stage area. One black man, carrying a stack of the *Spare Change* newspapers that homeless people sell on the Boston streets, was agitated, bouncing on the balls of his feet and saying repeatedly, "This is bullshit, man!" Others were trying to calm him down.

The much-touted horizontal participatory democracy of Occupy general assemblies seemed to make space for some process-savvy people's voices but to shut out others, including some of those most personally affected by the financial crisis that triggered the movement. Realizing the powerful potential of Occupy and other future movement mobilizations will mean asking some hard questions about class cultures and learning what it takes to become truly cross-class and multicultural.

Implications of Understanding All Influences on Group Style

The metaphor of looking through lenses that I used in the introduction now seems too static to describe the active interplay of movement traditions with race, gender, and class cultures in the stories of how activists actually grappled with their groups' troubles. Like the metaphor of a toolkit (Swidler 1986), the lens metaphor implies that movement traditions, race and gender predispositions, and class cultures each provide a fixed, unchanging repertoire.

A better metaphor would include moving parts, gears meshing and gears grinding, or an interdependent ecosystem. I discovered no straightforward formula for what happened when an individual's class predispositions clashed with a group's usual modus operandi. I've spotlighted stories where movement tradition prevailed, where the activists with the highest social status prevailed, where the majority class prevailed, and where an innovative response to the particular situation was created.

But given how often the class-culture dimension goes unmentioned or underemphasized by both activists and academics,[1] my findings of powerful class predispositions are striking. Many things *didn't* correlate with class, such as the militant to moderate spectrum; how formal or informal meetings were; and how much meeting time was spent talking about wider political issues versus the group's business. Some items I tested had a greater correlation with race or gender than with class. But more than I expected, as I tested behavior after behavior, word after word, idea after idea, class patterns appeared. In the absence of explicit class identities and class talk, it was remarkable to see how durable, even stubborn, class predispositions could be.

The thoughts and behavior of the 362 activists in the study were not, of course, rigidly determined by their childhood class socialization. Rather, those predispositions provided the jumping-off point for their actions in the group, some of which were deliberate strategic choices, some of which involved blending into the pre-existing group practices, and only some of which were individuals' old habits. Our attitudes toward our own class conditioning and other inherited behavioral expectations can vary from unawareness to enthusiastic justification to skepticism to fierce resistance. Greater awareness of how we've been socialized into a class culture can make us more flexible and can strengthen our resistance to the harmful parts of our childhood conditioning.

When we know that our individual predispositions are woven together with social structures and with unfolding situations to generate our conscious and unconscious strategies for reaching our goals, such an understanding enables us to struggle with what we've inherited in a more conscious way. Becoming aware of the patterns of class, race, gender, and other predispositions shaping ourselves and our groups, we can choose to strengthen or transcend them; becoming aware of the institutionalized group norms of a movement tradition, we can celebrate them or work to change them; becoming aware that activists' interactions have the power to create behavior expectations and group style, we can become more mindful of the effects of our speech.

For many groups, the most neglected of these discussions is about internal class dynamics and what gifts members can bring from their class cultures. What would it look like to openly discuss class, claim class identities, and tap all class cultures to strengthen a group? I'm fortunate to have seen such transformative discussions in practice.

Identifying Class-Cultural Strengths and Limitations

The nonprofit organization Class Action has a workshop exercise that I've done dozens of times: participants meet in caucuses according to their class backgrounds, discuss what they took from their upbringing, and look for commonalities. Each caucus brings back to the whole group two written lists, one of the strengths and one of the limitations bestowed by their class backgrounds. I've never yet found a class caucus that couldn't generate two long lists, nor a group where the class caucuses' lists weren't quite distinct from each other. Almost always the list of strengths goes beyond the material realm (e.g., "Can cook dinner for four on two dollars"; "International travel = learning about other cultures") into the subtle cultural realm (e.g., "Resilience in crisis"; "Bold 'cuz we feel safe in the world.")

So before I began the research for this book, I already took it as axiomatic that every activist class culture brings distinct gifts to the coalition table and that each has its own particular limitations. Once the class lens is made available and the facts of everyone's life story are shared, these distinct strengths and weaknesses can become visible to the group.

The purpose of naming our class-cultural limitations is not to be self-deprecating, and not to denigrate the people we come from, but to acknowledge that the unjust class system damages everyone, and for all of us, it's a struggle to regain our full humanity. As long as there's an attitude of respect for every person, in particular for working-class and poor people, but also for those with more class privilege, open discussion of how to tap all class-cultural strengths can be transformative.

Class Action's founding story attests to this potential for transformation. Six Western Massachusetts activists—three who grew up working class or in poverty, three from multimillionaire owning-class families—formed a cross-class dialogue group and spent one day a month together for six years (Koch-Gonzalez, Ladd, and Yeskel 2009). They dug deep into how their class conditioning had affected them, and in particular how it continued to thwart their dreams. The members from working-class backgrounds changed their lives most dramatically, as all three began to pursue their heart work in a way they had not felt entitled to do before. But the owning-class members changed their lives as well. Owning-class pioneer Jennifer Ladd teamed up with proudly working-class Felice Yeskel to found Class Action in 2004. Their intention was to bring their own profound experience to as many people as possible. I hope this book will help inspire such cross-class dialogue within more social change groups.

Toward a Resurgence of Class Consciousness and a Class-Multicultural Movement

How could future progressive movements become more powerful and effective by tapping all class-cultural gifts? To explore this question, let's do a thought exercise and imagine a mixed-class activist group with all the strengths of the class cultures revealed in this book and none of the limitations. With the caveat that specific class-culture traits vary across decades, geography, intersecting identities, and movement traditions, it's nevertheless revealing to ask what such a group would be like.

In this idealized group, the working-class and poor members have taught the others how to create a warm, familylike group style through food, teasing and laughter, mutual aid, and one-on-one bonding among leaders and members. But when personal bonds go sour or leaders prove untrustworthy, all the working-class members keep their eyes on the prize, valuing the group for its social change goals, and speak up instead of quitting. All powerhouse working-class leaders have apprentices in training, mentoring them for leadership transitions to come.

The working-class preference for action toward short-term winnable goals has caught on in the whole group. But the working-class and other members with a distaste for meetings and organizational-management topics nevertheless bite the bullet and engage with them, because they know that ceding that territory to the managerially oriented college graduates would create a power imbalance in the group.

The straddlers in the group bring in deeply held moral principles, sharing with the group the values and the class loyalty that they kept from their working-class childhoods and the ideals they formulated in college—but all of them do it flexibly, without self-righteousness or hostility toward group members who see things differently.

The voluntarily downwardly mobile activists create egalitarian alternative institutions and suggest ways for the group to prefigure its ideals in its operations and tactics, but without erecting ideological or subcultural barriers between themselves and other activists. They matter-of-factly describe themselves as coming from class-privileged backgrounds and choosing to use their cultural capital for movement building. VDM members build warm, trusting relationships with other members, even with leaders and with new recruits, despite their assumption that paid informants are present in the group.

The professional-middle-class process-junkies-in-recovery have realized that facilitators of many classes and movement traditions will feel more competent using simpler forms of decision making and that discussions that are more similar to everyday conversational patterns will foster more creativity. They suggest innovative processes but accept defeat graciously if the group doesn't take their suggestions.

The lower professionals have learned to speak up more boldly and directly, their tongues unbitten, even during conflicts. The LP and PMC behind-the-scenes workhorses are not just pillars of the organization but can also speak from the heart, express anger, make people laugh, and reveal their lively minds.

Thanks to mentoring from some class-bicultural straddlers, all the college graduates have figured out how to contribute the useful theories and historical parallels they've read about by speaking briefly and without jargon, not using their knowledge to dominate but humbly offering it as one gift among many. Self-assured upper-middle-class, owning-class, and high-PMC members in particular have found ways to share their informed hope and heightened sense of efficacy with other members without arrogance. As they help turn their self-confidence into group confidence, they do it with no presumption that this valuable gift entitles them to be in charge.

The college graduates have also learned from the working-class people and from the labor movement to subordinate their individual agendas to a greater solidarity so that everyone pulls together as a team. There's room in this group for many people to take on leadership roles without being shot down for stepping forward, but there are no uncritical, passive followers either.

Food and other short-term material incentives are used to get new recruits in the door, but the group also systematically discusses which issues and frames are most likely to catch on with the media and with potential constituencies. As new disempowered and especially multiply marginalized people arrive, all hands are on deck to encourage them to gain skills and confidence; but everyone recognizes that straddlers and working-class powerhouses have a special role to play as role models who can teach them to become class-bicultural without losing their working-class strengths. The group has explicit goals of empowering marginalized and inexperienced people, affirming and drawing from working-class culture, and having a high percentage of lifelong-working-class people in leadership.

The group has a culture of candor: conflicts are discussed openly but don't break up the group, because loyalties to both people and ideals are strong. Members are assertive but not aggressive in raising their ideas and concerns. Unrooted activists grow new roots in the group and in the informal networks around it, which hold them accountable for their behavior. But if extreme behavior breaches do happen, they are met with a full range of responses drawn from all movement traditions, including both private and group discussion, both informal reactions and a formal mediation process.

The group spends a modest amount of time away from its wide-world struggles to build its sense of community, to educate members on the political context, to talk about "isms," and to evaluate and improve the organization—but without bogging down in looking inward. When windstorms of opposition and failure shake the group, members hold on tight to their political ideals *and* to their relationships with one another, and refuse to let the group be blown apart.

If such class-multicultural groups exist, I haven't encountered them. How could they come into being? I know one necessary (though not sufficient) first step: talk openly about class. Share class life stories, without pretense and without any shame or blame about the hidden hardships and privileges that are revealed. Define class by differences in education and other cultural and social capital as well as finances, and then have some reality-based conversation about who's present in the group and who's not. Respectfully put into words the specific class-culture differences found in the particular group, as well as all race, gender, age, and other intersecting cultural differences. And then take action to reach out across class, form alliances, and incorporate missing class-cultural strengths.

Coalitions and cross-class movements would be much easier to form among such class-aware and class-multicultural groups. No single movement tradition, and no one activist class culture, has all the elements needed for building a mass progressive movement, especially in today's daunting political environment. But groups that draw on the best of each class culture and each movement tradition will have a better shot at building powerful cross-class movements.

ACKNOWLEDGMENTS

It truly takes a village to raise a book. For the first two years of fieldwork, I had a wonderful research collaborator, Erin Balleine, and a skilled interviewer, my friend and Class Action colleague Jerry Koch-Gonzalez. The peerless transcriber Jack Danger created extremely accurate transcripts of the taped meetings and interviews, distinguishing voices at even the biggest and most chaotic meetings.

In the Boston College sociology department I was fortunate to find storehouses of relevant wisdom in Bill Gamson, Lisa Dodson, and Eve Spangler. Many thanks to them and to the groundbreaking cultural sociologist Francesca Polletta for their feedback and for the inspiration of their work. The department gave me innumerable types of support. A summer research fellowship covered the travel costs to the convention cities, and a fellowship gave me two semesters for writing. A departmental seminar led by Natasha Sarkisian, Leslie Salzinger, and Zine Magubane provided a supportive home base and peers who reviewed my drafts. Stephanie Howe, John Williamson, Natasha Sarkisian, Sandi Propp-Gubin, and the ever-generous Sara Moorman guided me through the statistical rapids. For uncovering the mysteries of Bourdieusian theory, I offer thanks to David Swartz, Juliet Schor, and the Harvard Bourdieu Study Group.

Many thanks to the Sociological Initiatives Foundation (SIF) for a grant to Class Action (www.classism.org) to cover the expenses of the fieldwork, and to the Class Action staff who administered the grant. For help with data entry and data management, I owe much appreciation to Carmen Lee, Roy MacKenzie, Rachie Lewis, Allison Stieber, Naomi U, Chris Bowker, Sandra Herforth, Laura Tennenhouse, Daniel Verinder, and Rahima Sage.

Many friends and colleagues read drafts and gave me savvy advice: Rafe Ezekiel; Kathy Modigliani; Bob Irwin; Anne Ellinger; Susan Legere; Charlotte Ryan; Penny Lewis; and the labor activists Maynard Seider, Steve Early, and Suzanne Gordon. Numerous other friends and family members listened to findings-in-progress and gave me support and encouragement. I especially thank Jack Metzgar, a gifted editor and supporter of writers, who read and critiqued every draft chapter. Taking his advice was always the right thing to do.

Many thanks to editor Fran Benson, a pioneer in the field of Working-Class Studies, and to Ange Romeo-Hall, Katy Meigs, Katherine Hue-Tsung Liu, and others at Cornell University Press whose efforts improved the book.

No writer has ever had a more supportive spouse than I have in Gail Leondar-Wright. She gave me insightful feedback on drafts; her sage counsel was sometimes informed by her book publicity experience. She graciously accepted sacrifices in my time availability and breadwinning capacity. But I'm grateful to Gail for more than just tangible support. At a deeper level, relaxing into such an exceptionally happy marriage released me to dream of doing something ambitious. As Stephen Sondheim wrote, "It only gets better and stronger, and deeper and nearer, and simpler and freer, and richer and clearer."

Finally, my thanks to the hundreds of activists who let a researcher observe their meetings and to the interviewees who shared their stories and ideas. They are my inspiration.

APPENDIX: METHODOLOGY NOTES

Like much social science research, this book began with a burning curiosity about a question that couldn't be answered any other way: What are the class-culture differences among progressive US activists? The tools of social research allowed me to listen to the voices of hundreds of activists and to hear them collectively give answers that neither I nor any one of them could have articulated. The statistics and the qualitative analysis reinforced each other; both were evocative and both were rigorous. Electronically coding the transcripts and then sorting the coded portions by class was like putting on 3D glasses: patterns popped out that were invisible to the naked eye.

I was able, to some degree, to create grounded theory (Charmaz 2005); that is, I drew the themes inductively from the meetings and interviews themselves. I had some initial hypotheses, but almost all were abandoned along the way. Many group troubles and class-culture traits were suggested by the activists themselves. Overtalking, for example, was not on my list of topics until I discovered that it was what activists most wanted to talk about.

In this appendix I offer suggestions for those who might want to do a similar study. I especially recommend that anyone tackling a large, multiyear research project read Robert Boice's *Advice for New Faculty Members: Nihil Nimus* (2000, esp. 103–202).

Seven Steps in the Research Process

While weighing options and eventually deciding to use a research design that included observing meetings, a written survey and follow-up interviews, I found the most useful tips in Michael Quinn Patton's *Qualitative Evaluation and Research Methods* (1990), a pragmatic and funny book.

1. Finding the Groups

The study design depended on observing a varied sample of activist groups. To make sure the class patterns we found were not particular to any one movement tradition, in late 2006 Erin Balleine and I generated a list of currently active issues[1] from progressive magazines and websites.[2] Then we looked for membership-based groups working on those issues. Within a two-hour-drive around our hometowns in Massachusetts and Florida, we gathered contact info for over fifty activist groups that relied primarily on volunteer efforts, prioritizing mixed-class groups. We reached out to all those groups, but the list shrank rapidly; while only two groups said no to being observed, often there was no upcoming meeting or we never successfully connected with the group.

2. Going Out into the Field

We wanted the survey and interview questions to draw out as much from activist informants as possible, yet to take a realistically small amount of their time and to yield consistent, comparable answers. Once we had drafted the survey (see online appendix 1), interview questions, field notes form, and consent form, we got Institutional Review Board approval and began attending meetings. We would explain the study, get consent forms signed, and ask permission to tape the meeting. Whether or not we were able to record, we took field notes (Emerson, Fretz, and Shaw 1995). Immediately after meetings, we typically spent longer than the meeting itself writing up our impressions and reactions.

At almost every meeting (except for a few large, open direct action–planning gatherings) almost all the participants filled out the survey. A piece of insider social science lore was responsible for this high response rate. Social psychologist Rafe Ezekiel kindly reviewed the research design and proclaimed it workable except for one missing element: chocolate. Why would activists linger after a meeting to fill out a survey? Some irresistible incentive was needed. Sure enough, if we pulled out surveys and chocolates simultaneously at the end of the meeting, all eyes were riveted in our direction; once we explained that the chocolate was a reward for filling out a survey, the surveys practically flew from our hands.

At the bottom of the survey was an offer of twenty-five dollars for a one-hour interview. If four or fewer people in a meeting gave their contact information for an interview, we attempted to interview them all. If more than four people signed up to be interviewed, we sorted the surveys by race and approximate class, picked surveys randomly from each pile and contacted those people first. This resulted in oversampling working-class and poor people and people of color, since for most groups those piles were smaller than the college-graduate and white piles.

The interviews were semistructured, with a set of starter questions and unstructured follow-ups. In all cases the interviewer was the same researcher who had observed the meeting(s). Most interviews lasted about sixty to ninety minutes, but a few were mini-interviews and a few lasted over three hours. Interview locations included the group's meeting space, the interviewee's home or workplace, or a fast-food restaurant; a few took place over the phone.

The target amount of fieldwork per group was two meetings and interviews with four diverse members of each group. In most cases a smaller amount of data was collected, for various logistical reasons.

At some point during 2007 I began to feel that the sample of groups was problematic. Without intending to, I had found myself studying during a time of movement abeyance. It was striking how many of the groups we contacted had no next meeting planned. As a result, the groups that welcomed us to observe their meetings were almost all long-standing, stable groups. In meeting after meeting, we met combinations of people who had been activist colleagues for five, ten, or even thirty years, which did not seem ideal for learning how diverse activists negotiate class-culture differences. The ideal sample would include both newer and older groups.

To find newly formed groups where strangers would interact, in early 2008 I contacted all the groups organizing protest events at the Republican and Democratic National Conventions. In the six months before the conventions, I attended planning meetings of seven protest-planning groups, as well as a few ongoing groups in the convention cities. During the two convention weeks, I observed last-minute meetings and spokescouncils, interviewed meeting participants, and was a participant-observer at the protests themselves, which gave me a deeper understanding of those groups.

3. Drawing a Circle around the Subjects of the Study and Disguising Their Identities

After seventeen months of fieldwork, we had collected data on thirty groups, but in five cases I decided the amount of data was too small to consider the group as part of the study. For twenty-five groups we had sufficient data to be included in the study, eighteen with full data (one or two meetings and multiple interviews) and seven with partial data (for example, a meeting but only one interview). Within this final pool of twenty-five groups, we observed thirty-four meetings and did sixty-one interviews.

The twenty-five groups, in eight cities in five states, were varied in every almost way I had hoped: by issue, movement tradition, geography, size, race and gender composition, and, most relevant, class composition. While no sample of twenty-five groups could be fully representative of the tens of thousands of US social movement groups, I am confident that the class commonalities I found in the sample don't actually reflect another variable, such as a certain region or race.

To assign pseudonyms for groups, towns, issues, and people, I tried to mimic cultural style without giving any clues to actual identities. I came up with a pseudonymous issue for each group, matching not just movement tradition but how common or uncommon, controversial or mainstream, technical or populist the actual issue was. To assign pseudonyms to group members, I drew from online lists of the most common names given in each decade to baby boys and girls by white, African American, and Latino families, so that most informants' pseudonyms are typical of their age, race, and gender. To respect certain interviewees' concerns about being identified by fellow group members, in a few cases I falsified additional details that might give away identities, without changing any quotes.

4. Categorizing Survey Respondents by Class

The success of the study hinged on creating valid class categories and on accurately and consistently assigning the 362 survey respondents to those class categories.

The first step was to assign numeric values to class-indicator variables (parents' income source, education, and housing when the respondent was age twelve; respondent's occupation, education, employer, and housing) and load them into a database in the PASW statistical program. Then we combined class-indicator variables to create two index variables, class background and current class, with values ranging from 1 to 7 for poor, working-class, lower-middle-class, lower-professional, professional-middle-class, upper-middle-class, and owning-class respondents. For scoring survey data on these index variables (Warner 2008: chap. 4), we wrote up a protocol (see online appendix 2) for how to treat various answers, including missing data.

When occupation and education both indicated the same class, then that became the informant's score. If education and occupation were scored three or more degrees apart on the 7-step scale, or two degrees apart but crossing the class divide between lower middle class and lower professional, then that informant was categorized as mixed-class and treated as missing data in statistical analyses. One example of a mixed-class informant was a custodian with a law degree.

When education and occupation fell just one degree apart, on the same side of the class divide, then informants' housing (rented or owned) and their employers' status were taken into consideration. Homeownership tipped respondents up into the higher category, while renting tipped them down, as did being in foreclosure proceedings; homelessness and public housing pulled the score down even further than just renting. A large, high-status employer (such as a name-brand national corporation, big hospital or university, or a state or national agency) tipped respondents up into the higher category; a tiny or informal employer (such as a domestic employer or a three-person office) tipped them down.

To see the effect of using homeownership and employer status to tip the balance in ambiguous cases, consider this example. Two high school graduates (education score of 2, working class) worked as human services case managers (occupation score of 3, lower middle class). The case manager who was a homeowner working at a large state agency was categorized as lower middle class (3) despite his lower educational attainment; the renter on the four-person staff of a small group house for mentally disabled people was categorized as working class (2) despite her relatively high job title.

Rental housing did not tip the score of class-ambiguous people between eighteen and thirty years old (for whom renting is common in all classes), or of those who fell between professional and upper middle class (who were all homeowners except for a few with special circumstances).

For those who listed two or more sources of income (such as those circling "wages" *and* "salary" for parents' main income source when informant was age twelve), the mean of the two was used as the occupation score. Small business income was scored as lower middle class unless the business was specified as a professional practice, such as a law office.

When someone's parents' or guardians' education levels differed, the protocol depended on respondents' age. For younger respondents, their current-class score rose for each additional degree in the family, as children can absorb more cultural capital depending on how many caretakers they learn it from. But for older respondents, born in the 1950s or earlier, an era when women tended to get less formal education, if the father's education level was higher, only his was used in calculating the score.

This class-categorizing protocol was so complicated that there was a risk of error; and it required so many judgment calls that there was a risk of rater bias, especially concerning informants who fell into the gray areas between two class categories. The scoring had to be done without knowing anything about the informants except for their class indicators. To prevent scorers' assumptions based on race, gender, or other survey answers from distorting the class categorization of respondents, a stripped-down spreadsheet was created with only the pseudonym and the class indicator survey answers. I oriented two people to the class-scoring protocol, and each of them and I scored the 362 survey respondents using the same sequence of rules. Respondents who did not get identical or very close scores from all three scorers were given an ambiguous class value and treated as missing data in statistical analyses. An example of someone the scorers disagreed about was a guitar maker: one person thought that making guitars was a manual labor occupation, which bumped the score down, while another saw it as a professional art form, which raised the score up.

To check the validity of the class-scoring system, inter-rater reliability was tested with Cohen's kappa for each pair of scorers; kappa ranged from .795 to .763, very high levels, all significant at the .001 level ($N = 362$). All three raters agreed on class categorizations 77 percent of the time.

For the other 23 percent of cases, usually two raters agreed and the third scored either class background or current class just one degree away on the 7-point scale, on the same side of the class divide; in those cases the majority vote prevailed. But in the cases with any greater discrepancy than that (in other words, where any two scores were two or more degrees apart or crossed the class divide, or where all three raters disagreed), they were given the ambiguous class value and omitted from statistical analyses.

Some informants who in my opinion were very strong examples of a certain class culture disappeared from the quantitative analyses because one or both of the other raters interpreted survey data differently than I did. In a few cases, I had extra information from interviews, meetings, or informal conversation and knew that another rater had misinterpreted a survey response, so I rescued someone from the discard pile and put him or her back into one of the class categories. For example, one survey respondent wrote that her parents neither owned nor rented a home, and one rater took this as a sign of homelessness, which contradicted other background indicators, requiring categorization as mixed class; however, I had heard the informant say that her father was a minister and they lived in a parsonage owned by the church, so I kept her in the PMC-background category where the other rater and I had placed her.

After the background scores and current class scores were determined, they were then combined to put respondents into one of four class-trajectory categories: lifelong in the working-class range; lifelong in the professional range; upwardly mobile straddler; or downwardly mobile. All undergraduate students and other very young adults were put into the lifelong trajectory for their class background, as they were closer to their childhood experience and hadn't yet had enough adult experience with the class system to be considered upwardly or downwardly mobile.

For downwardly mobile respondents, I went over their surveys, their meeting participation, and (for interviewees) their interview transcripts, seeking indications as to whether the downward mobility was voluntary (VDM) or involuntary. The VDM category encompassed the 22 people who described making choices after college that led to downward mobility into the working-class range. Another 21 fell into the involuntary category because of a story of an addiction, a disability, a layoff, or other misfortune. For a few downwardly mobile people, there were no clues either way. In statistical analyses, the downwardly mobile for involuntary or unknown reasons were treated as missing data.

From a total of 364 survey respondents, 309 people ended up assigned to one of the four class-trajectory categories compared throughout the book.

Once respondents were assigned to class categories, three numeric scores were entered into the PASW data file: two ordinal (ranked) variables for class background and current class, and a nominal (unrankable) variable for class trajectory.

It was also important to characterize the *groups* in terms of class. For each group I calculated the mean, mode, and median of members' class backgrounds and current class. (See center column of table 9.1 for modes and online figure 4.7 for medians and distribution.)

5. Creating and Coding the Transcripts

A transcriber created exact transcripts for nineteen of the thirty-four meetings and more than fifty of the interviews, using a composite linguistic transcription marking system to indicate simultaneous speech, laughter, sounds, pauses, tone of voice, and emphasis.

I created demographic summary tags and attached them to the pseudonyms throughout the transcripts. For example, each time Martina spoke in a meeting, the transcript said "Martina WC22imBlF80s," meaning that Martina was an African American immigrant female born in the 1980s who was categorized as lifelong-working-class because both her childhood and adult class scores were 2. This enabled me to see at a glance the ethnicity, class, gender, and age of all meeting participants as I read.

I read the transcripts with these demographic pseudonyms, along with the field notes—over one thousand pages in all—and wrote notes about my observations. After this open coding (Charmaz 1983), I organized the themes in my notes into a codebook with thirteen categories and over five hundred items. For example, the category "Humor" included the item "Laughing at fake bad behavior." I entered the codebook and the transcripts into HyperResearch, qualitative-coding software that lets researchers mark their material with codes and then run reports that assemble all instances of any given code. I went through transcript by transcript and applied the codes to the text. As I coded, I wrote memos about patterns and hypotheses (Emerson, Fretz, and Shaw 1995: chap. 6).

6. Looking for Class-Culture Patterns

From my memos and codebook I created a menu of analysis options, covering all my questions and hypotheses, and ran HyperResearch reports on each. The coded bits came up sorted by class of interviewee, so I could read, for example, all the straddlers' quotes marked with a certain code, which enabled me to catch nuances of class similarities. For example, I don't think I would have noticed how often lifelong-working-class activists criticized the leaders of the groups they had quit in the past if I hadn't read all the working-class excerpts related to leadership at one sitting.

My aim was to include statistics whenever possible to confirm that the patterns I saw were unlikely to have appeared by coincidence. However, many measures can be used only with sufficiently large Ns and with variables with the appropriate levels of measurement, and on many topics I had small Ns and only nominal variables, such as class trajectory. Often only descriptive statistics were applicable, not inferential statistics. I applied techniques to correlate nominal and ordinal variables with low and medium-sized Ns (Chen and Popovitch 2002), finding the highest-level statistic possible for each analysis (Warner 2008: chaps. 7–8).

I was able to use the Pearson's r correlation only in a few cases where I had two ordinal (rank-order) variables for all survey respondents, such as correlating class background with current class. Similarly, analysis of variance (ANOVA) could usually not be used, but in one case, testing ANOVA for activists' racism frames gave me confidence that I had found a very strong difference among classes.

But sometimes my quantitative data qualified for no inferential statistic at all; I compared raw numbers, rates, or means. For example, only the means of the frequency of laughter per hour and the mean number of criticisms of interviewees' own groups could be presented; there was no way to test how likely it was that the class differences had happened by chance. Usually I used the middle range of statistics, such as chi-square to test the relation between two dichotomous variables; a t-test to see whether differences in word-use rates were significant; or Spearman's rho to correlate an ordinal variable with another variable.

To analyze frequency of speech at meetings, I went through the meeting transcripts and tallied how often each person spoke and then calculated and compared rates per hour. To calculate wordiness, I used the word count tool in Word to measure how many words participants spoke in meetings, finding for each person their longest speech turn.

To do vocabulary-rate comparisons, I compiled all the interview transcripts of activists of each class trajectory, then used the Simple Concordance Program to call up and count that class's use of significant words.[3] The frequencies of each word were divided into the total number of words spoken by all interviewees of that class trajectory, then divided by 10,000 to get rates. I used an online t-test calculator to test ratios between rates for significance.[4]

Despite the limitations of the data, statistical analyses let me assert class-culture traits much more strongly, confident that what I saw was not just based on anecdotal patterns that would disappear in a larger study.

7. Writing up the Findings

I found hundreds of items that correlated with class, but most of them ended up on the cutting-room floor. I had two criteria for what made it into the book: first, whether I could understand the finding in a bigger context, explain it, and tie it to other findings to make an argument; and second, whether it seemed to have action implications for strengthening social change groups.

A useful resource on the revision process is Zerubavel 2001: chap. 3, evocatively titled "A Mountain with Stairs."

William Faulkner said, "Kill all your darlings," meaning edit out the bits of writing you're most attached to. (Lamott 1995 gives similar advice.) I left some of my favorite interviewees and even entire groups unmentioned.

This editing process increased my respect for every focused, concise social science book. Behind every incisive new theory lies a big, messy swamp of data.

Notes

Introduction

1. All names of groups, individuals, and cities are pseudonyms.

1. Why Look through a Class Lens?

1. The issue is pseudonymized here as job creation and job training, funded through the community-benefits payments required of big developers. The actual issue has similar technical complexity.

2. Applying Class Concepts to US Activists

1. Neo-Marxists tend to see a flaw in sociologists' methods of defining classes in terms of indicator similarities. For example, Aronowitz mocks sociological class analysts as mere ahistorical "map-makers" (2003: 48). Some say that socioeconomic-status categories are missing the element of power relations between classes, of class consciousness (the collective awareness of being a class), and of organizations acting on behalf of an entire class's self-interest (Aronowitz 1992: 127; Wright 1985: 35; Grusky 2005: 51–66). These are good points. However, following the last two criteria, there are no classes-for-themselves in the United States today, except perhaps a ruling class, only classes-in-themselves (unorganized, un-self-aware aggregates sharing some class indicators). Thus the sociological way of categorizing individuals is more practical for the purposes of this book.

2. Bourdieu coined the word "habitus" for these inculcated attitudes and practices. To avoid academic jargon, I use "predispositions" as a synonym.

3. In his later work (1998, 2001), Bourdieu began acknowledging gender and ethnic habitus as well as class (Swartz 1997: 154–56).

4. One exception is Fantasia's (1988) analysis of working-class cultures of solidarity.

3. Four Class Categories of Activists and Their Typical Group Troubles

1. Jensen (2012) uses the term "crossovers" for straddlers, which emphasizes the adult experience of assimilating into PMC culture. I use Lubrano's term to emphasize how straddlers often remain class bicultural.

2. The Pearson correlation between class background and current class is $r = .522, p < .001$, significant at the .01 level, one-tailed, $N = 246$. Mixed-class and ambiguous-class survey respondents in either background or current class are treated as missing data.

3. Since founding Women Safe from Violence, Elaine had risen into the straddler category because she had finally earned a college degree in a vocational field after twenty years of taking courses while working full time. See the straddler section for more about the distinct roles played by activists in the gray area between the lifelong-working-class and straddler categories.

4. While generally the outlaw/respectable spectrum aligned with the empowered/disempowered spectrum, a few disempowered outlaws were also observed, such as Olivia, the young Parecon Collective member featured in chapter 1. There were also some empowered respectable activists, such as Alonzo from the Local 21 Organizing Committee.

5. Spearman's rho for ordinal class background variable and dichotomous variable religious/nonreligious: rho = .227, p < .001, significant at the .01 level, one-tailed, N = 235. For current class and religious dichotomy: rho = .129, p = .024, significant at the .05 level, one-tailed, N = 235. Test of the relation between dichotomous class-trajectory variable (working class/college educated) and dichotomous religious/nonreligious variable: χ^2 (1, N = 249) = 7.66, p = .006. Clear-cut yes and no answers to the question "Are you religious?" were included in the dichotomous variable; ambiguous write-in answers such as "Spiritual but not religious" were omitted as missing data.

6. Details have been changed here to obscure which convention was being protested by what groups. Confidentiality about tactics that could provoke prosecution was the greatest concern expressed by direct action planners in considering whether to be interviewed, so some references to tactics include falsified details. In this case, the man's quote is his exact words, but the account of what we saw and our past contacts with direct action groups has been altered.

7. Those lifelong within the broad professional range are sometimes referred to by the shorthand "PMC" for brevity's sake, even though some were more precisely upper middle class or lower professional or had moved up or down within the professional range.

8. One reason the VDM number is low is that participants in large spokescouncils (open preprotest meetings) during the conventions were the most likely of all meeting attendees to decline to be surveyed. Most likely some VDM activists were among them, along with students and temporary protestors with day jobs. In some cases informal sources indicated that certain unsurveyed meeting participants were VDM. A conservative estimate of the number of VDM activists actually observed at meetings is 70.

4. Movement Traditions and Their Class-Cultural Troubles

1. Correlating class background and movement tradition, Spearman's rho = .260, p < .001, one-tailed, N = 289. For current class, rho = .265, p < .001, one-tailed, N = 286.

2. http://www.industrialareasfoundation.org/, accessed March 7, 2012.

3. http://www.jwj.org/, accessed March 7, 2012.

4. http://www.unitedforpeace.org; http://www.codepink.org; http://www.350.org; http://www.soaw.org/, all accessed March 7, 2012.

5. http://www.answercoalition.org/national/index.html; http://www.workers.org; http://www.unitedforpeace.org/, all accessed March 7, 2012.

6. Personal experience is my source here. I was at the demolished MOVE house on the day of the 1978 shoot-out and spoke with many West Philadelphia neighbors, then and later.

7. http://abcf.net/, accessed February 15, 2011.

8. http://www.foodnotbombs.net/, accessed March 7, 2012.

9. http://critical-mass.info/, accessed March 7, 2012.

5. "Where Is Everybody?"

1. Using the concordances of interview transcripts, frequencies of the word "kids" were divided into the total number of words spoken by all interviewees of each class trajectory, then divided by 10,000 to get rates. The t-test for significant differences between working-class interviewees' (N = 35) and all college-educated interviewees' rates of saying "kids" per 10,000 words (N = 42) shows t = 10.19, p < .001, extremely statistically significant. *Any* higher rate of a word by working-class interviewees is unusual, because they used so many more specific names of people, places, and organizations, making *all* general terms a smaller share of their speech. However, since working-class activists are more likely to be parents, and since most interviews included reviewing answers to the survey, which included questions about numbers and ages of children, some of the working-class references to children were in the context of these factual descriptions of family configuration.

2. In all word counts, all variations of the words were included, such as "kids," "grandson," "granddaughter(s)," "grandkid(s)," etc.

3. The working-class rate of 6.5 times saying "help" per 10,000 words contrasts with 4.7 times by PMC interviewees, 4.4 times by straddlers, and only 3.6 times by VDM interviewees.

4. "The Festival of Activist Street Bands," http://www.honkfest.org, accessed July 15, 2011.

Class Speech Differences I: Humor and Laughter

1. The total number of group laughs was divided into the meeting's total number of minutes. Because of some untaped meetings, as well as a few transcriptions that didn't include notes on laughter, N = 15 (out of the 34 total meetings observed): 5 working-class-majority, 8 PMC-majority, 3 straddler-majority, and 1 VDM-majority groups.

2. The median was a very similar 8.47, suggesting that outliers are not distorting the mean for working-class-majority groups.

3. The median was 11.86, suggesting that a few high-laughter groups pulled up the mean for PMC-majority groups.

4. I wasn't able to calculate an exact average for the VDM-majority groups since some didn't allow taping, but at one meeting zero group laughs were heard, and two others inspired field notes about the strange dearth of laughter.

5. Incidences of laughter at individual foibles were counted and divided by the length of the meeting to get an hourly rate. In all transcripts of lifelong-working-class-majority groups (N = 5 meetings), the mean was 3 times per hour, compared

with a mean of 1.3 times in lifelong-PMC-majority groups (N = 9 meetings), a 2.26:1 ratio. When class-mobile categories are combined with lifelong categories, the rate of laughing at individual foibles at meetings of working-class background (straddlers plus lifelong-working-class) groups (N = 8 meetings) was 3.2 times per hour, compared with 1.2 times in PMC-background (VDM plus lifelong-PMC) groups (N = 10), a 2.09:1 ratio.

6. The mean rate of snafu laughter was very close to 2 per hour of meeting for all class categories. The few groups with very high numbers of laughter at snafu comments, 4 to 8 per hour (the Parecon Collective, City Power, and Green Homes Green World) were very different from each other in class, race, and gender composition, and in movement tradition. This kind of humor seems to be a feature of certain groups' organizational styles, regardless of class.

7. When class background is included, the PMC/working-class ratio of mean rates per hour of meeting laughter about word play and cultural references is 2.9:1 (working-class/straddler N = 8; PMC/VDM N = 10). The ratio is 3:1 when only lifelong-PMC-majority groups (N = 9) are compared to lifelong-working-class-majority groups (N = 5).

6. Activating the Inactive

1. www.warresisters.org, highlandercenter.org, and ncbi.org, all accessed March 28, 2012.

2. www.trainingforchange.org, accessed February 15, 2011.

3. Fisher Lavell, a Canadian straddler, told me that such direct responses by a leader would be considered offensively patronizing in her rural working-class community, particularly among indigenous people; silent listening would be the respectful response. This feedback was helpful in showing me that some of the class-culture patterns I observed were specific to the United States.

Class Speech Differences II: Abstract and Concrete Vocabulary

1. Test of the relation between the dichotomous variable indicating lifelong PMC or not PMC and the dichotomous abstract/concrete speech variable: χ^2 (1, N = 27) = 12.71, p < .001. For lifelong working class or not working class: χ^2 (1, N = 27) = 8.13, p < .004. For straddler/not straddler, χ^2 (1, N = 27) = 3.14, p = .076. The dichotomous variable indicating VDM or not does not have a statistically significant association with abstract or concrete speech, because the number of VDM interviewees is too small, only seven.

2. Correlation between class background and dichotomous variable of interviewees' notably abstract or concrete speech: rho = .526, p = .002, significant at the 0.01 level, one-tailed, N = 29.

3. Correlation between current class and dichotomous variable of interviewees' notably abstract or concrete speech: rho = .412, p < .013, significant at the 0.03 level, one-tailed, N = 29.

4. Test of the relation between the dichotomous variables male/not male and female/not female and the dichotomous abstract/concrete speech variable: χ^2 (1, N = 29) = .017, p = .897.

5. Test of the relation between the dichotomous variable white/not white and the dichotomous abstract/concrete speech variable: χ^2 (1, N = 29) = 1.42, p = .233. For black/not black, χ^2 (1, N = 29) = 3.02, p = .082. For Latino/not Latino, χ^2 (1, N = 29) = 0.05, p = .823. For Asian/not Asian, χ^2 (1, N = 29) = .842, p = .359.

6. Test of the relation between the dichotomous variable community-needs group/not community-needs group and the dichotomous abstract/concrete speech variable: χ^2 (1, N = 29) = .057, p = .811. For labor/not labor, χ^2 (1, N = 29) = .3.02, p = .082. For progressive cause/not progressive cause, χ^2 (1, N = 29) = .607, p = .436. For anarchist/not anarchist, χ^2 (1, N = 29) = 2.43, p = .119. For staff advocacy/not staff advocacy, χ^2 (1, N = 29) = .738, p = .390. Only one interviewee in a militant anti-imperialist cause group was notably abstract or concrete, so χ^2 couldn't be calculated. Younger activists were somewhat more likely to speak notably abstractly than older activists. Correlation between notably abstract or concrete speech and decade born: rho = .326, p = .042, significant at the .05 level, one-tailed, N = 29.

7. Working-class interviewees as a group used approximately 450 distinct words per 10,000 words spoken; PMC interviewees used approximately 400 distinct words per 10,000; straddlers used approximately 500 distinct words per 10,000.

8. To find the rate of nonrepeated words, I sorted the concordances for each class trajectory's interview transcripts by decreasing frequency of word use, found the cut-off rank for words used twice or more per 10,000, divided the total number of vocabulary words by the cut-off rank to get the rate of multiple uses, and subtracted this percent of two or more uses from 100 to get the percent of rarely used words.

Class Speech Differences III: Racial Terms

1. There may be similar class differences in terminology for Native Americans ("indigenous" and "Native American" versus "Indian") and for Asian Americans ("Asian" versus nationality words), but the total number of references is too small to be sure.

2. The small N for working-class references to people of color generally, just 15, virtually guaranteed that the class difference would not be statistically significant, but the small N itself is evidence of how working-class people tended to talk about race, with more specificity and fewer general references.

3. Transgender references were too few to correlate with class or race. It appeared that people in more radical groups and in groups with transgender members were more likely to mention gender identities such as "genderqueer," "transsexual," and "transgender."

7. Diversity Ironies

1. www.faireconomy.org, accessed February 15, 2011.
2. www.pisab.org/, accessed May 16, 2013.
3. http://www.ctwo.org/, accessed February 15, 2011.
4. www.whiteprivilegeconference.com, accessed May 16, 2013.
5. Analysis of variance shows that informants in different class trajectories vary statistically significantly in the race frames they invoke: F = 8.85, df between groups = 3, p < .001. Post-hoc Tukey tests show that the statistically significant variations are

between lifelong working-class activists and each of the three college-educated class trajectory groups: working class and straddler, $p < .001$; working class and PMC, $p < .001$; working class and VDM, $p < .05$. The voluntarily downwardly mobile trajectory had a smaller N, not just because they are the smallest group of informants, but also because they talked about race least often.

Class Speech Differences IV: Talking Long, Talking Often

1. The three working-class-majority groups are City Power (half black, half white), median number of words in longest speaking turn during meetings = 36; Local 21 Organizing Committee (mostly black), median = 65; and Neighbors United (majority white, several Latinos), median = 58. The three PMC-majority groups are the Workforce Development Task Force (half black, half white), median number of words in longest speaking turn during meetings = 364; The People's Convention (all white), median = 183; and Easthaver Demands Justice (majority white, several blacks), median = 151. This subset of six was selected because they are the only meetings with such clear-cut class compositions at the two ends of the class spectrum for which complete word-for-word transcripts are available (excluding extremely small or large meetings, which tend to have atypical conversation patterns). These meetings each had between five and twenty people who weren't playing a speaking role such as chair, staff, or presenter. Speakers in such roles were excluded from the word counts.

2. Easthaver Demands Justice was the exception to this pattern, with 238 speaking turns per hour. However, as chapter 8 describes, one overtalker from a working-class background drove this number up, which is evidence strengthening the overall class pattern.

3. This comparison also excludes all chairs, staff, and guest speakers, those with a responsibility to speak extra at the meeting.

4. Minimal responses such as "right, right"—also known as "response tokens," "continuers," and "back-channel responses" (Gardner 2001)—were counted as turns if they included words, but not counted if they were only sounds such as "mmm-hmmm." These responses were more common among working-class women and people of color. But only a few people frequently chimed in with such conversational supports; the vast majority of the speech turns tallied in the utterance counts involved actually taking the floor.

5. Again, this comparison excludes all chairs, staff, and guest speakers.

6. All race/gender combinations in the overall pool have at least one long-talker except for Latino men. Percent using more than 174 words in their longest speaking turn: 31% of men, 22% of women, 25% of whites, 28% of African Americans, 20% of Latinos, 17% of those born after 1960, 30% of those born before 1960.

8. Overtalkers

1. To measure frequency of talking, the number of total speaking turns in each meeting (excluding speech within the roles of guest speaker, staff, or chair/facilitator) was divided by the number of attendees to determine an equal share of airspace, the number of times each person would have spoken if participation had been divided equally. Then a ratio was calculated for the 143 participants for whom exact turn

counts and complete demographic information was available, by dividing their number of speaking turns by the equal share. Twenty-four meeting participants (17% of the 143) spoke at a rate twice or greater than their share.

2. The resented overtalkers were four women, seven men; one black, one Latina, one Asian American, eight whites; five professional middle class, three working class, one straddler, and two involuntarily downwardly mobile; born in five different decades.

3. Three were lifelong-working class in mostly professional-range or VDM groups. Another was the only straddler in a mostly PMC group. Two overtalkers were lifelong PMC, one in a group with a LMC majority and one in a group that was mostly straddlers. And three overtalkers in mostly working-class groups came from professional backgrounds; two of them were involuntarily downwardly mobile, perhaps for reasons related to their overtalking.

4. Asperger's syndrome is a mild form of autism characterized by poor skills at reading social cues.

5. It should be noted again that almost all people of color were observed in mixed-race groups. Only one meeting made up entirely of people of color was observed. Thus, these observations might not reflect how people of color would interact without any whites present. For one interpretation of this race difference, see Penelope Brown (1980) on politeness as the expression of social distance or subordination.

Class Speech Differences V: Anger, Swearing, and Insults

1. College-educated (PMC, voluntarily downwardly mobile (VDM), and straddler) rate of saying "pissed off" per 10,000 words was .8, compared with lifelong-working-class rate of .2, a 4.1:1 ratio; for "angry," the college-educated rate was 1.4, compared with a working-class rate of 1, a 1.4:1 ratio.

2. For the words "shit" and "bullshit," the PMC rate per 10,000 words was .10, compared with .56 for lifelong working class and 1.69 for straddlers; the working-class/PMC ratio was 3.9:1. For "fuck(ing)/(ed)," the PMC rate was .67, compared with .08 for working class and .65 for straddlers; the working-class/PMC ratio was .19:1. For all swear words, working-class/PMC ratio was 1.35:1.

3. The extremely high rate of swear words by VDM interviewees, 17.58 per 10,000 words, is not a reliable finding for two reasons: the small number of VDM interviews, just 8; and one outlier, Zorro, who peppered almost all her sentences with swear words, in particular "fucking."

4. The PMC rate per 10,000 words of all intelligence-based insults was .92, compared with the working-class rate of .40, a 2.33:1 ratio.

5. In all other cases, I obscure geographical locations of groups by using city pseudonyms; the Denver DNC protest groups here and in chapter 9 are an exception. My reason is that there were only two 2008 convention cities, and in the Twin Cities, the RNC protest groups agreed to a unity pledge, vowing not to speak publicly against other activist groups. There were also some antagonisms among RNC convention protest groups, but they were successfully kept confidential, almost never visible in the media or online. Several Twin Cities interviewees expressed pride in how well the pledge of solidarity worked. It would be an unfair betrayal of my Twin Cities informants to write vaguely of activists attacking each other in "one of the

convention cities," placing suspicion on them for the intramovement hostilities in Denver. Elsewhere in this book, less-controversial Denver convention-protest stories are told with their location obscured.

9. Activists Behaving Badly

1. More specifically, DNC activists' accusations of unacceptable behavior included three threats of violence; two threats to sue; drowning out another group's rally by shouting into an amplified bullhorn; a hate-blog almost entirely devoted to profanity-filled trashing of The People's Convention; "spies" who attended meetings only to report on them to rival groups or to the hate-blogger; denouncing activists publicly (in the media, online, or from a rally stage), including two public accusations that someone was a government informer without evidence given and one false accusation of posting violent content online; "stealing bands" and speakers from one rally for another (several accusations, at least some probably unfounded); a threat to change an event time deliberately to conflict with another group's event; a threat to cancel a keynote speaker's plane ticket secretly; and many e-mail and listserv messages using harsh language (e.g., "shut up," "Stalinist") toward or about other activists.

2. In several groups, a member was believed to be drunk or drugged at a meeting or public event; in two groups, someone spent the organization's money in unauthorized ways; in another group, members stole money; in one group, a member hit another member; in several groups, members abused power, such as stacking a meeting to win a vote or hiding a financial conflict of interest; members of several groups yelled, swore, said insult words, or were verbally hostile in ways that offended other members.

3. Survey respondents were scored by whether they shared their parents' religion; whether they lived near where they were born (in the same metropolitan area or within one hundred miles); whether they were born near where one or both parents were born; whether they had dependent children; and whether they worked for an employer. Those with three or more of those factors were categorized as very rooted. Those with one or none of those factors were categorized as very unrooted. An intermediate score of two became a middle value in a three-value variable; this intermediate value was omitted from a dichotomous ordinal variable with very-rooted and very-unrooted values. For the correlation between this dichotomous rooted/unrooted variable and a dichotomous variable of working class or not working class, rho $= -.159$, $p = .003$, significant at the .01 level, one-tailed, $N = 305$. Three dichotomous variables were also created: very unrooted or not, very rooted or not, and medium rooted or not. Only 15% of college graduates ($N = 221$) were very rooted, compared with 30% of working-class activists ($N = 84$). Test of relationship between dichotomous working-class/college-graduate variable and very rooted or not: χ^2 $(1, N = 305) = 8.69$, $p = .003$. Of college graduates, 59% were very unrooted, compared with 45% of lifelong-working-class activists. Test of relationship between dichotomous working-class/college-graduate variable and very unrooted or not: χ^2 $(1, N = 305) = 4.86$, $p = .028$. Relationship with medium rooted was not significant.

4. Decade born significantly correlated with dichotomous variable of rooted or unrooted: Spearman's rho $= -.360$, $p < .001$, one-tailed, $N = 270$.

5. For example, one of only two members from working-class backgrounds in a VDM-majority group, the only steadily employed lifelong-PMC person in a VDM-majority anarchist group, and three lone straddlers in PMC-majority groups were accused of extreme misbehavior.

6. Rothschild and Leach (2007) have a third, more conflict-positive category, "fight cultures," which I'm omitting for two reasons: first, no group in my sample had a full-blown fight culture by their definition, although some in SUFB and other groups advocated it; and second, Leach informed me in e-mail correspondence that she had changed the definitions and redrawn the line between cultures of candor and fight cultures since publishing the article.

7. Action Against Empire and Safety Net for All shrank in size during the observation period; the Workforce Development Task Force disbanded after the observed meeting.

Class Speech Differences VI: Missing Class Talk

1. "Class" as counted here excludes other meanings such as classrooms and class action suits; just the sense of social class was tallied.

2. One of the exceptions is the uncommon term "working class," which college-educated people said as infrequently as working-class people did. All working-class interviewees were 1.15 times as likely as others to say "working class." But when outlier Dorothea was excluded, working-class interviewees were then slightly less likely to use "working class" than college-educated interviewees. In addition, in some cases the interviewer used "working class" as a prompt, and some working-class interviewees said the phrase only in agreement with this prompt. Unprompted uses of "working class" by working-class people other than Dorothea were extremely rare.

3. The interview protocol fished for class awareness and class terminology in several ways. First came an open question along the lines of "How are the members of your group similar and how are they different?," sometimes including the word "diversity." If no demographic identities were mentioned, interviewees were then prompted with a gender observation, such as "It seems that there are more women than men" and a question such as "What else?" About half of the sixty-one interviews included these opportunities to bring up class unprompted, with no prior mention of class by the interviewer; in the other half of the interviews class had already been mentioned by interviewer or interviewee. If the interviewee didn't mention class or any class indicators (such as education or occupation) in answering those first questions, they were then asked explicitly, "How would you describe the people at the meeting in terms of their social class?," followed if needed by a prompt, "For example, who might be the richest and who might be the poorest?" Then in the last portion of more than three-quarters of the interviews, while going over what the person wrote on the paper survey, the interviewer asked, "How would you describe yourself in terms of your social class?" The answers to these questions were coded for conventional and unconventional class terms, and whether class mentions were prompted or unprompted.

4. A dataset of 304 times when informants either mentioned class or were asked a class or diversity question but answered with a nonclass, resistant, or garbled

answer was analyzed for correlations with the class trajectory, race, gender, age, and movement tradition of the group member. Class trajectories were compiled into a dichotomous variable of lifelong-working-class versus college-graduate variable (including the PMC, VDM, and straddler trajectories) (shorthand term "WC/college graduate"). A dichotomous variable was created distinguishing resistant or garbled class responses (shorthand term below "nonclass responses") from all other class mentions. Test of the relation between the dichotomous WC/college graduate and the dichotomous variable of giving nonclass responses: χ^2 (1, N = 301) = .6.42, p = .011. Crosstabs for nonclass responses and the WC/college-graduate variables show that 17% of working-class class-talk opportunities but only 7% of college graduates' class-talk opportunities were nonclass responses.

5. χ^2 shows no significant difference in giving nonclass responses and dichotomous variables for each race, gender, and movement tradition, except that Latinos were less likely to give nonclass responses: for Latino/not-Latino variable, χ^2 (1, N = 303) = 4.05, p = .044. Spearman's rho is not significant for decade born: rho = .056, p = .167, one-tailed, N = 299.

6. Test of relationship between dichotomous working-class/college-graduate variable and dichotomous variable of mentions or failures to mention class in answer to questions about identities of others in the group: χ^2 (1, N = 303) = 1.86, p = .173.

7. Test of relationship between dichotomous white/not-white variable and dichotomous variable of mentions or failures to mention class in answer to questions about identities of others in the group: χ^2 (1, N = 131) = 3.95, p = .047. For black/not-black variable: χ^2 (1, N = 131) = 4.84, p = .028. For Latino/not-Latino variable, χ^2 (1, N = 131) = 1.05, p = .305. χ^2 is not significant for dichotomous variables for each gender, decade born, and movement tradition.

8. Test of relationship between dichotomous working-class/college-graduate variable and dichotomous variable of mentioning concrete proximate class facts: χ^2 (1, N = 300) = 4.43, p = .035. There was no significant relationship between any race, gender, or movement tradition and such concrete class talk.

9. "Poor" as counted here excludes other meanings such as "did a poor job"; only the sense of low income was tallied. Working-class interviewees used "poor" 4.92 times per 10,000 words compared with 1.7 times for all college-educated interviewees. Straddlers said "poor" only .5 times per 10,000 words.

10. "Low income" was said by all interviewees 1.2 times per 10,000 words.

Conclusion

1. Eliasoph (1998: 264–68) devotes an appendix to justifying her decision neither to categorize her informants by class nor to describe the cultural themes she found as class cultures.

Appendix: Methodology Notes

1. The issues on which we found social change group activity in 2006 were labor solidarity and antisweatshops; environmental justice; post-Katrina reconstruction; antiwar; welfare rights and antipoverty (including fighting budget cuts in human

services such as day care, affordable housing, and health care); living wage and minimum wage; immigrant rights and civil liberties; climate change; racial profiling and police brutality; reproductive rights; gay, lesbian, bisexual, and transgender rights; and prison reform.

2. Sources of current activist issues included the magazines *ColorLines, Z,* the *Progressive, In These Times, Nation, Ms., Yes, Utne Reader, Mother Jones,* and the websites *Common Dreams, Alternet, Black Commentator,* and *Racewire.*

3. Simple Concordance Program, http://download.cnet.com/Simple-Concordance-Program/3000–2279_4–4577501.html.

4. Online t-test calculator, www.graphpad.com/quickcalcs; standard deviations calculated online, http://www.quantitativeskills.com/sisa/statistics.

REFERENCES

Abramovitz, Mimi. 2000. *Under Attack, Fighting Back: Women and Welfare in the United States*. New York: Monthly Review Press.

Adams, Maurianne, and Lee Bell, eds. 2007. *Teaching for Diversity and Social Justice*. 2nd ed. New York: Routledge.

Adilkno, Foundation for the Advancement of Illegal Knowledge. 1990. *Cracking the Movement: Squatting beyond the Media*. Brooklyn, NY: Autonomedia.

Alinsky, Saul. 1971. *Rules for Radicals*. New York: Random House.

Anner, John. 1999. *Beyond Identity Politics: Emerging Social Justice Movements in Communities of Color*. Boston: South End Press.

Anzaldúa, Gloria. 1987. *Borderlands/La Frontera: The New Mestiza*. San Francisco, CA: Spinsters/Aunt Lute.

Aronowitz, Stanley. 1992. *The Politics of Identity: Class, Culture, Social Movements*. New York: Routledge.

———. 2003. *How Class Works: Power and Social Movement*. New Haven: Yale University Press.

Atlas, John. 2010. *Seeds of Change: The Story of ACORN, America's Most Controversial Antipoverty Community Organizing Group*. Nashville: Vanderbilt University Press.

Bageant, Joe. 2008. *Deer Hunting with Jesus: Dispatches from America's Class War*. New York: Random House.

Bailey, Benjamin. 1997. "Communication of Respect in Interethnic Service Encounters." *Language and Society* 26(3): 327–56.

Bales, Robert. 1950. *Interaction Process Analysis: A Method for the Study of Small Groups*. New York: Addison-Wesley.

Bartels, Larry. 2006. "What's the Matter with *What's the Matter with Kansas?*" *Quarterly Journal of Political Science* 1(2): 201–26.

Belenky, Mary Field, Lynne A. Bond, and Jacqueline S. Weinstock. 1997. *A Tradition That Has No Name: Women's Ways Of Leading*. New York: Basic Books.

Benjamin, Joan, Judith Bessant, and Rob Watts. 1997. *Making Groups Work: Rethinking Practice*. St. Leonards, Australia: Allen and Unwin.

Bernstein, Basil. 1971. *Class, Codes, and Control*. Vol. 1. New York: Routledge & Kegan Paul.

Bettie, Julie. 2003. *Women without Class: Race, Girls, and Identity*. Berkeley: University of California Press.

Binkley, Sam. 2007. *Getting Loose: Lifestyle Consumption in the 1970s*. Durham: Duke University Press.

Bobo, Kim, Jackie Kendall, and Steve Max. 2001. *Organizing for Social Change: Midwest Academy Manual for Activists*. 2nd ed. Santa Ana, CA: Seven Locks Press.

Boice, Robert. 2000. *Advice for New Faculty Members: Nihil Nimus.* Needham Heights, MA: Allyn & Bacon.

Bonilla-Silva, Eduardo. 2010. *Racism without Racists: Color-Blind Racism and Racial Inequality in Contemporary America.* 3rd ed. New York: Roman and Littlefield.

Bookchin, Murray. 1982. *The Ecology of Freedom: The Emergence and Dissolution of Hierarchy.* Palo Alto, CA: Cheshire Books.

Bourdieu, Pierre. 1983. "The Field of Cultural Production: The Economic World Reversed." *Poetics* 12(4–5): 311–56.

———. 1984. *Distinction: A Social Critique of the Judgement of Taste.* Cambridge, MA: Harvard University Press.

———. 1990. *The Logic of Practice.* Stanford: Stanford University Press.

———. 1998. *Pascalian Meditations.* Stanford: Stanford University Press.

———. 2001. *Masculine Domination.* Stanford: Stanford University Press.

Breen, Richard. 2005. "Foundations of Neo-Weberian Class Analysis." In *Approaches to Class Analysis*, ed. Erik Olin Wright, 31–50. New York: Cambridge University Press.

Breines, Wini. 1989. *Community and Organization in the New Left, 1962–1968: The Great Refusal.* 3rd ed. New Brunswick, NJ: Rutgers University Press.

Breslin, J. William, and Jeffrey Z. Rubin. 1995. *Negotiation Theory and Practice.* 3rd ed. Cambridge: Harvard Law School, Program on Negotiation.

Brooks, David. 2001. *Bobos in Paradise: The New Upper Class and How They Got There.* New York: Simon and Schuster.

Brown, Elaine. 1992. *A Taste of Power: A Black Woman's Story.* New York: Anchor Books.

Brown, Penelope. 1980. "How and Why Are Women More Polite: Some Evidence from a Mayan Community." In *Women and Language in Literature and Society*, ed. Sally McConnell-Ginet, Ruth A. Borker, and Nelly Furman, 111–36. New York: Praeger and Greenwood.

Bryson, Bethany. 1996. "Anything but Heavy Metal: Symbolic Exclusion and Musical Dislikes." *American Sociological Review* 61(5): 887–99.

Buck, John, and Sharon Villines. 2007. *We the People: Consenting to a Deeper Democracy: A Guide to Sociocratic Principles and Methods.* Washington, DC: Sociocracy.info.

Butler, C. T. 1981. *Building United Judgment: A Handbook for Consensus Decision-Making.* Madison, WI: Center for Conflict Resolution.

Carlsson, Chris. 2008. *Nowtopia: How Pirate Programmers, Outlaw Bicyclists, and Vacant-Lot Gardeners Are Inventing the Future Today.* Oakland, CA: AK Press.

Charmaz, Kathy. 1983. "The Grounded Theory Method: An Explication and Interpretation." In *Contemporary Field Research*, ed. Robert M. Emerson, 109–26. Prospect Hills, IL: Waveland Press.

———. 2005. "Grounded Theory in the 21st Century: Applications for Advancing Social Justice Studies." In *Strategies of Qualitative Inquiry*, ed. Norman K. Denzin and Yvonna Lincoln, 507–36. Thousand Oaks, CA: Sage.

Chen, Peter Y., and Paula M. Popovich. 2002. *Correlation: Parametric and Nonparametric Measures.* Thousand Oaks, CA: Sage.

Clarke, Philippa, Patrick M. O'Malley, Lloyd D. Johnstone, and John E. Schulenberg. 2008. "Social Disparities in BMI Trajectories across Adulthood by Gender, Race/Ethnicity, and Lifetime Socio-Economic Position: 1986–2004." *International Journal of Epidemiology* 38(2): 499–509.

Cluster, Dick. 1979. *They Should Have Served That Cup of Coffee.* Boston: South End Press.

Cohen, Cathy. 1999. *The Boundaries of Blackness.* Chicago: University of Chicago Press.

Collins, Patricia Hill. 1990. *Black Feminist Thought: Knowledge, Consciousness, and the Politics of Empowerment.* Boston: Unwin Hyman.

ColorLines. 2011. "#Occupy." Accessed January 12, 2012. http://colorlines.com/occupy/.

Conley, Dalton. 1999. *Being Black, Living in the Red.* Berkeley: University of California Press.

Cornell, Andrew. 2011. *Oppose and Propose! Lessons from Movement for a New Society.* Oakland, CA: AK Press.

Converse, Philip. 1964. *The Nature of Belief Systems in Mass Publics.* New York: The Free Press.

Crenshaw, Kimberlé, Neil Gotanda, and Garry Peller. 1995. *Critical Race Theory: The Key Writings That Formed the Movement.* New York: The New Press.

Croteau, David. 1995. *Politics and the Class Divide: Working People and the Middle-Class Left.* Philadelphia: Temple University Press.

Cummings, Claire. 2003. "Class Lessons." PhD. diss., University of Massachusetts, Boston.

Delvino, Nick. 2011. "Horizontal Participatory Democracy Is Worth the Wait." Accessed January 19, 2012. http://www.classism.org/horizontal-participatory-democracy-worth-wait.

Derber, Charlie, William Schwartz, and Yale Magrass. 1990. *Power in the Highest Degree.* New York: Oxford University Press.

DiMaggio, Paul. 2012. "Sociological Perspectives on the Face-to-Face Enactment of Class Distinction." In *Facing Social Class: How Societal Rank Influences Interaction,* ed. Susan T. Fiske and Hazel Rose Markus, 15–38. New York: Russell Sage Foundation.

Dyson, Michael Eric. 1997. *Race Rules: Navigating the Color Line.* New York: Vintage.

———. 2005. *Is Bill Cosby Right, or Has the Black Middle-Class Lost Its Mind?* New York: Basic Civitas Books.

Early, Steve. 2009. *Embedded with Organized Labor: Journalistic Reflections on the Class War at Home.* New York: Monthly Review Press.

———. 2011. *The Civil Wars in US Labor: Birth of a New Workers' Movement or Death Throes of the Old?* Chicago: Haymarket Books.

Eliasoph, Nina. 1998. *Avoiding Politics: How Americans Produce Apathy in Everyday Life.* New York: Cambridge University Press.

Eliasoph, Nina, and Paul Lichterman. 2003. "Culture in Interaction." *American Journal of Sociology* 108(4): 735–94.

Ellsworth, Elizabeth. 1989. "Why Doesn't This Feel Empowering? Working Through the Repressive Myths of Critical Pedagogy." *Harvard Educational Review* 59(3): 297–324.

Emerson, Robert M., Rachel I. Fretz, and Linda L. Shaw. 1995. *Writing Ethnographic Fieldnotes.* Chicago: University of Chicago Press.

Epstein, Barbara. 1991. *Political Protest and Cultural Revolution.* Berkeley: University of California Press.

Evans, Sara. 1980. *Personal Politics: The Roots of Women's Liberation in the Civil Rights Movement and the New Left.* New York: Vintage.

Faderman, Lillian. 1999. *To Believe in Women: What Lesbians Have Done for America—a History*. Chicago: University of Chicago Press.

Fantasia, Rick. 1988. *Cultures of Solidarity: Consciousness, Action, and Contemporary American Workers*. Berkeley: University of California Press.

Ferree, Myra Marx, and Patricia Yancey Martin. 1995. *Feminist Organizations: Harvest of the New Women's Movement*. Philadelphia: Temple University Press.

Fine, Janice. 2006. *Workers Centers: Organizing Communities at the Edge of the Dream*. Ithaca: Cornell University Press/Economic Policy Institute.

Fisher, Roger, and William Ury. 1981. *Getting to Yes: Negotiating Agreement without Giving In*. New York: Penguin.

Fiske, Susan T., and Hazel Rose Markus, eds. 2012. *Facing Social Class: How Societal Rank Influences Interaction*. New York: Russell Sage Foundation.

Flacks, Richard. 1988. *Making History: The Radical Tradition in American Life*. New York: Columbia University Press.

Frank, Thomas. 2004. *What's the Matter with Kansas? How Conservatives Won the Heart of America*. New York: Henry Holt & Company.

Freeman, Jo. 1972. "The Tyranny of Structurelessness." *Second Wave* 2(1). Accessed September 30, 2008. http://www.jofreeman.com.

Freire, Paulo. 1970. *Pedagogy of the Oppressed*. New York: Continuum.

Furo, Hiroko. 2001. *Turn-Taking in English and Japanese: Projectability in Grammar, Intonation, and Semantics*. New York: Routledge.

Gamson, William A. 1990. *The Strategy of Social Protest*. 2nd ed. Belmont, CA: Wadsworth.

———. 1991. "Commitment and Agency in Social Movements." *Sociological Forum* 6(1): 27–50.

———. 1992. *Talking Politics*. New York: Cambridge University Press.

Gardner, Rod. 2001. *When Listeners Talk*. Philadelphia: John Benjamins.

Garfinkel, Harold. 1967. *Studies in Ethnomethodology*. Englewood Cliffs, NJ: Prentice Hall.

Gartman, David. 1991. "Culture as Class Symbolization or Mass Reification? A Critique of Bourdieu's Distinction." *American Journal of Sociology* 97(2): 421–47.

Gaventa, John. 1982. *Power and Powerlessness: Quiescence and Rebellion in an Appalachian Valley*. Chicago: University of Illinois Press.

Gerstel, Naomi. 2011. "Rethinking Families and Community: The Color, Class, and Centrality of Extended Kin Ties." *Sociological Forum* 26(1): 1–20.

Gitlin, Todd. 1996. *The Twilight of Common Dreams: Why America Is Wracked by Culture Wars*. New York: Holt.

Goffman, Erving. 1955. "On Face-Work: An Analysis of Ritual Elements in Social Interaction." *Psychiatry: Journal for the Study of Interpersonal Processes* 18: 213–31.

———. 1959. *The Presentation of Self in Everyday Life*. New York: Doubleday.

Goldthorpe, John H. (with Catriona Llewellyn and Clive Payne). 1980. *Social Mobility and Class Structure in Modern Britain*. Oxford: Clarendon Press.

González, Juan. 2011. "Once Enemies, Now They March Together: Organized Labor Expected to Join Wall Street Protest." Accessed March 15, 2012. http://www.democracynow.org/blog/2011/10/5/once_enemies_now_they_march_together_organized_labor_expected_to_join_wall_street_protest.

Goodwin, Jeff, James M. Jasper, and Francesca Polletta, eds. 2001. *Passionate Politics: Emotions and Social Movements.* Chicago: University of Chicago Press.

Gosselin, Peter. 2008. *High Wire: The Precarious Financial Lives of American Families.* New York: Basic Books.

Gould, Deborah. 2009. *Moving Politics: Emotion and ACT UP's Fight against AIDS.* Chicago: University of Chicago Press.

Gouldner, Alvin W. 1979. *The Future of Intellectuals and the Rise of the New Class.* London: Macmillan.

Grusky, David. 2005. "Foundations of a Neo-Durkhemian Class Analysis." In *Approaches to Class Analysis,* ed. Erik Olin Wright, 51–81. New York: Cambridge University Press.

Hackman, J. Richard, and Charles G. Morris. 1978. "Group Process and Group Effectiveness: A Reappraisal." In *Group Processes: Papers from Advances in Experimental Social Psychology,* ed. Leonard Berkowitz, 57–66. New York: Academic Press.

Hall, Stuart, and Tony Jefferson. 1975. *Resistance through Rituals: Youth Subcultures in Post-war Britain.* London: Routledge.

Han, Hahrie. 2009. *Moved to Action: Motivation, Participation, and Inequality in American Politics.* Stanford: Stanford University Press.

Harding, Vincent. 1983. *There Is a River: The Black Struggle for Freedom in America.* New York: Random House.

Hart, Betty, and Todd Risley. 1995. *Meaningful Differences in the Everyday Experience of Young American Children.* Baltimore: Paul H. Brookes.

Hay, Jennifer. 2000. "Functions of Humor in the Conversations of Men and Women." *Journal of Pragmatics* 32: 709–42.

Heath, Shirley Brice. 1983. *Ways with Words: Language, Life, and Work in Communities and Classrooms.* Cambridge: Cambridge University Press.

Hebdige, Dick. 1979. *Subculture: The Meaning of Style.* New York: Routledge.

Helgesen, Sally. 1990. *The Female Advantage: Women's Ways of Leadership.* New York: Doubleday.

Heller, Frank A. 1973. "Leadership, Decision Making, and Contingency Theory." *Industrial Relations* 12: 183–99.

Heritage, John. 1984. *Garfinkel and Ethnomethodology.* New York: Polity Press.

Hersey, Paul, and Kenneth H. Blanchard. 1977. *Management of Organizational Behavior.* 3rd ed. New York: Prentice Hall.

Hertz, Thomas. 2006. "Understanding Mobility in America." Center for American Progress. Accessed September 30, 2010. www.americanprogress.org/kf/hertz_mobility_analysis.pdf.

Hirschman, Albert. 1970. *Exit, Voice, and Loyalty: Responses to Decline in Firms, Organizations, and States.* Cambridge: Harvard University Press.

Holt, Douglas. 1997. "Distinction in America? Recovering Bourdieu's Theory of Tastes from Its Critics." *Poetics* 25(2–3): 93–120.

———. 1998. "Does Cultural Capital Structure American Consumption?" *Journal of Consumer Research* 25(1): 1–25.

hooks, bell. 1981. *Ain't I a Woman: Black Women and Feminism.* Boston: South End Press.

——. 2000. *Where We Stand: Class Matters*. New York: Routledge.

Iannello, Kathleen. 1992. *Decisions without Hierarchy: Feminist Interventions in Organization Theory and Practice*. New York: Routledge.

Jacobs, Elisabeth, and Jacob Hacker. 2008. "The Rising Instability of American Family Incomes, 1969–2004: Evidence from the Panel Study of Income." Accessed September 29, 2010. http://www.epi.org/publications/entry/bp213/.

Jasper, James. 1997. *The Art of Moral Protest: Culture, Biography, and Creativity in Social Movements*. Chicago: University of Chicago Press.

Jensen, Barbara. 2012. *Reading Classes: On Culture and Classism in America*. Ithaca: Cornell University Press.

Johnston, Hank, and Bert Klandermans, eds. 1995. *Social Movements and Culture*. Minneapolis: University of Minnesota Press.

Kahn, Si. 1991. *Organizing: A Guide for Grassroots Leaders*. Silver Spring, MD: National Association of Social Workers.

Kivel, Paul. 1998. *Men's Work: How to Stop the Violence That Tears Our Lives Apart*. New York: Ballantine.

——. 2002. *Uprooting Racism: How White People Can Work for Racial Justice*. Gabriola Island, BC: New Society.

——. 2004. *You Call This a Democracy? Who Benefits, Who Pays and Who Really Decides*. New York: Apex Press.

Klandermans, Bert. 1997. *The Social Psychology of Protest*. Oxford: Blackwell.

Koch-Gonzalez, Jerry, Jennifer Ladd, and Felice Yeskel. 2009. *Talking across the Class Divide: A Manual for Cross-Class Dialogue and Learning*. Boston: Class Action.

Kochman, Thomas. 1981. *Black and White Styles in Conflict*. Chicago: University of Chicago Press.

Kornbluh, Felicia. 2007. *The Battle for Welfare Rights: Politics and Poverty in Modern America*. Philadelphia: University of Pennsylvania.

Kurtz, Sharon. 2002. *Workplace Justice: Organizing Multi-Identity Movements*. Minneapolis: University of Minnesota Press.

Kutz-Flamenbaum, Rachel. 2010. "Evaluating the Importance of the National Political Opportunity Structure: Comparing 2004 and 2009 Protestors' Ideology, Experience, and Issue Priority." Paper presented at the Eastern Sociological Society conference, March 20, 2010, Boston, Massachusetts.

Lakey, Berit, George Lakey, Rod Napier, and Janice Robinson. 1996. *Grassroots and Nonprofit Leadership: A Guide for Organizations in Changing Times*. Gabriola Island, BC: New Society.

Lakoff, Robin. 1975. *Language and Women's Place*. Oxford: Oxford University Press.

Lamont, Michèle. 1992. *Money, Morals, and Manners: The Culture of the French and the American Upper-Middle Class*. Chicago: University of Chicago Press.

——. 2000. *The Dignity of Working Men: Morality and the Boundaries of Race, Class, and Immigration*. Cambridge: Harvard University Press.

Lamont, Michèle, and Annette Lareau. 1988. "Cultural Capital: Allusions, Gaps, and Glissandos in Recent Theoretical Developments." *Sociological Theory* 6(2): 153–68.

Lamott, Anne. 1995. *Bird by Bird: Some Instructions on Writing and Life*. New York: Knopf Doubleday.

Lareau, Annette. 2003. *Unequal Childhoods.* Berkeley: University of California Press.

Leach, Darcy. 2009. "An Elusive 'We': Antidogmatism, Democratic Practice, and the Contradictory Identity of the German Autonomen." *American Behavioral Scientist* 52(7): 1042–68.

Leach, Darcy, and Sebastian Haunss. 2009. "Scenes and Social Movements." In *Culture, Social Movements, and Protest,* ed. Hank Johnston, 255–76. Farnham, UK: Ashgate.

Leondar-Wright, Betsy. 2005. *Class Matters: Cross-Class Alliance Building for Middle-Class Activists.* Gabriola Island, BC: New Society.

Lichtenstein, Nelson. 2002. *State of the Union: A Century of American Labor.* Princeton: Princeton University Press.

Lichterman, Paul. 1996. *The Search for Political Community: American Activists Reinventing Commitment.* Cambridge: Cambridge University Press.

Liddicoat, Anthony J. 2007. *An Introduction to Conversation Analysis.* New York: Continuum.

Likert, Rensis. 1961. *New Patterns of Management.* New York: McGraw-Hill.

Lipset, Seymour Martin. 1960. *Political Man: The Social Bases of Politics.* New York: Doubleday.

Lofland, John. 1993. *Polite Protestors: The American Peace Movement of the 1980s.* Syracuse, NY: Syracuse University Press.

———. 1995. "Charting Degrees of Movement Culture: Tasks of the Cultural Cartographer." In *Social Movements and Culture,* ed. Hank Johnston and Bert Klandermans, 188–216. Minneapolis: University of Minnesota.

Lubrano, Alfred. 2004. *Limbo: Blue-Collar Roots, White-Collar Dreams.* Hoboken, NJ: John Wiley & Sons.

Lui, Meizhu, Barbara Robles, Betsy Leondar-Wright, Rose Brewer, and Rebecca Adamson. 2006. *The Color of Wealth: The Story behind the US Racial Wealth Divide.* New York: New Press.

Lukes, Steven. 1974. *Power: A Radical View.* London: Macmillan.

Macaulay, Ronald K. S. 2005. *Talk That Counts: Age, Gender, and Social Class Differences in Discourse.* Oxford: Oxford University Press.

Martinez, Elizabeth. 2000. "Where Was the Color in Seattle? Looking for Reasons Why the Great Battle Was So White." *ColorLines.* Accessed April 3, 2012. http://colorlines.com/archives/2000/03/where_was_the_color_in_seattle looking_for_reasons_why_the_great_battle_was_so_white.html.

Mayer, Brian. 2008. *Blue-Green Coalitions: Fighting for Safe Workplaces and Healthy Communities.* Ithaca: Cornell University Press.

McAdam, Doug. 1988. *Freedom Summer.* New York: Oxford University Press.

McCarthy, John D. 2005. "Persistence and Change among Nationally Federated Social Movements." In *Social Movements and Organization Theory,* ed. Gerald F. Davis, Doug McAdam, W. Richard Scott, and Mayer N. Zald, 193–225. New York: Cambridge University Press.

McKinnon, Neil Joseph. 1994. *Symbolic Interactionism as Affect Control.* Albany: State University of New York Press.

Melucci, Alberto. 1995. "The Process of Collective Identity." In *Social Movements and Culture,* ed. Hank Johnston and Bert Klandermans, 41–63. Minneapolis: University of Minnesota Press.

Meredith, Judith. 2001. *Lobbying on a Shoestring*. Boston: Massachusetts Continuing Legal Education.

Mesthrie, Rajend, Joan Swann, Andrea Deumert, and William L. Leap. 2000. *Introduction to Sociolinguistics*. Amsterdam: John Benjamins.

Metzgar, Jack. 2003. "Politics and the American Class Vernacular." *WorkingUSA* 7: 49–80.

———. 2010. "Are 'the Poor' Part of the Working Class or in a Class by Themselves?" *Labor Studies Journal* 35(3): 398–416.

Miller, Peggy J. 1986. "Teasing as Language Socialization and Verbal Play in a White Working-Class Community." In *Language Socialization across Cultures*, ed. Bambi B. Schieffelin and Elinor Ochs, 199–212. Cambridge, UK: Cambridge University Press.

Miller, S. M., and Frank Riessman. 1961. "Working Class Authoritarianism: A Critique of Lipset." *British Journal of Sociology* 12: 263–76.

Moraga, Cherrié, and Gloria Anzaldúa. 1981. *This Bridge Called My Back: Writings by Radical Women of Color*. Watertown, MA: Persephone Press.

Morris, Aldon. 1984. *The Origins of the Civil Rights Movement: Black Communities Organizing for Change*. New York: The Free Press.

Munson, Ziad W. 2008. *The Making of Pro-Life Activists: How Social Movement Mobilization Works*. Chicago: University of Chicago Press.

Myers, Daniel J. 2008. "Ally Identity: The Politically Gay." In *Identity Work in Social Movements*, ed. Jo Reger, Daniel J. Myers, and Rachel L. Einwohner, 167–88. Minneapolis: University of Minnesota Press.

Norrick, Neal R. 2010. "Humor in Interaction." *Language and Linguistics Compass* 4(4): 232–44.

O'Brien, Erin E. 2008. *The Politics of Identity: Solidarity Building among America's Working Poor*. Albany: State University of New York Press.

O'Connor, Alan. 2008. *Punk Record Labels and the Struggle for Autonomy: The Emergence of DIY*. Lanham, MD: Rowman and Littlefield.

Ostrander, Susan A. 1984. *Women of the Upper Class*. Philadelphia: Temple University Press.

Patton, Michael Quinn. 1990. *Qualitative Evaluation and Research Methods*. Thousand Oaks, CA: Sage.

People's Institute for Survival and Beyond. 2002. *Training manual*. Accessed February 7, 2011. http://www.pisab.org/.

———. 2011. *Our Approach*. Accessed February 7, 2011. http://www.pisab.org/.

Peterson, Richard, and Roger M. Kern. 1996. "Changing Highbrow Taste: From Snob to Omnivore." *American Sociological Review* 61(5): 900–907.

Piatelli, Deborah. 2008. *Stories of Inclusion? Power, Privilege, and Difference in a Peace and Justice Network*. Lanham, MD: Lexington Books.

Piven, Frances Fox, and Richard Cloward. 1979. *Poor People's Movements: Why They Succeed, How They Fail*. 2nd ed. New York: Vintage.

Polletta, Francesca. 2002. *Freedom Is an Endless Meeting: Democracy in American Social Movements*. Chicago: University of Chicago Press.

Pollin, Robert, and Stephanie Luce. 1998. *Building a Fair Economy*. New York: New Press.

Ransby, Barbara. 2005. *Ella Baker and the Black Freedom Movement: A Radical Democratic Vision.* Chapel Hill: University of North Carolina Press.

Reed Jr., Adolph. 1999. *Stirrings in the Jug: Black Politics in the Post-Segregation Era.* Minneapolis: University of Minnesota Press.

Reed-Danahay, Deborah. 2005. *Locating Bourdieu.* Bloomington: University of Indiana Press.

Robinson, Dawn T., and Lynn Smith-Lovin. 2001. "Getting a Laugh: Gender, Status, and Humor in Task Discussions." *Social Forces* 80(1): 123–58.

Rose, Fred. 2000. *Coalitions across the Class Divide.* Ithaca: Cornell University Press.

Rothenberg, Paula, ed. 1995. *Race, Class, and Gender in the United States: An Integrated Study.* New York: St. Martin's Press.

Rothschild, Joyce, and Darcy Leach. 2007. "Avoid, Talk, or Fight: Alternative Cultural Strategies in the Battle against Oligarchy in Collectivist-Democratic Organizations." In *Handbook of Community Movements and Local Organizations,* ed. Ram A. Cnaan and Carl Milofsky, 346–61. New York: Springer Handbooks.

Sacks, Harvey. 1992 [1972]. *Lectures on Conversation.* Vol. 2, ed. Gail Jefferson. Oxford: Blackwell.

Schmidt, Jeff. 2000. *Disciplined Minds: A Critical Look at Salaried Professionals and the Soul-Battering System That Shapes Their Lives.* Lanham, MD: Rowman and Littlefield.

Sen, Rinku. 2011. "Race and Occupy Wall Street." *Nation.* November 14, 2011. Accessed January 12, 2012. http://www.thenation.com/article/164212/race-and-occupy-wall-street.

Shartle, Carroll L. 1956. *Executive Performance and Leadership.* New York: Prentice Hall.

Shelton, Jason E., and George Wilson. 2006. "Socioeconomic Status and Racial Group Interests among Black Americans." *Sociological Spectrum* 26: 183–204.

Smith, Tom. 1992. "Changing Racial Labels: From 'Colored' to 'Negro' to 'Black' to 'African American.'" *Public Opinion Quarterly* 56(4): 496–514.

Somma, Nicolás M. 2009. "How Strong Are Strong Ties? The Conditional Effectiveness of Strong Ties in Protest Recruitment Attempts." *Sociological Perspectives* 52(3): 289–308.

Starhawk. 1979. *The Spiral Dance: A Rebirth of the Ancient Religion of the Great Goddess.* New York: Harper and Row.

——. 1988. *Truth or Dare: Encounters with Power, Authority, and Mystery.* San Francisco, CA: HarperSanFrancisco.

——. 2008. "Singing in Spite of Fear: Overcoming Violence at the Republican National Convention" in *Peacework* 389. American Friends Service Committee. http://www.peaceworkmagazine.org/singing-spite-fear-overcoming-violence-republican-national-convention.

Starr, Amory. 2005. *Global Revolt: A Guide to the Movements against Globalization.* New York: Zed Books.

Stout, Linda. 1996. *Bridging the Class Divide and Other Lessons for Grassroots Organizing.* Boston: Beacon.

Strobel, Margaret. 1995. "Organizational Learning in the Chicago Women's Liberation Union." In *Feminist Organizations: Harvest of the New Women's Movement,* ed. Myra Marx Ferree and Patricia Yancey Martin, 199–219. Philadelphia: Temple University Press.

Strolovitch, Dara Z. 2007. *Affirmative Advocacy: Race, Class, and Gender in Interest Group Politics*. Chicago: University of Chicago Press.

Swartz, David. 1997. *Culture and Power: The Sociology of Pierre Bourdieu*. Chicago: University of Chicago Press.

Swidler, Ann. 1986. "Culture in Action: Symbols and Strategies." *American Sociological Review* 51(2): 273–86.

Tannen, Deborah. 1990. *You Just Don't Understand: Women and Men in Conversation*. New York: Ballantine.

———. 1994. *Talking from 9 to 5: Women and Men at Work*. New York: Avon.

———. 1996. *Gender and Discourse*. Oxford: Oxford University Press.

Taylor, Verta, and Nancy Whittier. 1995. "Analytical Approaches to Social Movement Culture: The Culture of the Women's Movement." In *Social Movements and Culture*, ed. Hank Johnston and Bert Klandermans, 163–87. Minneapolis: University of Minnesota Press.

Teixeira, Ruy, and Joel Rogers. 2000. *America's Forgotten Majority*, 2nd ed. New York: Basic Books.

Teske, Nathan. 1997. *Political Activists in America: The Identity Construction Model of Political Participation*. University Park: Penn State University Press.

Thompson, Becky. 2001. *A Promise and a Way of Life: White Antiracist Activism*. Minneapolis: University of Minnesota Press.

Vaid, Urvashi. 1996. *Virtual Equality: The Mainstreaming of Gay and Lesbian Liberation*. New York: Doubleday.

van Dijk, Teun A. 2008. *Discourse and Context: A Sociocognitive Approach*. Cambridge, UK: Cambridge University Press.

Veblen, Thorstein. 1994 [1899]. *The Theory of the Leisure Class: An Economic Study of Institutions*. New York: Penguin.

Ward, Jane. 2008. *Respectably Queer: Diversity Culture in LGBT Activist Organizations*. Nashville: Vanderbilt University Press.

Warner, Rebecca M. 2008. *Applied Statistics: From Bivariate through Multivariate Techniques*. Thousand Oaks, CA: Sage.

Warren, Mark. 2001. *Dry Bones Rattling: Community Building to Revitalize American Democracy*. Princeton: Princeton University Press.

———. 2010. *Fire in the Heart: How White Activists Embrace Racial Justice*. New York: Oxford University Press.

Willis, Paul. 1981. *Learning to Labor: How Working Class Kids Get Working Class Jobs*. New York: Columbia University Press.

Wise, Tim. 2004. *White Like Me: Reflections on Race from a Privileged Son*. New York: Soft Skull Press.

Wright, Erik Olin. 1985. *Classes*. New York: Verso.

———, ed. 2005. *Approaches to Class Analysis*. New York: Cambridge University Press.

Yates, Michael, David Bacon, Warren Mar, Stephen Lerner, and John Borsos. 2008. "SEIU: Debating Labor's Strategy." *MRZine*. Accessed March 17, 2010. http://mrzine.monthlyreview.org/2008/seiu140708.html.

Yuen, Eddie, Daniel Burton-Rose, and George Katsiaficas, eds. 2004. *Confronting Capitalism: Dispatches from a Global Movement.* New York: Soft Skull Press.

Zerubavel, Eviatar. 2001. *The Clockwork Muse: A Practical Guide to Writing Theses, Dissertations, and Books.* 2nd ed. Cambridge: Harvard University Press.

Zweig, Michael. 2011. *The Working-Class Majority.* 2nd ed. Ithaca: Cornell University Press.

INDEX